TOM'S Big DINNERS

ALSO BY TOM DOUGLAS

TOM DOUGLAS' SEATTLE KITCHEN

TOM'S Big DINNERS

BIG-TIME HOME COOKING FOR FAMILY AND FRIENDS

TOM DOUGLAS

WITH ED LEVINE, SHELLEY LANCE, AND JACKIE CROSS

WM
WILLIAM MORROW
An Imprint of HarperCollinsPublishers

HarperCollins books may be purchased for educational, business, or sales
promotional use. For information please write: Special Markets Department, HarperCollins Publishers Inc., 10 East 53rd Street, New York, NY
10022.

FIRST EDITION

Designed by Mary Sarah Quinn

Photographs by Robin Layton

Printed on acid-free paper

Library of Congress Cataloging-in-Publication Data

Douglas, Tom, 1958—
    Tom's big dinners : big-time home cooking for family and friends /
Tom Douglas, with Ed Levine, Shelley Lance, and Jackie Cross.
        p. cm.
      ISBN 0-06-051502-3 (hc.)
      1. Dinners and dining.   2. Menus.   3. Cookery, American—Pacific
Northwest style.   I. Title.

    TX737.D68 2003
    642'.4—dc21

                                                                    2003045886

03   04   05   06   07   WBC/RRD   10   9   8   7   6   5   4   3   2   1

TO OUR GRANDMAS,
WHO COULD ALWAYS SQUEEZE
A FEW MORE CHAIRS AROUND THE TABLE

CONTENTS

ACKNOWLEDGMENTS

The friends and family who sit at our dining room table year after year are really the heart and soul of *Big Dinners*. I owe my parents, Bob and Mary Douglas, my brother, Bob, and my sisters, Kate, Mary Lou, Laurie, Chere, and Michelle thanks for making the big family meal an indispensable element of my life.

For their help, advice, and good-natured patience, I particularly want to thank my in-laws, Dot, Jim, and Sharon Cross. Extra thanks go to Mike Teer for his help with wine recommendations, as well as Pam Hinkley who is stuck drinking beer only. I also want to thank Susan and Peter Cipra; Peter, Peggy, and Molly Dow; Kay Simon and Clay Mackey; and Dale Chihuly, Joanna Sikes, and the boathouse crew for letting us make them part of this book.

Many thanks to those who did the *mise en place* for this book—my cowriters Shelley Lance and Ed Levine, our in-house artistic director Jackie Cross, and recipe testers Chris Fitzgibbon and Mikal Czajkowski. Thanks to Robin Layton for her awesome photographs, and the very patient Brian Smale for his cover shot. Also thanks to my daughter, Loretta, who had to pretend she liked my cooking whenever the photographer was around.

While I'm gallivanting around the country promoting my books, sauces, rubs, and radio show, there are many folks minding the stove, greeting the customers, and paying the bills. Pam Leydon, Colleen Kennelly, Eric Tanaka, and Steven Steinbock, along with two hundred dedicated staff, run the business in a way that I couldn't be more proud of.

Of course there could be no *Big Dinners* cookbook without my agent Judith Riven, who takes all my phone calls and makes a mean brunch, and the hard-working team at William Morrow Cookbooks—my editor, Harriet Bell, who, while brilliant, beautiful, and rich, screens all my calls; Carrie Bachman, the p.r. diva; Kate Stark, the queen of marketing; Roberto de Vicq de Cumptich, art director; Leah Carlson-Stanisic, interior design; Karen Lumley, production; and Ann Cahn, who catches all our mistakes.

All of you please stand up and take a bow.

INTRODUCTION

The Douglas family is a big family, and the house in Newark, Delaware, where I grew up is a big house. It seems as though we had a big dinner every night of the week. In many ways it was like a bustling restaurant with three meals a day not only for a family of ten but often for friends in the neighborhood, boyfriends, girl-friends, even exchange students from the nearby University of Delaware, home of the "Fighting Blue Hens," as well. There was only one difference between our house and a restaurant: There were no menu choices. You either ate what was on the table or you went hungry.

Our big dinners were punctuated by house rules. Hands were washed and sometimes even inspected before dinner. No tele-phone calls. It didn't matter if it was my sister Kate's newest squeeze calling to ask her out or my mom's friends checking on bridge club dates. Absolutely no talking with your mouth full. No elbows on the table. The tines on my dad's fork were particularly sharp when dug into an unsuspecting forearm.

There was certainly enough food for everybody. Mom would always be thinking ahead to the next meal, making an extra meat loaf to be used for school brown bag lunches as long as she was making one anyway. (To this day I often use that lesson. When fir-ing up the grill, I'll cook an extra chicken for leftovers the next day.) You would never know by the bounty on the table the actual state of the household finances.

Conversation was constant, often boisterous. With twenty years' difference between my oldest brother, Bob, and my youn-gest sister, Michelle, there was a wide variety of subjects to discuss, ranging from "Sesame Street" to which of Bob and Kate's friends were going to be drafted and sent to Vietnam. There were no dis-tractions from a TV or radio, because they weren't allowed during dinner.

We each had jobs to do before and after the big dinner. For me, it was sweeping up the kitchen floor and taking out the garbage after dinner. The younger sisters were assigned setting the table, while the older kids dealt mostly with loading the dishwasher and then washing and drying anything that wouldn't fit—which was usually about the same amount that did fit. My mother often served on melamine dishes, for good reason with all of us kids doing the dishwashing. Since my dad was a traveling salesman, our glassware often consisted of whatever Esso or Shell was giving away with a full tank of gas. As with many families at the time, juice glasses were leftover Kraft pimiento cream cheese spread jars collected, saved, and passed along by the grandmas.

Mom would always sit next to the baby, and it seemed like there was *always* a baby. Even when hers were grown, she took on some to baby-sit and gladly transitioned to grandkids. Gert, as my dad called her—a nickname from her middle name, Gertrude—was the cook of the house. Bob Senior was often on the road Monday through Friday, and on the weekends, her menus reflected his favorites—like chili noodles (ground beef mixed with diced tomatoes and mild, mild chili powder, then stirred into well-cooked egg noodles) or huge hunks of roast beef with her delicious pan gravy. Sloppy joes, fried chicken, and mac and cheese were staples when he was gone—the joes heaped on spongy white buns served with our favorite Herrs thick-cut potato chips and finely diced creamy coleslaw.

At the table, my dad's job was to carve the roast, usually with his deer-antler-handles carving set, then take the bowls of food that my mom had cooked so carefully and, with a stack of warm plates in front of him, serve us one by one around the table. Portions were based on your physical size and age, not necessarily your appetite. For me, this was never a problem, but for my waist-size-minded sisters, it was often a battle. There were never any options, such as "Could I skip the spinach?" or "I'm not eating any red meat at this time in my life." You had some of everything, like it or not. It was curious, though, that the veggies always seemed to run out before my dad served himself. The final rule, which all the kids were most concerned with, was no dessert unless you finished what was on your plate. Grandma Fogarty often baked silky but-

terscotch meringue pies or one-two-three-four cakes with cocoa powder frosting. They loomed on the counter next to the table like the devil himself daring you not to finish.

Our dinners were always big but rarely formal unless it was a holiday. On these special occasions we would move from the kitchen table, where most of our daily meals happened, to the dining room table, which, with a couple of Samsonite card tables, extended to seat twenty. Now Mom would break out her fancy wedding china—Franciscan Apple—cut-crystal stemware, and monogrammed silver from the red velvet–lined chest.

Nobody could touch a bite until everyone was served. You can imagine hungry kids sitting there, looking at a full plate of food— steaming hot butter melting on the mashed potatoes, Thanksgiving turkey with salty crisp skin, and just-from-the-oven Parker House rolls . . . it was torture. Then, just when you thought you could dig in, Dad would abruptly call for "Grace, please." He didn't even go to church.

These big meals for six, eight, ten, or twelve every day—breakfast, lunch, and dinner—never seemed like anything out of the ordinary to me. Of course as a child I didn't know what a huge amount of work it was for my mom—budgeting, menu planning, shopping, and cooking. But I did know that these meals were the best part of my day! Even now, sitting down to a meal with my family and friends is the moment of the day that I treasure the most.

Three thousand miles away, my wife, Jackie, grew up in a Spokane house where big dinners were also the norm but more on a weekly basis. Every Sunday her grandmother Claire Elizabeth Dimico Cross would cook up an Italian storm for the extended Cross family, which could number as many as twenty, depending on who was around. At the Cross table a big dinner was likely to consist of a staggering selection of Italian specialties. There might be head cheese an amalgamation of all nonprime cuts (ears, tongue, feet, heart, etc.) of the hog held together in a loaf shape by the gelatinous stock made from bones of the animal. Fragrant hand-stuffed fennel-seed sausages cured and then hung from the attic rafters and lightly smoked were a favorite of Jackie's. Fat, ricotta-stuffed ravioli in meat sauce centered the table, along with rack of pork or shoulder of lamb and sometimes both.

Seasons dictated Grandma Cross's menus, with most vegetables coming from her impressive garden. Winter brought out the amazing results of summer and fall's canning. To this day Jackie's father, Jim, cans Grandma Cross's rightfully famous antipasto every year and spreads the wealth among his siblings, daughters, and granddaughter. Our daughter Loretta has now taken on the responsibility of learning the recipe and the craft.

When I started cooking professionally—at the Hotel DuPont in Delaware right out of high school and later, in 1977, at restaurant jobs in Seattle—it seemed that those restaurant dining rooms were extensions of the family dinner table. I loved the collective energy of the kitchen and the lovely hum and buzz that would emanate from a room full of people enjoying both the food and one another's company. When Jackie and I opened our first restaurant, the Dahlia Lounge, in the fall of 1989, my favorite place in the joint was standing beneath the stairs heading up to the mezzanine. I was in the dining room, but nobody could see me. I would just close my eyes and listen to the clang and clatter of a room filled with diners. At that moment it wasn't about money, success, or fame. It was about feeding people, making people happy, facilitating birthdays, anniversaries, engagements. I'm often asked, "What is your favorite part of the restaurant business?" And I will tell you, without hesitation, when somebody comes up to me and says "I've been trying to decide where to have my fortieth birthday or fiftieth anniversary meal for a month, and I chose you," it's a spectacular feeling.

Of course, big dinners don't happen only in our restaurants. Now, with my own family, working in our carefully remodeled kitchen, serving on our hand-built big table, with close friends, workmates, and even Loretta's friends, we carry on the tradition of big dinners. Big dinners at our house tend to be much more spontaneous than at either of our folks'. Both Jackie and I are at work all day, as are most of our friends. Typically a big dinner with everything made from scratch tends to be on a Saturday or Sunday. This doesn't stop us from having big dinners during the week.

A quick call to our friends Pam and Mike, as well as Peter, Peggy, and their daughter, Molly, takes care of half of the menu, and we try to take some smart shortcuts.

Shrimp filling for tacos takes about ten minutes to cook, but homemade tortillas are much more time consuming, so we stop by our favorite Mexican restaurant on the way home and grab two or three dozen for $5. You might ask why we don't just stay and have tacos there, but you haven't tasted Jackie's shrimp tacos. The first order of business when we get home is to set the tone. I mean the Gypsy Kings, baby. As loud as the neighbors can stand it. For some reason this makes me cook faster—and better. It also makes sharing the kitchen with your wife a little sexy. Maybe you take a "salsa" turn around the kitchen—one that's not in a bowl on the table. Hey, if you haven't tried it, don't knock it.

We cut up half the tortillas into wedges and fry them to serve with the fantastic pico de gallo we learned at the restaurant from Big Eddie from Mexico, an incredible cook. Pam scores some ripe avocados and makes perfect guacamole—just a little salt and lime juice. I am in charge of watermelon margaritas. It takes only a second to puree the watermelon in the food processor, and the fresh juice adds a little sunshine to the table. Peggy Dow, who's been to Mexico many times and has taken classes with Diana Kennedy, contributes her savory pinto beans. Peter and Mike make sure there's plenty of wine, since none of us can drink more than one of those margaritas. A simple but delicious dessert for either an Asian or Mexican menu is to take ripe, juicy mango slices, sprinkle with sugar, and caramelize under the broiler or with a crème brûlée torch.

Out come the big platters. We have a collection picked up from our travels around the world or received as gifts from family and friends. If we're serving buffet style, we use the big platters and lay them out on our big kitchen island. When serving family style at the table, we prefer smaller platters or oversized dinner plates so people can easily and more comfortably pass the food around the table.

When it comes to cleanup, Loretta and Molly cheerfully (ha!) clear the table. Everything gets stacked by "my" dishwasher. In our house, Jackie does the laundry and I do the dishes—an arrangement Jackie has always been fond of.

Years ago I got into the bad habit of treating big dinners at home like we were at the restaurant. Whenever someone would offer to bring a course or make the salad or bring dessert, I would say "Oh, no, I got it," and dinners would end up being orchestrated in a way that stifled the essence of a big dinner. For another example, Jackie sets such a spectacular table, it's hard for her to let it go, even on a weeknight, but now we're trying to let Loretta learn how to set the table. It's important for everyone to have a job, to interact, to feel included, and, for the kids' sake, just be taught what needs to be done.

When I started thinking about what kind of book I wanted to write after *Tom Douglas' Seattle Kitchen,* the choice was easy. I loved whenever I heard that some readers of my book invited, say, five couples to their house, all having to bring one course out of our book. A genuine Tom Douglas big dinner. We are living in a time when fast food is king, when time pressures on kids and adults alike make cooking a big dinner seem more of a chore. Don't let it happen. It's too important. When times are tough, a big dinner is a meeting place, a place to share and comfort, and certainly better for your soul than reality TV.

BASICS

Working in restaurant kitchens, you get used to having lots of the basics around—buckets of cold chicken stock and tubs of duck fat in the walk-in refrigerator, batches of pastry dough in the freezer, and plenty of yesterday's bread to turn into crumbs, croutons, and crostini.

Although I never have quite the same wealth of basics around my home kitchen, I believe in the fundamental idea. Jackie and I both grew up in big families where any excess bounty was saved, preserved, and stored—never thrown away. Rather than just throwing the last of the fall garden's sugar pumpkins onto the compost pile, Jackie will spend an afternoon roasting them and passing the flesh through a food mill so she can put some bags of pumpkin puree in the freezer for making winter's pumpkin risotto and pies.

One of the secrets to great home cooking is always having a few sealable plastic bags of chicken stock stashed in the freezer, so Jackie and I start a batch of chicken stock whenever we have time. Last night's leftover shredded meat and cooked vegetables, plus the odd carrot and turnip hanging around the vegetable bin, can be turned into a pot of soup for tonight's dinner with the addition of some homemade chicken stock.

I buy good bread, and I almost never throw it away. The leftover part of a nice crusty loaf always gets sliced and sealed in a plastic bag in the freezer, where it's handy for making toasts at a later date. And I never, ever throw away bacon or duck fat. I keep a small, lidded porcelain pot of bacon fat in my refrigerator at all times, and anytime I roast a duck all of that fabulous fat gets saved in the refrigerator or freezer.

Whenever you put a little effort into some prep for a meal at a later date—whether it's making an extra batch of pastry dough for the freezer or a jar of dried bread crumbs from a leftover chunk of bread—you're cooking like a restaurant chef.

CHICKEN STOCK

MAKES 1 GALLON

I always keep my eyes open for a good deal on chicken wings, backs, and necks or cheap whole chickens when I'm shopping.

I get two things out of a pot of chicken stock. First, I strain the stock and freeze it in approximately 2-cup portions in sealable plastic bags. Then I pick the bones, chop up the vegetables, stir the skimmed chicken fat back in, and make my own doggone delicious homemade dog food for Ruby.

I've never found a canned or boxed chicken stock that even comes close to the homemade version. But you can substitute low-sodium canned chicken broth in our recipes. Regular canned chicken broth is too salty. To get a nice clear stock, don't let the stock boil hard. After it comes to a boil, reduce the heat to a steady simmer. Allow hot stock to cool before you chill it. It's best to put a larger container of hot stock in a larger bowl of ice water, stirring until cool, then cover and refrigerate.

I roast the bones and vegetables for a deeper flavor, but you can make a flavorful stock if you simply combine the bones and vegetables with the water in a large pot. If you're using a whole chicken instead of bones, skip the roasting step.

4 pounds chicken bones or wings, backs, and necks

2 onions, roughly chopped

2 carrots, roughly chopped

2 celery ribs, roughly chopped

1 tablespoon olive oil

½ bunch fresh flat-leaf parsley

2 bay leaves

1 teaspoon black peppercorns

A STEP AHEAD Chicken stock can be stored, covered, in the refrigerator for a few days or in the freezer for several weeks. Bring to a boil before using.

Preheat the oven to 450°F. Roast the chicken bones on a baking sheet until browned, about 45 minutes to an hour. Toss the onions, carrots, and celery with the oil in a bowl. Spread the vegetables on another baking sheet and roast until browned, about 40 minutes. In a large pot over high heat, combine all the ingredients and add 6 quarts cold water. Bring to a boil, then reduce the heat and simmer for 2 hours, skimming occasionally to remove any foam from the surface. Strain the stock into a large bowl and discard the solids. Let the stock sit for 5 to 10 minutes so the fat floats to the surface, then skim off the fat, or refrigerate the stock overnight and remove the fat the next day.

CHICKEN DEMIGLACE

MAKES ¼ CUP

Demiglace is poultry or meat stock that has been boiled until it is reduced in volume, intensely flavorful, and thick enough to coat a spoon. (See "How to Make Reductions," page 79.) There are some pretty good packaged demiglace products on the market these days. They even make a vegetable demi (see Sources, page 265).

1 quart Chicken Stock

A STEP AHEAD Demiglace can be stored, covered, in the refrigerator for a few days or frozen longer.

Put the chicken stock in a heavy saucepan and bring to a boil over high heat. Continue to boil until the stock is thick and reduced to ¼ cup.

CHINOOK SALMON ROAST

Roasting a whole salmon is ceremonial, dramatic, and festive in a way cooking individual fillets of white fish can never be. I roast a chinook salmon in the round or a beautiful black-skinned sablefish stuffed with stalks of copper fennel and sweet Walla Walla onions.

There are two ways I get a fish for a salmon roast. I either go down and talk to Harry at Mutual Fish in Seattle and pick out some beautiful line-caught, boat-bled masterpiece tucked into a bed of ice. Or I go out with Keith Robbins, owner and guide of Spotted Tail Salmon Charter. While Harry's fish are beautiful, there's nothing quite like catching your own, which I've had a chance to do on several occasions with Keith.

Puget Sound is full of amazing sea life. The last time we went out we encountered a half-mile-long and quarter-mile-wide school of herring (bait), swirling, roiling, jumping out of the water. Thousands of gulls and a few sand sharks (which the local fisherman call *dogfish*) gleefully attack the bait. The salmon also lurk about the bait while keeping careful watch on the sea lions and porpoises chasing them. The result of all this fish commotion is a veritable tornado of sea life. Quickly baiting our hooks, we dropped lines to go after chinook, the king of salmon and my favorite. We spent all morning losing hook after hook to the feisty sand sharks, which indicated to Keith that our lines were out too deep. We persevered, changed our lines strategy, and ended up hooking a ten-pound silver, or coho salmon that is a little leaner than a chinook. By noon we headed back to the dock, serenaded by barking sea lions, thinking about what else to make with our salmon dinner.

MENU

MOM'S CRAB DIP ON RUSSET POTATO CHIPS

STE. MICHELLE RIESLING, WASHINGTON

WILD MUSHROOM PAN ROAST

WHOLE SALMON ON THE GRILL STUFFED WITH SEA SALT, LEMON, AND ONION

SWEET FENNEL BUTTER

HAZELNUT RICE SALAD WITH PARSLEY AND ARTICHOKES

CANOE RIDGE CHARDONNAY, WASHINGTON

BUTTERNUT SQUASH GINGERBREAD

DOMAINE DURBAN MUSCAT BEAUMES D'VENISE

MOM'S CRAB DIP ON RUSSET POTATO CHIPS

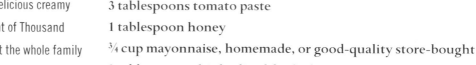

MAKES 8 TO 10 SERVINGS

My mom makes a delicious creamy crab dip reminiscent of Thousand Island dressing that the whole family loved. She served it on Ritz crackers, but I serve dollops of crab dip on my homemade potato chips.

While my mom would never add a pepper to her recipe, I've tweaked it with the classic Delaware sub shop pickled cherry peppers.

3 tablespoons tomato paste

1 tablespoon honey

¾ cup mayonnaise, homemade, or good-quality store-bought

2 tablespoons thinly sliced fresh chives

1 tablespoon freshly squeezed lemon juice

1 tablespoon seeded and minced sweet red cherry pepper (from a jar of vinegar-packed sweet cherry peppers)

2 teaspoons freshly grated lemon zest

1 teaspoon prepared horseradish

¼ teaspoon Tabasco sauce

1 hard-cooked egg, finely chopped

¾ pound fresh cooked Dungeness crabmeat, picked over for bits of shell and cartilage, with claw meat and large pieces of crab left whole

Kosher salt and freshly ground black pepper

½ lemon

Russet Potato Chips (page 14) or top-quality store-bought potato chips

A STEP AHEAD You can make the dressing a day ahead and store it, covered with plastic wrap, in the refrigerator. When you're ready to serve, mix the dressing with the crabmeat.

In a large bowl, whisk the tomato paste and honey together until smooth. Whisk in the mayonnaise, chives, lemon juice, cherry pepper, lemon zest, horseradish, and Tabasco. Using a rubber spatula, gently fold in the egg. Add the crabmeat to the bowl and toss it with the dressing. Season to taste with salt and pepper and a squeeze of lemon. Set a bowl of crab dip on a large platter and surround it with potato chips for dipping.

MAYONNAISE

I like to make my own mayonnaise, but if you prefer, or if you're concerned about egg safety, you can use good-quality store-bought mayonnaise instead. Be sure to buy "real" mayonnaise, such as Best Foods brand or Hellmann's, not something labeled "salad dressing."

You can use a mild-flavored vegetable oil, pure olive oil, or a mixture of the two. I don't like to use extra virgin olive oil in my mayonnaise because the olive flavor is too dominant.

2 large egg yolks
1 teaspoon freshly squeezed lemon juice
1 teaspoon Dijon mustard
⅔ cup vegetable oil, pure olive oil, or a mixture
Kosher salt and freshly ground black pepper

A STEP AHEAD Store mayonnaise in the refrigerator, covered, and use it the same day it is made.

Put the yolks, lemon juice, and mustard in the bowl of a food processor. Gradually pour in the oil with the machine running and process until emulsified. Season to taste with salt and pepper.

NOTE: It's important to be aware of the potential dangers of salmonella and other harmful bacteria and take precautions. Use very fresh grade A or grade AA eggs (check the expiration date on the carton before buying) and always keep your eggs refrigerated. Don't keep eggs at room temperature for more than an hour, and always wash your hands, work surface, and equipment thoroughly before and after using raw eggs. Use products that have been made with raw eggs within one day.

RUSSET POTATO CHIPS

MAKES 8 TO 10 SERVINGS

The extra work of making your own potato chips is very worthwhile, and you can do it a day ahead.

You can use a sharp knife to cut the potatoes, but a mandoline or slicer works best (see page 261).

2 to 3 large russet potatoes (about 2 pounds), peeled
Peanut, canola, or grapeseed oil for deep frying
Kosher salt

A STEP AHEAD You can fry the chips up to 1 day ahead and store them in an airtight container at room temperature.

Using a slicer or mandoline, cut the potatoes into almost-paper-thin slices, about $\frac{1}{16}$ inch thick or less. Place the potato slices in a container of cold water until you are ready to fry them. Before frying, drain the potatoes and blot them dry on paper towels.

To cook the potato chips, heat at least 2 inches of oil to 350°F in a straight-sided pot (see below), but be sure not to fill your pot more than halfway, because the oil will foam up during frying. Fry the potato chips in batches, stirring them around frequently with a slotted metal spoon to cook them evenly, until they are crisp and golden brown, 1 to 2 minutes. Transfer the chips to a baking sheet lined with paper towels and sprinkle them with kosher salt to taste.

HOW TO DEEP-FRY

Deep frying is extra work, but a deep-fried treat can make a meal special. Frying is not hard to do, and it's fast, but it does require all your attention while the food is in the oil.

I prefer peanut, grapeseed, or canola oil for deep frying because of its high smoke point and clean, neutral flavors. Olive oil can add a special flavor to some foods, but use pure olive oil, which has a higher smoke point than extra virgin.

While some people use an electric deep-fat fryer, I prefer a wide, heavy, straight-sided pot with deep sides and a clip-on frying thermometer. The frying thermometer is the most important element for success in deep frying. Usually you want to deep-fry foods at about 350°F, but the temperature of the oil will fluctuate. When you add a batch of food to the oil, it will lower the temperature, or the oil may get hotter the longer it is on the burner. Use your thermometer to check the temperature of the oil before you start frying and keep checking it throughout the frying process, adjusting the heat of your burner to keep the temperature consistent.

You'll need at least 1 to 3 inches of oil to deep-fry, but don't fill your pot more than halfway with oil because the hot oil will bubble up when you add food.

A skimmer (a small flat wire-mesh basket on the end of a long handle) is the perfect tool for removing foods from hot oil.

Frying is potentially dangerous. Work carefully and keep a box of salt or baking soda or a large lid on hand to smother a small fire. It's always a good idea to have a working fire extinguisher nearby.

WILD MUSHROOM PAN ROAST

MAKES 8 SERVINGS

A few years ago Jackie, Loretta, and I stayed at Anne Willan's Château du Fey in Burgundy with a group of our friends. It was an off week for Anne's school, so we had the La Varenne kitchens to ourselves. Most of the week was spent shopping the local markets and returning to the fabulous facilities to cook for our group of twelve. One of the few meals we did end up leaving the château for was lunch at the famed three-star Côte St. Jacques on the main highway through Joigny in central Burgundy. Our lunch consisted of seven courses enjoyed over three hours with the consensus highlight being a simple plate of roasted wild mushrooms, flavored with just a bit of veal stock, salt, pepper, and duck fat. This is my humble attempt to re-create this simple but fantastic dish.

2½ pounds assorted wild and cultivated mushrooms, such as shiitake, oyster, chanterelle, black trumpet, or portobello
2 tablespoons bacon fat, duck fat, or unsalted butter
2 tablespoons olive oil
Twelve 4-inch fresh thyme sprigs
Four 4-inch fresh rosemary sprigs
Kosher salt and freshly ground black pepper
¼ cup Chicken Demiglace (page 9), or store-bought demiglace (see Sources, page 265)
Eight ½-inch-thick Garlic Toasts, cut in half

Preheat the oven to 450°F.

Clean any dirt off the mushrooms by wiping them with a damp cloth and trim off the tough bottoms of the stems. Leave small mushrooms whole and cut the bigger ones into large attractive pieces. Set the mushrooms aside.

Put the fat and olive oil in the bottom of a roasting pan large enough to hold all the mushrooms in a single layer. (If you are using butter, add it to the pan when you add the mushrooms so the butter doesn't burn.) Place the pan in the oven for 5 minutes to get the pan and the fat hot. Remove the pan from the oven, add the mushrooms, thyme, and rosemary, and season to taste with salt and pepper. Shake the pan to distribute all the ingredients. Return the roasting pan to the oven and roast until the mushrooms are thoroughly cooked, about 25 minutes turning once with a spatula. The mushrooms may initially throw off a lot of juices, but as you continue roasting, much of the liquid will evaporate. Remove the pan from the oven and pour in the demiglace. Return the pan to the oven for a few minutes more to heat the demiglace and combine the flavors. Remove the pan from the oven and season to taste with salt and pepper. Pile the mushrooms onto a large platter and surround them with the garlic toasts.

NOTE: If you're making the whole menu, clean the grill with a grill brush after you remove the salmon, then grill your toasts for the wild mushrooms.

GARLIC TOASTS

Crunchy and aromatic, garlic toast is one of my favorite foods and the perfect garnish for many of the foods I love to eat. Try putting a grilled steak right on top of a crusty slice of garlic toast. It will soak up all the meat juices as you slice the steak.

Whenever I have leftover bread, I slice it up, throw it in a plastic bag, and put it in the freezer for toasts. Frozen bread slices are particularly good for making garlic toasts. The still-frozen bread acts like a piece of sandpaper when you rub the raw garlic across it.

Whole garlic cloves, peeled
Rustic bread, sliced $\frac{1}{2}$ to $\frac{3}{4}$ inch thick
Olive oil
Kosher salt and freshly ground black pepper

Grill method: Fire up your grill. Smash the garlic cloves with the side of your knife and rub a garlic clove over each slice of bread. Generously brush both sides of the slices with olive oil and season with salt and pepper. Grill the bread over direct heat with the lid off, until golden and crusty, about 1 minute per side.

Broiler method: Toast the prepared slices of bread under the broiler, turning once, until golden and toasted, a minute or two per side.

VARIATION: Another way to make garlic toast is to brush the bread with garlic oil. To make enough oil for 6 to 8 toasts, put 2 thinly sliced garlic cloves and ¼ cup olive oil in a small pan over medium heat. Heat the oil for a few minutes, just until the garlic bubbles, then remove from the heat and use the garlic oil to generously brush both sides of the bread slices before you grill or broil them.

WHOLE SALMON ON THE GRILL
STUFFED WITH SEA SALT, LEMON, AND ONION

MAKES 8 SERVINGS

Barbecuing a whole salmon on the grill is a Seattle tradition, especially when celebrating any significant event or holiday, from the Fourth of July to Christmas. Try cooking a whole fish once in a while; it's quicker and easier than you think. Jackie spends no more than ten minutes getting this salmon ready to go on the grill, then only about thirty minutes cooking it. Just wait until you carry this gorgeous, slightly charred, sizzling hot salmon to the table.

Some people don't like eating the salmon skin, but if you do want to eat it, be sure to remove the scales or ask your fishmonger to do it for you. A small sharp knife or a boning knife works well for scraping the scales off, though Jackie uses an Italian cheese knife.

Try to get a wild salmon for this recipe, rather than a farmed salmon, because a fish with a nice firm texture is best. A 3½- to 4-pound fish is the perfect size for grilling. You can grill the salmon with the head and tail on or ask your fishmonger to remove them. Instead of salmon, try substituting a steelhead, large trout, striped bass, or red snapper.

Sea salt
1 whole salmon, about 4 pounds, gutted, rinsed, and
    patted dry
½ medium onion, thinly sliced
½ lemon, thinly sliced
1 small bunch fennel fronds or fresh dill
All-purpose flour for dusting
Olive oil for brushing
Lemon wedges and fennel fronds or fresh dill for garnish
Sweet Fennel Butter, softened

A STEP AHEAD Stuff and tie the salmon early in the day and keep refrigerated.

Fire up the grill, with the coals lined up for direct heat about 5 to 6 inches below the fish. Sprinkle sea salt generously in the cavity of the fish and over the skin, then stuff the cavity with the onion, lemon, and fennel fronds. Tie kitchen string around the fish in three or four places to hold the stuffing in. In between the strings, make deep incisions with your knife through the thickest part of

the fish on both sides, all the way down to the spine, so the fish will cook more quickly and the smoke flavor will get inside the fish. Lightly dust one side of the fish with flour. Brush both the floured side of the fish and the grate with oil, then place the salmon on the grill, floured side down. Once the salmon is on the grill, lightly dust the other side of the fish with flour and brush it with oil.

Grill the salmon over medium-hot direct heat, with the lid on and the vents open. If your grill has a thermometer, maintain the heat at 300°F to 350°F. When the skin side facing the grill is nicely browned, after about 20 minutes, use two large grill spatulas to flip the fish to the other side. Slide your spatula under the fish in several places first, to help detach the skin from the grill. Then continue to grill until the fish is just cooked through and an instant-read thermometer inserted in the thickest part of the fish reads 125°F to 135°F, 10 to 20 minutes longer, for a total grilling time of 30 to 40 minutes. Remove the fish from the grill, place it on a large platter, cut off the string, and let rest for 10 minutes.

Garnish the salmon with lemon wedges and fennel fronds. Put the fennel butter in a small bowl and serve on the side.

If you like, peel off the skin so your guests can more easily help themselves to the salmon. Use a paring knife to make an incision at the head end of the fish, then peel off the skin. Sprinkle a little sea salt directly over the flesh of the fish. Use a metal serving spatula to lift each serving of salmon up off the backbone of the fish. When all the fish has been served from one side, flip the fish over and repeat with the other side.

SALMON SALAD SANDWICHES

If you have any leftovers from your whole grilled salmon, make salmon salad sandwiches the next day. Flake the leftover salmon, mix with some Ginger Mayonnaise (page 114), and serve between slices of toast or on split soft rolls. Tuck a few Bibb lettuce leaves into each sandwich.

SWEET FENNEL BUTTER

MAKES ABOUT 1 CUP

This soft butter will start melting as soon as it's spooned over a piece of warm salmon, creating a simple sauce.

$\frac{1}{2}$ pound (2 sticks) unsalted butter, softened

3 tablespoons chopped fresh fennel fronds or fresh dill

2 tablespoons freshly squeezed orange juice

2 teaspoons freshly grated orange zest

1 teaspoon honey

Kosher salt and freshly ground black pepper to taste

A STEP AHEAD You can make the butter up to 3 days ahead and store it, tightly wrapped, in the refrigerator. Bring it to room temperature a few hours before you plan to serve it.

Mix together the butter, fennel, orange juice, zest, and honey until smooth, either in a food processor, in an electric mixer, or by hand. Season to taste with salt and pepper. Scrape the butter into a decorative small bowl and serve.

HAZELNUT RICE SALAD WITH PARSLEY AND ARTICHOKES

MAKES 8 SERVINGS

Steven Steinbock, my co-worker for the last twenty-plus years, makes the perfect rice salad. The most important thing about this recipe is not to refrigerate the rice after it's cooked, or it will become chalky and pasty.

Basmati is a type of long-grain rice with a lovely fragrance. Other varieties of rice cook a little differently, so if you substitute another type of rice, the proportion of water to rice and the cooking time may vary.

2 cups basmati rice

Kosher salt and freshly ground black pepper

¼ cup champagne vinegar or other mild vinegar

½ cup olive oil

Artichoke Hearts Cooked in Court Bouillon

⅔ cup toasted and roughly chopped hazelnuts (see page 24)

½ cup chopped fresh flat-leaf parsley

½ cup pitted and chopped good-quality black olives, preferably oil-cured

¼ cup freshly grated Parmesan cheese

2 tablespoons freshly grated lemon zest

A STEP AHEAD Cook the rice an hour ahead and leave it at room temperature to cool. Make the vinaigrette and assemble all the other ingredients several hours ahead. Toss the salad shortly before serving.

Put the rice in a saucepan with 3 cups water and 1 teaspoon salt. Bring to a boil over high heat. Cover the pan and turn the heat down to very low. Cook for 20 minutes without removing the lid. The water should be absorbed and the rice should be just tender. Remove the pan from the heat, spread the cooked rice on a baking sheet, and let it cool to room temperature. When the rice is cool, scrape it into a large bowl.

In a small bowl, make the vinaigrette by whisking together the vinegar and oil and season to taste with salt and pepper. Pour the vinaigrette over the rice, then add the artichoke hearts, hazelnuts, parsley, olives, Parmesan, and lemon zest. Stir the salad with a rubber spatula until everything is well combined, then season to taste, with salt, pepper, and a little more vinegar if needed. Mound the salad on a large platter and serve.

ARTICHOKE HEARTS COOKED IN COURT BOUILLON

MAKES 1½ CUPS COOKED ARTICHOKE HEARTS (6 OUNCES)

Artichokes are tastiest when they're cooked in a court bouillon or flavorful broth. Baby artichokes are immature; they don't have a choke to remove, and they make beautiful hearts.

10 baby artichokes, about 1½ pounds

2 lemons

1 carrot, peeled and cut into rough chunks

1 medium onion, peeled and cut into rough chunks

1 cup dry white wine

½ teaspoon black peppercorns

A STEP AHEAD Cook the artichokes and trim them into quartered hearts up to 2 days ahead. Cover them with plastic wrap and store them in the refrigerator.

Using a sharp knife (a serrated knife works well), slice off and discard the top inch of the artichokes and place them in a large saucepan with enough cold water to cover. Cut one of the lemons in half and squeeze it into the water, then toss in the squeezed halves. Add the carrot, onion, wine, and peppercorns. To keep the artichokes submerged while they cook, put a piece of parchment or wax paper on the surface and weight it with a plate or small lid. Place the pan over high heat and bring to a boil. Reduce the heat to a simmer and continue to cook until the artichokes are tender and can be easily pierced with the tip of a paring knife, 10 to 15 minutes. Scoop them out of the water and allow to cool.

When the artichokes are cool enough to handle, pull off and discard all the outer leaves until you get to the tender, completely edible inner ones. With a paring knife, trim away any tough or discolored parts of the stem. Then cut each artichoke heart into quarters. Cut the other lemon in half and squeeze the juice over the artichokes as you work to keep them from discoloring.

HOW TO TOAST SEEDS AND NUTS

Toast seeds and nuts by placing them in a heavy skillet over medium heat for a few minutes until they are lightly browned and aromatic. Or place seeds or nuts on a baking sheet in a preheated 350°F to 375°F oven for 5 to 10 minutes. Sesame seeds and pine nuts brown quickly, while big nuts like pecan halves take a little longer. Stir the nuts or seeds occasionally and watch them carefully so they don't burn.

Hazelnuts have papery brown skins. After roasting hazelnuts, remove as much of the skins as you easily can by rubbing the still-warm nuts in a clean dish towel.

If you are chopping toasted nuts in a food processor, pulse on and off briefly, being careful not to turn them into a paste. Or just chop them with a sharp knife.

Nuts and seeds are high in oil and turn rancid quickly. I always store nuts and seeds in my freezer, in sealed plastic bags.

BUTTERNUT SQUASH GINGERBREAD

MAKES ONE 10-INCH CAKE, SERVING 10 TO 12

The thin wedges of squash that top this cake bake in a brown sugar and butter glaze until they're candied and almost translucent. Butternut squash has a thin skin that's easy to peel with a vegetable peeler. Or substitute peeled slices of sugar pumpkin, red kuri squash, or ripe pears for the butternut squash. If you use pears, there's no need to roast them first.

This gingerbread would also make a great Thanksgiving dessert.

FOR THE SQUASH TOPPING

1 medium butternut squash (about 2 pounds)

8 tablespoons (1 stick) unsalted butter, plus a little more for buttering the pans

1 cup firmly packed light brown sugar

½ cup coarsely chopped pecans

FOR THE CAKE BATTER

2½ cups all-purpose flour

2 teaspoons baking soda

1 teaspoon kosher salt

1 teaspoon ground cinnamon

¼ teaspoon freshly grated nutmeg

1 cup hot strong brewed coffee

½ cup molasses

2 teaspoons peeled and grated fresh ginger

2 large eggs

1 cup granulated sugar

½ pound (2 sticks) unsalted butter, melted and slightly cooled

Sweetened Whipped Cream (page 69)

A STEP AHEAD You can bake and unmold the cake early in the day and leave it at room temperature. Leftovers, if there are any, stay moist for a day or two, wrapped in plastic wrap.

Butter a 10-inch by 2-inch round cake pan and line the bottom with a circle of parchment paper. Preheat the oven to 375°F.

To prepare the squash topping, cut the peel from the squash, then cut the squash in half lengthwise and scrape out the seeds and fibers with a spoon. Slice the squash into wedges about ⅓ inch thick and place them on a lightly buttered baking sheet. Bake until tender when pierced with the tip of a knife, 20 to 25 minutes, turning the squash pieces over with a spatula halfway through the cooking time, then remove from the oven and set aside. Reduce the oven temperature to 350°F.

In a small saucepan over medium heat, melt the butter with the brown sugar, stirring until smooth. Pour the butter-sugar mixture evenly into the cake pan. Arrange the squash wedges in a decorative pattern (like the spokes of a wheel) over the bottom of the pan, trimming them to fit if necessary. You may have a few squash slices left over. Using your fingers, press down on the squash slices gently so you'll be able to see them through the sugar topping when the cake is unmolded. Sprinkle the pecans over the squash. Set the prepared cake pan aside.

To make the cake batter, mix together the flour, soda, salt, cinnamon, and nutmeg in a bowl. In another bowl, whisk together the coffee, molasses, and ginger. In a large bowl, lightly whisk together the eggs and granulated sugar, then whisk in the melted butter. To the egg-butter mixture, add the dry ingredients in two batches, alternating with the coffee mixture and beating with a wooden spoon or a rubber spatula until smooth. The batter will be thin. Pour the batter into the prepared pan. Place the cake pan on a baking sheet lined with foil to catch any brown sugar mixture that bubbles over as the cake bakes. Bake until a toothpick inserted in the center of the cake comes out clean, 50 to 60 minutes. If the cake is browning too quickly before it is done, cover it loosely with a piece of foil.

Remove the cake pan from the oven and let it cool on a rack for about 5 minutes. To unmold, run a thin knife around the cake to loosen it. Cover the cake pan with an inverted plate, then invert the whole thing. Remove the pan; the cake should slide right out onto the plate. Peel off the circle of parchment paper and replace any squash or pecans clinging to the paper. Cool the cake to room temperature before slicing. Slice the cake into wedges and serve with dollops of whipped cream.

A CHINESE FEAST

Like most other Chinatowns, Seattle's has become Pan-Asiatown, where Chinese restaurants and shops are joined by Vietnamese, Thai, Cambodian, and Malaysian establishments. Our International District (ID), which is what we call our Chinatown, is not one of the country's biggest, but it is substantial enough to have had an enormous influence on the cooking in our restaurants and, for that matter, home kitchens all over the Pacific Northwest. One of my favorite sensory experiences is to spend an hour wandering through our Asian market superstore, Uwajimaya.

My own Chinese cooking was profoundly influenced by the late Barbara Tropp, who owned the legendary China Moon in San Francisco. Both her restaurant (now closed) and her *China Moon Cookbook* gave me the confidence to take classic Asian food and put it into a non-Asian setting. Tropp's *The Modern Art of Chinese Cooking* remains my Chinese cooking bible.

Chinatown restaurants tend to become magnets for chefs and restaurant workers both in Seattle and other cities around the country because they serve fresh, intensely flavored food, they're usually cheap, and they tend to be open late. For a chef, that's the food trifecta. There's something so elemental about the Asian approach to cooking and food that just blows me away. When I want something quick for my family, it's hard to beat the barbecued duck and pork loins at King's.

Although I've made my share of solo forays to the ID for some barbecue and a stir-fried dish or two after work, I usually think of Chinese food in the context of a big, noisy, extended family dinner. Ours usually start by taking Loretta and a friend or two on a Chinatown shopping expedition and then coming back to our house and putting everyone to work cleaning, chopping, and prepping. Actually these forays almost always begin with a visit to one of Seattle's dim sum restaurants, where the steaming noi mai gai and the sticky lo bac oh are family favorites.

MENU

STAR ANISE VODKA DRAGONS

SWEET AND HOT FRIED ALMONDS

CRISPY SHRIMP ROLLS WITH SWEET CHILE SAUCE

WOK-FRIED CLAMS WITH CHINESE BLACK BEANS

SHIITAKE PEANUT NOODLES

STICKY-FINGER RIBS

FIVE-SPICE ROAST CHICKEN

BABY BOK CHOY WITH GARLIC OIL

AROMATIC STEAMED RICE

TSING TAO OR SLIGHTLY CHILLED BEAUJOLAIS FROM KERMIT LYNCH

MANGO SORBET

COCONUT MACAROONS

STAR ANISE VODKA DRAGONS

MAKES 2 SERVINGS

It can be a challenge to match dry wine with Chinese food, but the slight sweetness in many cocktails makes them perfect companions for spicy food.

The little star anise dragon in this cocktail—a long strip of orange zest tied around a whole star anise—is an exotic garnish. Use a channel knife (see page 263) to pull long narrow strips of zest from your orange.

Sambal oelek (see page 264), a Southeast Asian condiment of pureed red chiles, is an unusual addition to a cocktail. The tiny fragments of red chile float in the icy glass, and the small amount adds only a touch of heat.

We've tried this cocktail with more expensive orange liqueurs, but Triple Sec tastes best.

2 thin strips orange zest, about 4 inches long

2 star anise

2 small lime wedges (¼ lime)

½ cup lemon vodka

2 tablespoons Triple Sec

2 drops sambal oelek (less than 1/16 teaspoon)

Chill 2 martini glasses.

Rub the rims of the glasses with the strips of orange zest, then tie the zest around the star anise, leaving a long tail. Drop the "dragons" into the glasses.

Put the lime wedges in a cocktail shaker and muddle them with a bar stick. Add enough crushed ice or broken-up ice cubes to fill the shaker halfway. Add the vodka, Triple Sec, and sambal oelek. Shake, then strain into the chilled martini glasses and serve.

SWEET AND HOT FRIED ALMONDS

MAKES 1½ CUPS

The Chinese-style recipes for glazed, fried, and spiced nuts in Barbara Tropp's cookbooks inspired me to come up with these caramel-glazed almonds. They are nice and crisp with a sweet, salty, and spicy taste. I prefer the mahogany color of almonds with the skins on, and the skins help the caramel adhere.

It's important to have your pan hot enough to caramelize sugar, but not too hot or the sugar will burn as soon as it hits the pan. Use a heavy sauté pan, but not nonstick. You'll need a pan large enough (12 inch is perfect) for the almonds to spread out in a single layer. The caramelized sugar and sugar-coated nuts are extremely hot, so be careful.

A restaurant tip: To clean hardened caramel out of a pan, add some water and boil for several minutes. Allow the pan to cool, then pour out the water and wash the pan as usual.

1½ cups whole almonds, skin on
6 tablespoons sugar
2 teaspoons kosher salt
1 teaspoon cayenne pepper

A STEP AHEAD The almonds can be stored in an airtight container at room temperature for at least 3 days.

Line a baking sheet with parchment paper or foil and place it near the stove. Place measured ingredients near the stove, once the sugar starts to caramelize, the whole process will take only about 3 minutes.

Heat a large heavy sauté pan over medium-high heat for a few minutes until the pan seems hot, but not smoking-hot. You should feel some heat when you hold your hand a few inches above the bottom of the pan. Add the almonds and shake for a minute or two, until the nuts are slightly warm to the touch. Sprinkle about 1 tablespoon of the sugar into the pan, trying to get some of the sugar in the empty spaces between the nuts, where it will caramelize more quickly on the surface of the pan. Watch carefully until the sugar melts and begins to turn golden brown, then gradually start adding more sugar, a tablespoon or two at a time, shaking the pan occasionally to keep the nuts evenly coated. Use a long-handled spoon if you're more comfortable stirring the nuts than shaking the pan. A few nuts will stick to the spoon, but you can pull them off when they cool. Work quickly and be careful not to burn the sugar; lower the heat or raise the pan off the burner for a moment if you need to. When all the sugar has been caramelized, add the salt and shake or stir the nuts.

Remove the pan from the heat and shake or stir in the cayenne, averting your face from the spicy fumes, Pour the nuts onto the prepared baking sheet. Allow the nuts to cool, then pull apart any clumps of nuts that are stuck together. You can also pull off any nuts that are stuck to the spoon, if you used one, after they cool. Don't touch or taste the nuts until they're completely cool. Pile the cooled nuts into a colorful bowl to serve.

CRISPY SHRIMP ROLLS WITH SWEET CHILE SAUCE

MAKES ABOUT 18 SMALL SPRING ROLLS, SERVING 6 TO 8

Make and freeze these shrimp-stuffed fried spring rolls well ahead, but don't fry them until your guests arrive.

Keep the spring roll wrappers (see page 265) covered with a damp kitchen towel as you work to prevent them from drying out. If your wrappers are bigger than 6 inches square, you can cut them down to size, using a ruler and a sharp knife to cut through the entire (unwrapped) stack at once.

1 pound raw shrimp, peeled and deveined (see following page)
2 tablespoons finely chopped fresh cilantro
2 tablespoons finely chopped scallion, both white and green parts
1 tablespoon Chinese chile garlic sauce
1 tablespoon toasted sesame seeds (see page 24)
2 teaspoons peeled and grated fresh ginger
1 teaspoon minced garlic
¾ teaspoon kosher salt
1 large egg
18 to 20 spring roll wrappers, 6 inches square
Cornstarch for dusting
Peanut or vegetable oil for frying
Sweet Chile Sauce

A STEP AHEAD Form the spring rolls up to 4 hours ahead. Line them up, without touching each other, on a wax paper–lined baking sheet dusted lightly with cornstarch, cover them with plastic wrap, and keep them refrigerated.

Or form them up to a few weeks ahead and freeze them. Line them up on baking sheets as described and place them, uncovered, in the freezer. When they are frozen solid, remove them from the baking sheet, seal in a plastic bag, and store in the freezer.

Fry the spring rolls when you are ready to serve them. If they are frozen, fry them directly from the freezer, without thawing them. Frozen spring rolls will take about 5 minutes to fry.

Place the shrimp in the bowl of a food processor and process by pulsing a few times until very coarsely pureed. There should still be some chunks of shrimp. If the shrimp is wet, it is important to squeeze out as much liquid as possible before pureeing. In a bowl, combine the shrimp, cilantro, scallion, chile garlic sauce, sesame seeds, ginger, garlic, and salt. Mix thoroughly.

To make an egg wash, beat the egg with 1 teaspoon water. Set aside.

Place a spring roll wrapper diagonally on your work surface. Place about 1 tablespoon of filling, formed into a 3½-inch log, slightly below the center of the wrapper, leaving a 1-inch border without filling on either side of the log. Use a pastry brush to paint the two upper sides of the wrapper with egg wash. Pull the bottom point of the wrapper up over the filling, roll once, then fold in the sides, continue rolling, and seal. Repeat this procedure with the remaining wrappers and filling. Place the finished spring rolls, without touching each other, on a baking sheet lined with wax paper dusted lightly with cornstarch. Cover the spring rolls with plastic wrap as you are working so they don't dry out.

Preheat the oven to 200°F. Fill a straight-sided pot with at least 1½ inches of oil and heat to 350°F, checking with a frying thermometer (see page 14). Fry the spring rolls in small batches until golden, about 3 minutes, rolling them over occasionally with a skimmer or slotted spoon so they brown evenly. Remove them from the oil and drain on paper towels. Keep the spring rolls warm in the oven until all are fried.

Pile the spring rolls on a platter and serve hot with small ramekins of Sweet Chile Sauce.

HOW TO DEVEIN SHRIMP AND PRAWNS

To devein a shrimp or prawn, first remove the shell, then pass the tip of a sharp knife along the back and remove and discard the dark vein, which is actually the digestive tract.

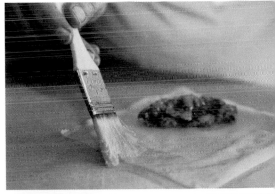

SWEET CHILE SAUCE

MAKES 1 CUP

A red jalapeño is the ripe version of a green jalapeño pepper. We like the red color here, but if you can find only a green jalapeño, use it instead. Wash your hands immediately after working with hot chile peppers or wear rubber or disposable gloves. Be especially careful not to touch your eyes after handling hot chiles.

Sambal oelek is an Indonesian condiment of ground fresh chiles (see page 264).

½ cup sugar

¼ cup freshly squeezed lime juice

3 tablespoons peeled, seeded, and finely diced cucumber

1 tablespoon plus 1 teaspoon seeded and minced red jalapeño pepper

1½ teaspoons sambal oelek

Kosher salt

A STEP AHEAD Make the sauce up to 1 day ahead and keep it covered and refrigerated, but don't add the cucumber until right before you plan to serve it.

Combine the sugar and ½ cup water in a small saucepan over high heat. Bring to a boil and cook, stirring, until the sugar is dissolved. Remove from the heat, pour into a small bowl, and cool. Stir in the lime juice, cucumber, jalapeño, and sambal oelek and season to taste with salt.

WOK-FRIED CLAMS WITH CHINESE BLACK BEANS

MAKES 6 TO 8 SERVINGS AS PART OF A MULTICOURSE FEAST

A hot wok full of gingery, aromatic clams in a glossy, bubbling sauce says Chinatown to me. Wok cooking is a last-minute task, but if you make the black bean sauce ahead, this dish can be finished in less than 10 minutes.

FOR THE BLACK BEAN SAUCE

1 tablespoon plus 2 teaspoons peanut or vegetable oil

1 medium red bell pepper, cut into 1-inch squares

1 teaspoon minced garlic

2 teaspoons peeled and grated fresh ginger

2 tablespoons Chinese fermented black beans, coarsely
   chopped

1/3 cup Chinese rice wine (Shaoxing) or dry sherry

1/4 cup soy sauce

1 tablespoon Chinese chile garlic sauce

2 teaspoons sugar

1 tablespoon cornstarch dissolved in 2 tablespoons cold water

FOR THE CLAMS

1 tablespoon peanut or vegetable oil

2½ pounds small steamer clams, scrubbed and rinsed

4 scallions, root ends and tough green ends trimmed, split in
   half lengthwise, and cut into 2-inch lengths

A STEP AHEAD Make the black bean sauce up to a day ahead and store, covered, in the refrigerator. Allow the sauce to come to room temperature before using.

To make the black bean sauce, heat 1 tablespoon of the oil in a sauté pan over high heat. Add the bell pepper and sear until wilted and slightly blackened in a few places, about 2 minutes. Remove the pan from the heat and, using a tongs or a slotted spoon, transfer the pepper to a bowl. Return the pan to medium-high heat and add the remaining 2 teaspoons oil. Add the garlic, ginger, and black beans and sauté, stirring, for a few minutes. Add the rice wine, soy sauce, chile garlic sauce, and sugar and bring to a boil for 1 minute. Add the dissolved cornstarch and simmer, stirring, until

the sauce thickens, about 1 minute. Remove from the heat. The sauce will be very thick at this point, but the clam juices will thin it. Scrape the sauce into the bowl with the bell pepper and set aside.

For the clams, put the oil in a wok or large pot and set it over high heat. When the oil is hot, add the clams, cover the wok with a lid, and cook over high heat, shaking the wok occasionally, just until the clams open, about 4 minutes.

As soon as the clams open, remove the wok from the heat. Holding the lid over the wok to keep the clams back, pour as much of the clam juice as you can into a large heatproof measuring cup. Reserve ½ cup of the clam juice and discard the rest. Return the wok to high heat and add the ½ cup clam juice, the black bean sauce, and the scallions. Cook, uncovered, shaking the wok or stirring with a rubber spatula to distribute the sauce evenly, just until the sauce bubbles and thickens, about 2 minutes. Pour the clams into a large shallow bowl and serve.

NOTE: If you're not making the Chinese feast, this recipe makes about 4 servings.

SHIITAKE PEANUT NOODLES

MAKES 6 SERVINGS AS PART OF A MULTICOURSE FEAST

I've been serving spicy peanut noodles at my restaurants for more than twenty years. The first time I tasted this dish wasn't in a Chinese restaurant. My good friend Debbie Gertz served it at an informal dinner party. This was typical of the way I was introduced to all kinds of foods, whenever friends experimented with a hot new cookbook or tried to re-create an interesting restaurant experience. In Seattle, Henry at the Tsue Chong Noodle Factory in the International District makes my favorite "Rose Brand" flat-cut lo mein noodles.

FOR THE PEANUT DRESSING

¼ cup smooth peanut butter

3 tablespoons water

3 tablespoons soy sauce

¼ cup tahini

2 tablespoons peanut or vegetable oil

2 tablespoons dark sesame oil

⅓ cup rice wine vinegar

2 tablespoons dry sherry

3 tablespoons honey

2 teaspoons chopped garlic

2 teaspoons peeled and grated ginger

½ teaspoon hot red pepper flakes

Kosher salt

FOR THE NOODLES

¾ pound Chinese wheat noodles

5 tablespoons peanut or vegetable oil

1 pound shiitake mushrooms, stems removed, caps wiped with a damp towel and left whole or cut in half if large

¾ cup fresh mung bean sprouts

¼ cup chopped roasted peanuts

¼ cup fresh cilantro leaves

A STEP AHEAD Make the peanut dressing up to a week ahead and store, covered, in the refrigerator. The noodles can be cooked early in the day, chilled, and stored, covered, in the refrigerator. The mushrooms can be roasted a few hours ahead and left at room temperature.

To make the peanut dressing, put the peanut butter in a bowl and, using a whisk, add the rest of the dressing ingredients in the order given, whisking well after each addition and seasoning with salt to taste. Set aside.

Bring a large pot of salted water to a boil. Cook the noodles, stirring occasionally, until soft, 4 to 5 minutes. Drain in a colander and rinse under cold water. Drain well. Toss the noodles with 1 tablespoon of the peanut oil to prevent them from sticking together and chill.

To roast the shiitakes, preheat the oven to 450°F. Put the mushrooms in a bowl, toss them with the remaining ¼ cup oil, and season with salt to taste. Spread the mushrooms in a single layer on a baking sheet. Roast in the oven until the mushrooms are cooked through and the edges are crisp and golden, about 25 minutes. Remove from the oven and set aside.

When you are ready to serve, place the cooked and chilled noodles in a large bowl and toss with the peanut dressing, then mound the dressed noodles onto a large platter. Scatter the bean sprouts over the noodles. Remove the shiitakes, either warm or room temperature, from the baking sheet (use a spatula if they stick to the pan) and arrange them over the noodles. Garnish with the peanuts and cilantro.

NOTE: If you're not making the Chinese feast, this recipe makes about 4 servings.

STICKY-FINGER RIBS

MAKES 6 SERVINGS AS PART OF A MULTICOURSE FEAST

These ribs have a sweet, sticky glaze and a deep, complex flavor. If possible, coat the ribs with the spice rub the day before you plan to cook them, but if you don't have time you can rub the ribs and cook them right away.

If you prefer, instead of broiling, finish the ribs on the grill over medium heat, brushing them with the glaze.

2 racks pork baby back ribs (about 2 pounds each)

FOR THE SPICE RUB
4 star anise, ground (see page 63)
1 tablespoon plus 1 teaspoon kosher salt
2 teaspoons freshly ground black pepper

¾ cup sake

FOR THE STICKY GLAZE
1 tablespoon peanut or vegetable oil
2 tablespoons minced garlic
2 teaspoons peeled and grated fresh ginger
⅔ cup honey
½ cup rice wine vinegar
¼ cup soy sauce
1 tablespoon Chinese chile garlic sauce

FOR GARNISHING THE RIBS
1 tablespoon toasted sesame seeds (see page 24)
2 tablespoons thinly sliced scallions, both white and green
   parts

A STEP AHEAD The dry rub and the sticky glaze can be prepared a few days ahead. Store the dry rub at room temperature and the glaze in the refrigerator. Reheat the glaze to thin it before brushing it on the ribs, or you can stir in a tablespoon or so of water to thin the glaze.

You can roast the ribs early in the day and keep them in the refrigerator until you are ready to glaze them.

You can glaze the ribs, cut them up, and keep them warm, loosely covered with a piece of foil, for about 20 minutes in a low oven (200°F) while you finish the rest of the dishes for this meal.

HOW TO REMOVE THE TOUGH MEMBRANE FROM THE RIBS

Place a rack of pork baby back ribs, bony side up, on a cutting board. Unless your butcher has already removed it, there will be a thin, tough, translucent membrane covering the bony side of the ribs. With a sharp knife, cut a slit through the membrane straight across the middle of the rack. Probing with the tip of a small knife or the stem end of an instant-read thermometer, find a place where you can loosen the membrane and slip your fingers under the slit, then pull the membrane off the bones. Repeat, pulling the membrane off from the other side of the slit.

A rack of spareribs has a similar membrane, which you remove in the same way, though it's a bit tougher to pull off. You may want to use the tip of a clean screwdriver to probe under the membrane and grab onto the membrane with a kitchen towel as you pull hard. It helps to have strong hands.

Remove the excess fat and the tough membrane from the backs of the ribs.

To make the dry rub, combine the star anise, salt, and pepper in a small bowl. Pat the dry rub all over both sides of the ribs. If you have time, allow the ribs to rest for 4 hours or overnight, refrigerated.

When you are ready to cook the ribs, preheat the oven to 325°F. Place the ribs, meaty sides up, on a rack in a roasting pan. Pour the sake into the pan and cover the pan with foil. Roast the ribs in the oven until the meat is tender and is starting to pull away from the bones, 1¼ to 1½ hours. Remove the ribs from the oven.

To make the glaze, heat the oil in a heavy saucepan over medium-high heat. Add the garlic and ginger and sauté, stirring occasionally, until the garlic starts to turn golden. Watch carefully so the garlic doesn't burn. Stir in the honey, rice wine vinegar, soy sauce, and chile garlic sauce and bring to a boil. Continue to boil the mixture until reduced and syrupy, about 10 minutes. You should have ¾ cup glaze. Remove the glaze from the heat and allow to cool to room temperature.

To finish the ribs, turn the broiler to high. Place the ribs, bony sides up, on a broiler pan lined with foil and brush with the glaze. Broil about 3 inches from the heat, rotating the pan once or twice, until the glaze is bubbling and browned, 2 to 3 minutes. Remove the pan from the broiler and turn the ribs meaty sides up, brushing with the glaze. Return the ribs to the broiler and continue to broil, rotating the pan as needed and brushing with the glaze another time or two until all the glaze is used. Broil until the meaty sides of the ribs are browned and caramelized, about 4 minutes. Watch carefully so the glaze doesn't burn.

Transfer the ribs to a cutting board and use a knife to cut between the bones. Pile the ribs on a platter. If there are any juices in the broiler pan, pour them over the top. Sprinkle with the sesame seeds and green onions.

NOTE: If you're not making the Chinese feast, this recipe makes 3 to 4 servings.

FIVE-SPICE ROAST CHICKEN

MAKES 6 SERVINGS AS PART OF A MULTICOURSE FEAST

Try this aromatic spice paste on other poultry, such as Cornish game hens. At the Dahlia Lounge we rub the paste on ducks, then cook them on a rotisserie over an applewood fire.

Buy your spices whole and grind them yourself in an electric coffee bean grinder set aside exclusively for that purpose. You can purchase cardamom as whole pods, hulled seeds, or ground. If you buy pods, crush them with the side of a knife, peel away and discard the pods, and remove the seeds, discarding the membrane. If using ground cardamom, stir it into the spice paste after the spices are ground.

For the best flavor, rub the spice paste on the chicken and refrigerate overnight before roasting.

FOR THE FIVE-SPICE PASTE

3 star anise

½ dried chipotle chile, or other dried hot chile such as chile arbol or pequin, stem and seeds removed

½ cinnamon stick, broken up into ½-inch pieces

2 teaspoons fennel seeds

¼ teaspoon whole cloves

¼ teaspoon hulled cardamom seeds

1 tablespoon peeled and grated fresh ginger

1 tablespoon minced garlic

¼ cup firmly packed light brown sugar

1 tablespoon kosher salt

1 teaspoon freshly ground black pepper

3 tablespoons peanut or vegetable oil

FOR THE CHICKEN

1 whole chicken, 3 to 3½ pounds, wing tips trimmed

¼ orange, cut into wedges, plus extra orange wedges for garnish

3 star anise

Kosher salt

2 tablespoons unsalted butter or bacon fat, melted

A STEP AHEAD Make the spice paste a few days ahead and keep it covered and refrigerated. After the chicken is roasted and carved, place the pieces in a pan, loosely covered with a piece of foil, and keep them warm in a low (200°F) oven for 15 to 20 minutes.

To make the five-spice paste, put the star anise, chile, cinnamon, fennel, cloves, and cardamom in a small pan over medium heat and toast for a few minutes until aromatic, shaking the pan. Let cool, then grind the toasted spices in a spice mill or clean coffee grinder. Transfer the ground spices to a small bowl. Add the ginger, garlic, brown sugar, salt, and pepper. Gradually add the oil,

stirring with a wooden spoon or rubber spatula to make a smooth paste. Trim the excess fat from the chicken and clean out the cavity. Rinse under cold water and pat dry. Use your hands to rub the spice paste all over the skin of the chicken. Set the chicken on a rack over a baking pan and place it, uncovered, in the refrigerator overnight.

The next day, preheat the oven to 425°F. Put the ¼ orange and star anise in the cavity of the chicken, season the bird with kosher salt, and place it on a rack in a roasting pan. For easier cleanup, line the roasting pan with foil because the spice paste that drips off may burn. Using a bulb baster instead of a brush, so you don't disturb the spice crust, baste the chicken with the melted butter or bacon fat and put the bird in the oven to roast. Baste the chicken with the fat collecting in the bottom of the pan every 20 minutes. The chicken is done when an instant-read meat thermometer inserted in the thickest part of the thigh reads 175°F and the juices run clear, about 1¼ hours. Remove the chicken from the oven and allow to rest for 5 to 10 minutes before carving.

To carve the chicken, cut off the legs and separate into leg and thigh. Using a knife or poultry shears, cut out the backbone, then separate the breasts by cutting through the breastbone. Cut off the wings, then cut each breast into 2 pieces. You should have 10 pieces: 2 legs, 2 thighs, 4 pieces of breast, and 2 wings. Pile the chicken pieces on a large platter and garnish with orange wedges

NOTE: This recipe would make about 4 servings if you're not making the Chinese feast.

OUR FAVORITE CHINESE FOOD WINES

When you serve a Chinese meal, there tends to be plenty of variety and flavors on the table, meaning you can't match a single wine to a single course. Try to avoid any pungent or overoaked wines, and you certainly don't want to waste intricate wines like first growths or expensive Barbarescos or Cabernets.

My rule of thumb for matching Western-style wines to Chinese food is to choose fruity wines that can complement many flavors, such as Spanish Albariño, German Riesling, or Alsatian Pinot Blanc. If I'm in the mood for Sauvignon Blanc, I serve a fruity type, like a Washington Sauvignon Blanc, rather than a steely version from New Zealand or the Loire Valley. Use the same rule with red wine and pour a fruity Beaujolais, a Nouveau style Zinfandel, or a Grenache-based Côtes-du-Rhône—something fresh tasting, not heavy like a Syrah.

BABY BOK CHOY WITH GARLIC OIL

MAKES 6 SERVINGS

The orange and ginger in the steaming water add a subtle fragrance to the bok choy. The smaller your bok choy, the more quickly and evenly it will steam. I use an inexpensive bamboo steamer.

½ orange, cut into wedges

4 unpeeled fresh ginger coins

1½ pounds baby bok choy, sliced in half or quarters if large, left whole if very small

3 tablespoons vegetable or peanut oil

3 garlic cloves, thinly sliced

1 tablespoon soy sauce

Set up your steamer, such as a large saucepan or wok with a Chinese bamboo steamer set over it. Put 2 cups water, the orange, and the ginger in the bottom of the steamer and bring to a boil over high heat. Put the bok choy in the steamer basket, cover, and steam until tender, 6 to 8 minutes.

A minute or two before the bok choy is tender, heat the oil in a sauté pan over medium-high heat. When the oil is hot, add the garlic and toast until light golden brown. Remove from the heat.

Arrange the bok choy on a platter, cut sides up. Drizzle first with the hot garlic oil, then with the soy sauce.

HOW TO MAKE GINGER COINS

Ginger coins add subtle flavor to a dish instead of the potent kick of grated ginger. Peel a knob of fresh ginger and cut it crosswise into slices ⅛ to ¼ inch thick. If you are using ginger coins in a marinade or a stock, or in any dish where the ginger is discarded before serving, it's not necessary to peel the ginger.

AROMATIC STEAMED RICE

MAKES 6 SERVINGS

A Chinese meal is not complete without rice, and this is my favorite steamed rice recipe. An electric rice cooker will cook rice perfectly, keep it warm, and doesn't require any attention on your part. Some people think rice cookers are an unnecessary appliance, but I like them so much I even bought my mom one for Christmas. If you buy one, get the kind with a nonstick interior.

2 cups Japanese short-grain rice

1 stalk lemon grass

3 unpeeled fresh ginger coins (see page 46)

3 star anise

Zest from 1 orange, cut into large strips with a vegetable peeler

A STEP AHEAD Assemble the cheesecloth bundle early in the day.

Place the raw rice in a fine-mesh strainer and rinse under cold running water until the water runs clear. Combine the rice and 2½ cups cold water in a saucepan. Smash the stalk of lemon grass with the back of a knife to release the aromatics and then slice thinly. Wrap the lemon grass, ginger coins, star anise pods, and orange zest in a small piece of cheesecloth and tie up the bundle with a piece of kitchen twine. Add the cheesecloth bundle to the pot of rice and bring to a boil. Reduce the heat to a simmer, cover the pot, and cook gently until all the water is absorbed, about 20 minutes. Turn off the heat and leave the lid on for 5 minutes to fluff the rice. Discard the cheesecloth bundle, mound the rice in a serving bowl, and serve hot.

NOTE: If you cook the rice in a rice cooker instead of a saucepan, you won't need as much water. Check the manufacturer's instructions for the best ratio of water to rice.

MANGO SORBET

MAKES ABOUT 1 QUART, SERVING 6 TO 8

Sweet, ripe, fragrant mangoes make an exquisite sorbet.

1 cup sugar

4 ripe mangoes (about 2½ pounds), peeled, pitted, and coarsely chopped

3 tablespoons freshly squeezed lime juice

Coconut Macaroons

A STEP AHEAD Store the sorbet in a tightly covered container in the freezer for about 5 days. If the sorbet gets too hard to scoop, leave the container out at room temperature for 10 to 15 minutes to soften before serving.

Combine the sugar and 1 cup water in a saucepan over high heat, bring to a boil, and stir occasionally until the sugar is dissolved. Remove from the heat and allow the simple syrup to cool.

Put the mango in the bowl of a food processor and puree as smooth as possible or pass the mango through a food mill. Pour the mango puree into a bowl and stir in the simple syrup and the lime juice. Chill the mixture completely, then freeze in an ice cream machine following the manufacturer's directions. Transfer the sorbet to a container, cover, and freeze for several hours or overnight until firm.

Put a scoop of sorbet into each of 6 colorful small dishes or Chinese-style ramekins and serve with a platter of macaroons.

COCONUT MACAROONS

MAKES ABOUT 20 COOKIES

If you're smart, you'll double this recipe, because once you taste them you'll want more.

2 large egg whites
Pinch of kosher salt
⅔ cup sugar
2 tablespoons all-purpose flour
1 teaspoon pure vanilla extract
2¼ cups sweetened shredded coconut

A STEP AHEAD The macaroons will stay fresh in an airtight container at room temperature for 1 day.

In the bowl of an electric mixer using the whisk attachment, or with a handheld electric mixer, combine the egg whites and the salt and whip to stiff peaks at high speed. Gradually add the sugar and continue to whisk for a few more minutes at high speed until the meringue is smooth and glossy and will form soft mounds. Add the flour and vanilla and whip briefly at medium speed until combined. Remove the bowl from the mixer and fold in the coconut with a rubber spatula. Cover the batter with plastic wrap and chill in the refrigerator at least 4 hours or overnight.

Preheat the oven to 325°F. Line a baking sheet with parchment paper, then spray the paper with vegetable oil spray, because this batter is quite sticky. (Or you can use a flexible nonstick baking sheet, such as Silpat, and you won't need to spray it.) Drop mounds of the batter, about 1 tablespoon each and about 2 inches apart, onto the baking sheet. A 1-ounce ice cream scoop works perfectly for this, or you can use a spoon, but keep the batter mounded up; don't flatten the cookies. Bake until the cookies are evenly light golden brown, about 25 minutes. Remove from the oven and allow the cookies to cool on the baking sheet before removing them with a metal spatula. Pile the cookies on an attractive platter to serve.

PIKE PLACE
MARKET MENU

For Jackie and me, the Pike Place Market is much more than just a market in the heart of Seattle. Pike Place Market has shaped our lives in more ways than we can count. I first became known in Seattle cooking at Café Sport, a restaurant on the northern edge of the market, in 1980. In 1995 we purchased the old Sport and created our second restaurant, Etta's Seafood, named after our daughter, Loretta. As a homesick young chef from Delaware trying to make his mark in the Pacific Northwest, I often took comfort from eating one of the all-time great Mid-Atlantic comfort foods, scrapple, which I miraculously found in the market at the Athenian Inn. Jackie and I met in the market while she was working at the Pike and Western Wine Shop owned by our friend Mike Teer. We spent many an evening courting in some of Seattle's most romantic restaurants: eating coq au vin at Chez Shea or slurping through bowls of steaming hot Penn Cove mussels at the cozy Place Pigalle. Many times the romantic spell would continue as we walked down Post Alley, its medieval ambience making us feel like we were somewhere in Italy or France. When we married, the perfect spot for a reception was the Pink Door, a quirky Italian café, where we must have had a hundred lunch dates over our favorite pasta and broccoli soup drizzled with extra virgin olive oil and dusted with mounds of Parmigiano Reggiano.

Although the market has undergone many changes in its ninety-five years of existence, it remains, in many ways, the epicenter of Seattle street life. Keeping the market growing and prosperous often seems to get bogged down in politics. But when you spend Sunday morning at Organic Day, a day of the week when local organic farmers have their own special area of the market, you feel all the trouble is worth it.

Special moments here last a lifetime. Like the August Sunset Supper, when the three-block-long cobbled street turns into

MENU

NEGRONI

GARLIC GREENS ON TOAST

CHILLED TOMATO SOUP WITH CUCUMBER BUTTERMILK PANNA COTTA AND BASIL OIL

L'ECOLE SEMILLON, WASHINGTON

FRESH CORN CRÊPES WITH GOAT CHEESE AND ROASTED PEPPERS, ANCHO CHILE SAUCE, AVOCADO-TOMATILLO SALSA, AND FRESH CORN SALSA

ARGYLE PINOT NOIR, OREGON

PEACH CARAMEL UPSIDE-DOWN CAKES

KIONA LATE HARVEST RIESLING

one fabulous banquet table, bursting with foods from thirty different restaurants. Another is our traditional Wednesday-before-Thanksgiving stroll. Jackie, Loretta, and I work our way from one end of the market to the other, snacking, tasting, and buying—picking out the best and the ripest for our turkey day feast.

I tell visitors that the best way to get a feel for Seattle is to stay at the Inn at the Market. Get up early to "wake up with the market" and watch the whole city come alive. The truck farmers unloading onto the low stalls. The buskers jockeying for the best spot to sing from the heart and collect from the appreciative. The market workers yelling jokes and insults to each other across the street as if they owned the place . . . and they do. As the day vendors shutter down, the nightlife begins to swell and a whole new vibe fills the air. Handsome couples scurry from bar to restaurant and back. Ninety kitchen exhaust hoods fog the air with cooking aromas from Morocco to Russia to good old Seattle.

Though the Pike Place Market is no longer the only place to shop in Seattle for a big dinner, it remains our favorite. Make a day of it, or hell, make a lifetime of it, as we have.

HOW TO SHOP THE PIKE PLACE MARKET FOR A PICNIC IN YOUR HOTEL ROOM

❖ Hard smoked salmon from Pike Place Fish or Pure Food Fish Market. Learn to love kippered salmon again; forget about lox.

❖ Acorn-fed jamon from The Spanish Table. While you're there, also pick up a little wedge of Cabrales or Manchego cheese and maybe some boquerones, Spanish anchovies that are pickled in tubs, not canned.

❖ Pâté fromage blanc, and roasted peppers from DeLaurenti's. Also pick up a package of La Panzanella's flat rosemary crackers.

❖ A jar of delicious, locally grown pickled asparagus, green beans, or carrots from the Made in Washington store.

❖ Have Michael Teer from Pike and Western Wine Shop help you pick out both a red and a white bottle of Washington wine. He even sells cheap corkscrews.

❖ A couple of perfect oh-so-French baguettes and some friand cookies for dessert from Le Panier. Don't forget to stop at the Pike Place Market Creamery for some French butter.

❖ Keep an eye open for a bouquet of fresh flowers from the low stalls in the market, while grabbing some creamy, ripe pears and crisp apples from one of the many produce stands.

❖ Stop at Sur La Table for keepsake napkins and a tablecloth to spread on the bed. Take them home with you so you'll always remember your fabulous Pike Place Market picnic.

❖ Pick up a bag of Holmquist hazelnuts from the low stalls to snack on as you carry your market picnic back to the hotel.

NEGRONI

This icy, bittersweet, ruby-red cocktail is the perfect companion to a crisp toast topped with savory, garlic-scented greens. Certain cocktails are best when made in small quantities.

2 narrow strips lemon zest, about 2 inches long

2 ounces gin

2 ounces Campari

2 ounces sweet vermouth

Chill 2 martini glasses by placing them in the freezer for several minutes. Rub the rims with the strips of lemon zest, then drop the zest into the glasses. Pour the gin, Campari, and vermouth into a cocktail shaker half-filled with ice cubes. Shake, then strain into the chilled martini glasses and serve.

GARLIC GREENS ON TOAST

MAKES 6 SERVINGS

There are many of varieties of kale, such as Lacinato and Red Russian, in a range of colors from deep blue-green to purple-red, some with frilly or crinkled leaves and others with flat leaves. Substitute chard, mustard, or beet greens, although the blanching time will vary.

Garnish the toasts with thin shavings of Parmesan cheese. Use a vegetable peeler to shave the cheese.

1 pound kale

½ cup dry sherry

¼ cup golden raisins

¼ cup extra virgin olive oil, plus a little more for drizzling

½ cup finely chopped onion

1 tablespoon minced garlic

3 anchovies, chopped

⅓ cup freshly squeezed orange juice

1 teaspoon freshly grated orange zest

½ to 1 teaspoon hot red pepper flakes, to taste

Kosher salt and freshly ground black pepper

12 toasts (see following page)

¼ cup shaved Parmesan cheese

A STEP AHEAD You can blanch, shock, squeeze, and chop the greens a few days ahead. Store in the refrigerator, covered with plastic wrap. Do the final cooking a few hours ahead and leave the greens at room temperature until you're ready to serve them.

Stem and wash the kale, shaking off excess water. In a large pot of boiling salted water, cook the kale until tender, 5 to 10 minutes. Drain the kale, then plunge it into a large bowl of ice water. Drain again and, using your hands, squeeze most of the water out. The greens don't need to be completely dry. Roughly chop the kale and set aside.

In a small saucepan, combine the sherry and the raisins over medium heat. Bring to a simmer, then remove from the heat and set aside to steep for at least 10 minutes.

In a sauté pan, heat the olive oil over medium heat. Add the onion and cook until soft and translucent, about 4 minutes. Add the garlic and cook until aromatic, another minute or two. Add the kale, sherry, raisins, anchovies, orange juice and zest, and red pepper flakes. Cover the pan, turn the heat to low, and cook until the flavors are blended, about 10 minutes. Remove the cover, raise

the heat to medium-high, and boil away most of the excess liquid. Remove from the heat. Season to taste with salt, pepper, and a drizzle of olive oil.

Top each of the toasts with some of the greens, either warm or at room temperature, and top with shavings of Parmesan. Arrange the toasts on a platter and serve.

HOW TO MAKE TOASTS

Cut a French baguette or Italian bread on the diagonal into slices about ⅓ inch thick. Lightly brush both sides with olive oil. Place the slices under the broiler, turning once, until golden and toasted.

CHILLED TOMATO SOUP WITH CUCUMBER BUTTERMILK PANNA COTTA AND BASIL OIL

MAKES 6 SERVINGS

The success of this soup depends entirely on using ripe, juicy, delicious tomatoes, in season. (I hope your local tomato season is longer than our three-day season.)

Pour the basil oil into a clean plastic squirt bottle, the kind usually filled with ketchup or mustard, and drizzle the oil decoratively over the soup.

2 tablespoons extra virgin olive oil

2 pounds (about 4 large) ripe tomatoes, roughly chopped

½ shallot, roughly chopped

6 fresh basil leaves

Kosher salt and freshly ground black pepper

Cucumber Buttermilk Panna Cotta, unmolded into 6 shallow soup bowls

Basil Oil

6 thin slices cucumber

A STEP AHEAD Make the soup a day or two ahead and store it in the refrigerator, covered with plastic wrap.

Heat the oil in a large sauté pan over medium heat. Add the tomatoes, shallot, and basil and sauté just until the tomatoes are warmed through and releasing their juice, about 2 to 3 minutes. Remove from the heat, transfer the contents of the pan to the bowl of a food processor, and puree until smooth. Pour the puree through a fine strainer set over a bowl, pressing on the solids with a rubber spatula to get as much of the tomato through the strainer

as possible. Discard the solids. Season the soup to taste with salt and pepper. Put the soup in the refrigerator to chill, or you can chill it more quickly by setting the bowl of soup into a larger bowl of ice water.

Ladle some soup around the panna cotta in each bowl, then, using a small spoon or a squirt bottle, drizzle a little basil oil over the soup. Garnish the top of each panna cotta with a cucumber slice.

CUCUMBER BUTTERMILK PANNA COTTA

MAKES 6 SERVINGS

Panna cotta is traditionally an Italian dessert custard that sets up with gelatin instead of eggs, but this nontraditional savory version is creamy and soft, with a nice bright cucumber taste. English cucumbers have a thin, mild-tasting skin, so you don't need to peel them, and the peel adds color and flavor. If you substitute another kind of cucumber, peel it first if the skin is bitter or waxed.

I'm continually inspired by the chefs I work with every day. This particular recipe was inspired by Duskie Estes, former chef at Palace Kitchen and now owner of Zazu restaurant in Santa Rosa, California.

Vegetable oil spray or flavorless vegetable oil
1 English cucumber, about 1 pound
$\frac{1}{2}$ cup buttermilk
$\frac{1}{2}$ cup heavy cream
$1\frac{1}{2}$ teaspoons unflavored gelatin (less than 1 envelope)
Kosher salt and freshly ground black pepper

A STEP AHEAD The panna cottas can be made 1 day ahead and stored, covered with plastic wrap, in the refrigerator. They lose some of their fresh cucumber flavor if they're stored longer.

Set out 6 demitasse cups or 4-ounce ramekins and spray the interiors with vegetable oil spray or brush lightly with a flavorless vegetable oil.

Chop the cucumber roughly and liquefy in a blender or food processor. Strain the puree through a strainer set over a bowl, pressing on the solids with a rubber spatula. Discard the solids. Measure out $\frac{1}{2}$ cup cucumber juice. Discard any excess cucumber juice. Pour the cucumber juice into a bowl and stir in the buttermilk.

Pour the cream into a small saucepan and sprinkle with the gelatin. Let the mixture stand a few minutes to soften the gelatin. Then place the pan over medium heat and bring the cream just to a simmer. Cook the cream gently for a few minutes, stirring occasionally, until the gelatin is completely dissolved. Pour the cream into the cucumber-buttermilk mixture and stir to combine. Season to taste with salt and pepper. Pour the mixture into the prepared cups, dividing it evenly. Cover the cups with plastic wrap and chill until set, at least 6 hours or overnight.

To unmold a panna cotta, run a small knife around the edge of the custard. Invert a shallow soup plate over the top of the cup, then flip the whole thing over, giving the cup a sharp shake. The custard should flip right out into the soup plate.

BASIL OIL

MAKES 2 TABLESPOONS

Try this deep green herb-flavored oil drizzled over a bowl of white bean soup or minestrone.

⅓ cup lightly packed roughly chopped basil leaves
¼ cup extra virgin olive oil
Kosher salt

A STEP AHEAD Make the basil oil a few hours ahead and store it, covered with plastic wrap, in the refrigerator. A squeeze of lemon will help hold the color if you're not using the oil immediately.

Combine the basil and olive oil in a blender and puree until smooth. (Or chop the basil in a mini–food processor and gradually add the oil while processing.) Pour through a strainer, pressing on the solids with a rubber spatula to extract as much oil as possible. Season to taste with salt.

FRESH CORN CRÊPES WITH GOAT CHEESE AND ROASTED PEPPERS, ANCHO CHILE SAUCE, AVOCADO-TOMATILLO SALSA, AND FRESH CORN SALSA

MAKES 6 SERVINGS

When my friend Shelley (also my co-writer) first put this dish on the menu at the Dahlia Lounge, I ate it every day for a week.

Use any combination of mild to medium-hot peppers that appeals to you, such as red, orange, and yellow bells, Anaheims, and poblanos.

1½ pounds (about 6 or 7) assorted mild to medium-hot peppers, roasted and peeled (see page 60)

2 tablespoons olive oil

1 medium onion, halved and thinly sliced

1 teaspoon minced garlic

Kosher salt and freshly ground black pepper

6 ounces soft fresh goat cheese

3 tablespoons heavy cream

1 tablespoon chopped fresh cilantro

6 Fresh Corn Crêpes

2 tablespoons unsalted butter, melted, plus more for the baking sheet

Avocado-Tomatillo Salsa

Fresh Corn Salsa

Ancho Chile Sauce

A STEP AHEAD The pepper mixture and the mashed goat cheese can be made a few days ahead and refrigerated, covered with plastic wrap. Reheat the pepper mixture until warm before assembling the crêpes. Also, the filled crêpes can be placed on a buttered baking sheet and left at room temperature a few hours before baking.

Cut the peppers into ½-inch strips and set aside. You should have about 2½ cups.

Heat the oil in a sauté pan over medium high heat, then add the onion. Sauté until the onion begins to brown, then reduce the heat to medium and continue to cook until soft, 6 to 8 minutes. Add the garlic and sauté for a few minutes, until aromatic. Add the pepper strips and sauté until the flavors are blended, about 5 minutes. Season to taste with salt and pepper.

Using a wooden spoon, mash the goat cheese in a bowl with the cream and cilantro. Season to taste with salt and pepper.

Preheat the oven to 425°F. Place a crêpe on a work surface, prettiest side down. Dollop a sixth of the cheese mixture over the bottom half of the crêpe. Cover the goat cheese with a sixth of the pepper mixture and fold the crêpe over, like a half-moon. When all of the crêpes are filled, place them on a generously buttered baking sheet and brush the tops of the crêpes with the melted butter. Bake until the edges are crisped and browned, the filling is warmed, and the goat cheese is starting to ooze, about 12 minutes. Remove the crêpes from the oven and carefully transfer them to dinner plates, using a large spatula.

Place a generous spoonful of avocado salsa and another of corn salsa alongside each crêpe, then, using a ladle or a spoon, drizzle some of the ancho sauce over each crêpe and around the plate. Pass any extra salsa or sauce at the table.

HOW TO ROAST AND PEEL CHILES OR BELL PEPPERS

Place the peppers directly over the open flame of a gas burner, turning them with tongs until the skin is blackened, blistered, and charred all over. Or place the peppers on a baking sheet under a hot broiler, turning as needed. Place the charred peppers in a bowl, cover tightly with plastic wrap, and allow them to steam for about 10 minutes to loosen the skins. Take the peppers out of the bowl and scrape away all the skin with a paring knife. Remove the stems and split the peppers in half. Remove and discard the seeds and veins.

FRESH CORN CRÊPES

MAKES 6 TO 10 CRÊPES

This hearty crêpe batter takes a little more cooking than thinner batters. If you attempt to flip a crêpe before it is cooked on the first side, it will tear and fall apart. Cook the first side for about a full minute, then use a small rubber spatula to lift the crêpe gently to check that the underside, not just the edges, is browned lightly before you flip it to the second side.

It often takes a few crêpes before you get your pan to the perfect temperature, so this recipe makes enough batter to get 6 perfect ones.

3 large eggs

1½ cups fresh corn kernels (about 2 ears)

½ cup all-purpose flour

1 cup milk

⅓ cup medium-ground yellow cornmeal

1 teaspoon kosher salt

¼ teaspoon freshly ground black pepper

Pinch of cayenne pepper

3 tablespoons unsalted butter, melted, plus more for cooking the crêpes

3 tablespoons finely chopped scallion, both white and green parts

2 tablespoons finely chopped fresh cilantro

A STEP AHEAD Crêpe batter keeps for a day or two, covered, in the refrigerator. Or wrap the stack of cooked crêpes in plastic wrap with wax paper in between and store them in the refrigerator for a day.

In a food processor or a blender, combine the eggs, corn, flour, milk, cornmeal, salt, pepper, and cayenne. With the motor running, slowly pour in the melted butter. Then add the scallion and cilantro and pulse briefly. The mixture will look like a thin but slightly chunky pancake batter.

Heat a 10-inch nonstick sauté pan over medium-high heat. Brush with melted butter. Ladle about ⅓ cup crêpe batter into the pan as you tilt the pan so the batter completely coats the bottom. Cook each crêpe until lightly browned on one side, about a minute, then flip to cook the other side, about ½ minute more. Repeat until all of the crêpes are cooked. If your pan gets too hot while you are cooking the crêpes, reduce the heat to medium. Set the cooked crêpes aside with wax paper in between.

AVOCADO-TOMATILLO SALSA

MAKES ABOUT 2 CUPS

When I first encountered tomatillos, I couldn't figure out what the heck that papery skin was all about. Even now I think it's weird that there's a sticky sap underneath the paper when you peel them, but boy, are they delicious. They add a great acid kick wherever they're used.

The easiest way to peel an avocado is to cut it in half, remove the pit, and scoop the flesh right out of the skin, using a large spoon. Also try serving this salsa with tortilla chips for dipping.

$\frac{1}{2}$ pound tomatillos (about 8), husked and cut into quarters

1 tablespoon plus 2 teaspoons freshly squeezed lime juice

1 tablespoon finely chopped fresh cilantro

$\frac{1}{2}$ teaspoon minced garlic

2 ripe medium avocados, peeled, pitted, and cut into $\frac{1}{4}$-inch dice

Kosher salt and freshly ground black pepper

A STEP AHEAD You can make this an hour or two ahead and store it, covered, in the refrigerator. Or you could make the salsa without the avocado up to a day ahead, refrigerate it, and stir in the diced avocado shortly before you are ready to serve.

Put the tomatillos in the bowl of a food processor and process until coarsely pureed. Pour the puree into a strainer set over a bowl and drain briefly, discarding the liquid. (The puree doesn't need to be completely dry.) Put the drained puree into a bowl and stir in the lime juice, cilantro, garlic, and avocado. Season to taste with salt and pepper.

FRESH CORN SALSA

MAKES ABOUT 2 CUPS

This simple salsa features the sweet flavor of corn perked up with a little lime and cumin. Try spooning this over grilled salmon.

2 cups fresh corn kernels (2 to 3 ears)
3 tablespoons freshly squeezed lime juice
2 tablespoons olive oil
2 tablespoons minced scallion, both white and green parts
¼ teaspoon toasted and ground cumin (see below)
Kosher salt and freshly ground black pepper

A STEP AHEAD You can cook the corn early in the day and store it, covered, in the refrigerator. Combine the corn with the other ingredients an hour or two ahead and leave it at room temperature.

To cook the corn, bring a saucepan of salted water to a boil and have a bowl of ice water ready. Add the corn to the saucepan and cook for a minute or two. Strain the corn and immediately plunge it into the bowl of ice water. Drain the corn well and place it in a bowl. Add the lime juice, olive oil, scallion, and cumin and stir to combine. Season to taste with salt and pepper.

HOW TO TOAST AND GRIND SPICES

I generally buy whole spices and grind them myself for better flavor. The flavor of some spices, like cumin and coriander seeds, can be heightened by briefly toasting them before grinding.

To toast spices, place them in a small heavy skillet over medium heat for a few minutes, shaking or stirring constantly, just until they are very lightly browned and aromatic. Spices burn easily, so watch them carefully.

I use a clean electric coffee grinder for grinding spices. I keep one for my coffee and one just for spices. You can also use a mortar and pestle, which is fun to use, though it takes more muscle.

ANCHO CHILE SAUCE

MAKES ABOUT ¾ CUP

Ancho chiles are dried poblanos, and they have a fruity sweetness that really comes out in this sauce.

5 ancho chiles

3 tablespoons unsalted butter

1½ cups finely chopped onion

1 tablespoon minced garlic

1½ cups freshly squeezed orange juice, plus more for thinning the sauce

Kosher salt and freshly ground black pepper

A STEP AHEAD Make this 3 or 4 days ahead and store in the refrigerator, covered with plastic wrap. If the sauce is cold, reheat it gently before serving.

Split the chiles open and discard the stems and seeds. Place the chiles in a small saucepan and cover them with water. Bring to a boil, then remove the saucepan from the heat. Allow the chiles to soak until soft, about 10 minutes. Drain, discarding the soaking water, and set the chiles aside.

Melt the butter in a saucepan over medium heat. Add the onion and sauté until softened and translucent, about 5 minutes. Add the garlic and sauté until aromatic, another minute or two. Add the orange juice and the chiles. Simmer over medium-high heat until the mixture is reduced and looks like a very wet paste, stirring occasionally, 10 to 15 minutes. Remove from the heat and scrape into the bowl of a food processor. Puree until smooth, then pour through a strainer set over a bowl, pressing on the solids with a rubber spatula to pass as much of the sauce through the strainer as possible. Season to taste with salt and pepper. If the sauce seems too thick, add a little more orange juice, a tablespoon at a time, until it is thin enough to drizzle from a spoon.

PEACH CARAMEL UPSIDE-DOWN CAKES

MAKES 6 SERVINGS

There are two tricky parts to this recipe—caramelizing the sugar (see page 67), and unmolding the ramekins as soon as they come out of the oven, while they are still quite hot. Use a kitchen towel to protect your hands.

If you don't have a stand mixer, use a handheld electric mixer to make the cake batter, but cream the butter and sugar several minutes longer and scrape down the sides of the bowl several times.

There's only a little bit of cornmeal in this cake batter, but it adds texture to the delicate crumb.

A restaurant tip: Use an ice cream scoop instead of a spoon to neatly fill the prepared ramekins with cake batter.

TO PREPARE THE RAMEKINS AND TOPPING

2 tablespoons unsalted butter, melted, plus more for brushing the ramekins

⅔ cup sugar

2 peaches, peeled (see page 66), halved, pitted, and thinly sliced

FOR THE CAKE

1 cup plus 2 tablespoons all-purpose flour

2 tablespoons medium-ground yellow cornmeal

1 teaspoon baking powder

½ teaspoon kosher salt

6 tablespoons unsalted butter, softened

¾ cup plus 2 tablespoons sugar

3 large eggs, separated

2 teaspoons pure vanilla extract

½ cup whole milk

Vanilla ice cream or Sweetened Whipped Cream

A STEP AHEAD Make the cakes early in the day, but you must unmold them while they are still hot or they will stick to the ramekins. Cover the unmolded cakes loosely with a piece of plastic wrap when they are cool and leave them at room temperature. The cakes are delicious served either at room temperature or warm. If you would like to rewarm them, use a spatula to place the unmolded cakes on a parchment-lined baking sheet and heat in a 400°F oven for 6 to 8 minutes.

Preheat the oven to 350°F. Set six 8-ounce, 4-inch-diameter, straight-sided ovenproof ramekins on a baking sheet near the range where you are planning to caramelize the sugar. Brush the insides of the ramekins with melted butter, then pour 1 teaspoon melted butter into the bottom of each ramekin.

To make the caramel, combine the sugar with 3 tablespoons water in a small heavy saucepan. Stir over low heat until the sugar

HOW TO PEEL A PEACH

The easiest way to peel peaches is to blanch them briefly. Cut a small X in the bottom of each peach, fill a bowl with ice water, and bring a saucepan of water to a boil. Add the peaches to the boiling water until the skins begin to pull away, about 1 minute—less if the peaches are very ripe and juicy. Remove the peaches from the boiling water and immediately plunge them into the ice water for a few minutes. Remove the peaches from the ice water and peel them with a paring knife.

If substituting nectarines for peaches, you don't need to peel them.

is completely dissolved. Raise the heat to high and cook without stirring until the sugar turns a dark golden brown. Swirl the pan occasionally to distribute the color evenly. Remove the pan from the heat and carefully pour the caramel into the ramekins, dividing it evenly. Wait a few minutes for the caramel to cool. Then cover the caramel in each ramekin with as many peach slices as will fit in a single layer, trimming them to fit if necessary. (You may have some peach slices left over.) Set the prepared ramekins aside.

To make the cake, combine the flour, cornmeal, baking powder, and salt in a bowl and set aside. In the bowl of an electric mixer with the paddle attachment, cream the butter with the ¾ cup sugar until smooth and light, about 2 minutes on medium speed. Add the egg yolks and vanilla and mix on medium speed until smooth, about 2 minutes. Add the dry ingredients in three additions, alternately with the milk in two additions, beating briefly after each addition just until incorporated. Scrape the batter into a large bowl. Clean the electric mixer bowl, then, using the whisk attachment, whip the egg whites with the 2 tablespoons sugar until stiff. Using a rubber spatula, fold a third of the egg whites at a time into the batter. Fold gently but thoroughly, until all the whites are incorporated, being careful not to overmix.

Scoop the cake batter into the prepared ramekins. Smooth the tops and bake in the middle rack of the oven until the tops are light golden and a skewer inserted into the center of each cake comes out clean, 30 to 35 minutes. Remove from the oven. Unmold the ramekins immediately, while they are still hot, or the caramel will cool and stick.

To unmold, run a small knife around the edge of each cake. Invert a dessert plate over the top of the ramekin and, using a kitchen towel to protect your hands, flip the whole thing over, giving the ramekin a sharp shake. Remove the ramekin, and the cake should slide out onto the plate. Allow the cake to cool for at least 5 to 10 minutes before serving.

Serve with a scoop of ice cream or a dollop of whipped cream.

HOW TO CARAMELIZE SUGAR—SAFELY

You can caramelize dry sugar or dissolve it first in a little water. I've done it both ways many times, but generally, unless you're caramelizing only a few tablespoons of sugar, it's a little easier to control the process if you dissolve the sugar first. In a pan over low heat, stir the sugar and water until you have a clear solution, then turn the heat up to high to allow the sugar to caramelize. After the heat is turned up, don't disturb the solution by stirring, or you may cause crystallization. It's important to prevent crystals from forming because if they do the mixture will seize up, forming a slushy clump, and you'll have to throw it away and start over.

If a dark brown color forms in one corner of the pan, carefully swirl the pan to distribute the color. When the syrup is uniformly golden brown, immediately remove the pan from the heat. Sugar burns quickly, and it will continue darkening even after removed from the heat.

Making caramel is potentially dangerous, because hot sugar can give you a serious burn. Never touch hot sugar, and keep a bowl of ice water nearby in case you accidentally get some hot sugar on yourself.

FAVORITE BITES AT THE PIKE PLACE MARKET

❖ Cha gio with lettuce wrap at Saigon Restaurant

❖ Ham and butter sandwich at Le Panier

❖ Hot, greasy, tiny doughnuts by the dozen from the doughnut stand

❖ Peach samples at Sosio's Produce, during the season

❖ Espresso at the original Starbucks

❖ Warm crumpets with Deer Mountain gooseberry jam from the Crumpet Shop

❖ Handmade corn tortillas from El Puerco Lloron

❖ Normand Brook's eggnog from the Pike Place Market Creamery

❖ Half dozen Kumomoto oysters at Emmett Watson's

❖ A slice of acorn-fed jamon at The Spanish Table

❖ Deep-fried chicken gizzards at Chicken Valley

❖ Cantaloupe gelato at Procopio Gelateria

❖ A cold hot dog snack at Bavarian Meats while you're shopping for the best smoked bacon, bockwurst, and everything else they sell

❖ Dried cherry mix at the Chukar Cherry stand

❖ Icy cold bottle of fresh-pressed Woodring Orchard apple cider

SWEETENED WHIPPED CREAM

MAKES ABOUT 3 CUPS

Very cold cream whips best. Put your bowl and whisk in the refrigerator to chill for a while before whipping cream.

1½ cups heavy cream
3 tablespoons sugar
1½ teaspoons pure vanilla extract

Place the heavy cream, sugar, and vanilla in the bowl and whip with an electric mixer until soft peaks form. Serve immediately.

PERFECT PEACHES

Biting into a perfectly ripe peach is truly one of life's great sensual pleasures. Some people love their peaches stabbingly sweet, but I love mine to have that exquisite balance between sweetness and acidity. The Pacific Northwest produces some of the best peaches in the country. The Yakima Valley gets the combination of sunlight, heat, and cool nights that peach growers need to produce peaches that end up fragrant, juicy, and utterly delicious. At the market, at the height of peach season, mid- to late August, I head straight for Socio'o for my peach fix. They often have locally grown Red Haven peaches that are so juicy I end up wearing them as well as eating them. Make sure you ask for a taste, because all peaches, even those bought at a trusted purveyor, are not created equal. Peaches should smell . . . well, exceedingly peachy and have a slight softness. They need to ripen on the tree bathed in sunlight. Peaches picked before their time will never ripen fully off the tree. They'll get softer, but they won't get appreciatively sweeter. My favorite way to taste peaches in Seattle is at the local Thriftway chain during their August peach festival. They set out boxes of peaches from Pence Orchards (from Washington) and Frog Hollow (from northern California) and invite you to taste at your leisure. It's fascinating to taste the difference in both kinds of peaches from week to week (the festival lasts for a month). If I come upon perfectly ripe peaches, I don't try to cook with them. I just eat them, one incredible bite at a time.

WINE CELLAR DINNER

Wine is a consuming passion in our restaurants, in our house, and in our lives. In fact I met Jackie when she was working the floor at a local wine store, Pike and Western, and I was a wholesale wine salesman on one of my hiatuses from the stove. I sold some wine, and I also got the girl.

Yakima and the Columbia River Valley feel very much like the Old West, complete with desertlike vistas and tumbleweed. Five years ago Columbia Crest Winery flew a group of chefs from Boeing Field, near downtown Seattle, to their winery in the small town of Patterson for a luncheon. We were awestruck when we landed on a tiny airstrip right in a sea of grapevines. Columbia Crest's intention was to show off how well their wines worked with food, but for me the visit also drove home just how large the industry had become. As we walked through this tremendous operation—a million square feet under one roof—to the magnificent winery trimmed with old redwood barrel staves, with huge windows overlooking the glorious Patterson Ridge and Horseheaven Hills, I had a chance to chat with the winemaker, Doug Gore.

I've always been impressed with wineries that can make good wines at reasonable prices. Amazingly, Columbia Crest has had more top-one-hundred wines in the *Wine Spectator* than any other winery in the world. Doug is well aware that his wines will be judged, first and foremost, as Washington wines and thus will carry the torch for the whole Washington wine industry. I asked him how he can make so much wine, some 2½ million cases, and still be winning awards and selling it at prices that are half of the competition's. He said the secret is that Washington grapes have a unique intensity and are varietally correct and therefore need little manipulation. His secret barrel techniques help too.

When Jackie and I cook dinner for friends, we spend just as much time thinking about the wine we'll put in the glass as the food we'll put on the plate. One time we made a syrupy sweet-

MENU

GOAT CHEESE FONDUE WITH TOASTED BREAD AND APPLES

COLUMBIA CREST GRAND ESTATE CHARDONNAY

HEIRLOOM TOMATOES, GRILLED CORN RELISH, AND BASIL VINAIGRETTE

VINE-ROASTED SQUAB WITH SYRAH JAM

DUCK-FRIED JO JOS

SUMMER SQUASH AND EGGPLANT TIAN

COLUMBIA CREST RESERVE SYRAH

CHOCOLATE CRÊPES WITH GEWÜRZTRAMINER SYRUP

COLUMBIA CREST SEMILLON ICE WINE

and-savory jam from onions, sugar, and a bottle of Syrah. As soon as we tasted the intensely winey jam with a bite of grilled salt and pepper squab and then took a sip from a glass of peppery, full-flavored Washington Syrah, we knew we had a transcendent food and wine match. The following menu is our tribute to the infinite pleasures of delicious food matched with Washington state wines.

SALT

Mined salt comes from salt deposits left by dried salt lakes throughout the world. Table salt, iodized salt, and kosher salt are all produced from mined salt. Table salt is fine grained and may have additives to make it free flowing. Iodized salt has iodine added. Kosher salt is coarse grained for use in the koshering process of meat (i.e., raw meat is salted to remove blood) and contains no additives. Rock salt is less refined and comes in large crystals, making it good to use as a bed for shucked oysters or in your ice cream maker.

Kosher salt is the salt I use most of the time because I think it's less harsh on the palate than table salt and the coarse grains make it easier to season "by feel." However, I also enjoy the briny ocean flavor of sea salts and tend to sprinkle them on foods at the last minute, as finishing salts.

Sea salt, which may be in the form of flakes or crystals, comes from the evaporation of sea water, by either artificial or traditional methods. The traditional methods especially are a slower and more costly process than for mined salt—at least part of the reason for the high price of many sea salts. Some of the finest sea salts are French, such as fleur de sel, which only comes from crystals that have not been in contact with the sea bottom and therefore are pure white.

My favorite salt bite ever: Fran's Gray Salt Caramels—hand dipped in dark chocolate and sprinkled lightly with sea salt. The magic of salt and chocolate—these are fantastic!

FRAN'S CHOCOLATES
2594 N.E. University Village
Seattle, WA 98105
(206) 528-9969
www.franschocolates.com

GOAT CHEESE FONDUE WITH TOASTED BREAD AND APPLES

Sharing a pot of fondue is a friendly and companionable activity, perfect for creating a party mood. In addition to the toasted bread and apples, set out chunks of ripe pears and fennel bulbs for dipping.

If you don't own a fondue pot, and don't want to buy a trendy new one, they can be found at garage sales. A double boiler works well, too.

1 cup whipping cream or a little more if needed
11 ounces soft fresh goat cheese, broken into chunks, or a little more if needed
1 tablespoon sliced fresh chives
½ teaspoon freshly ground black pepper
Toasted Rustic Bread
3 unpeeled Granny Smith apples, cored and cut into wedges

Slowly warm the whipping cream in a heavy saucepan until hot but not boiling. Gradually add the goat cheese and whisk until smooth. The thickness of the fondue may vary due to the particular brand of fresh goat cheese that you use. It should be thick enough to coat a spoon. If too thin, add a little more cheese; if too thick, add a little more cream. Remove the fondue from the heat and stir in the chives and black pepper.

Pour the warm fondue into a fondue pot and serve with chunks of toasted rustic bread and apple wedges for dunking.

TOASTED RUSTIC BREAD

MAKES 6 TO 8 SERVINGS

Use a good yeasty, crusty bread for this recipe. If all you can get is squishy supermarket sandwich bread, it's not worth making.

If you're not making the fondue as part of a grilling menu, you can brush the bread with oil and toast it under the broiler, turning as needed until golden brown on both sides.

8 slices rustic bread, 1 inch thick

½ cup olive oil or as needed

Fire up the grill. Brush the slices of bread generously on both sides with the olive oil, then grill them, turning, until golden brown, a few minutes per side. Watch carefully and move the slices around so the bread toasts evenly and does not burn. Remove from the heat and use a serrated knife to cut the bread into bite-size cubes.

Pile the chunks of toasted bread on a colorful platter and pass regular or fondue forks to your guests for dunking the bread in the fondue.

HEIRLOOM TOMATOES, GRILLED CORN RELISH, AND BASIL VINAIGRETTE

The funny-looking, incredibly juicy and luscious fruits Jackie's grandma grew in her backyard are now called *heirloom tomatoes*, grown from seeds saved year after year like precious antiques. You can find heirlooms, in various shapes, sizes, and colors— red, pink, yellow, white, green, and even striped—at farmer's markets or, increasingly, in some supermarkets. But being labeled an heirloom doesn't necessarily make a tomato good. Like every other tomato you buy, it should be firm, unrefrigerated, and smell like a tomato. If you have ripe, flavorful tomatoes from your garden or anywhere else, use them here, whatever the variety.

If you have opal basil growing in your yard, or any basil that has gone to flower, use it to garnish this salad.

FOR THE BASIL VINAIGRETTE

⅓ cup chopped fresh basil leaves

⅓ cup extra virgin olive oil

1 tablespoon freshly squeezed lemon juice

½ teaspoon minced garlic

Kosher salt and freshly ground black pepper

FOR THE LEMON VINAIGRETTE

2 tablespoons plus 2 teaspoons freshly squeezed
    lemon juice

1 tablespoon minced shallot

2 teaspoons freshly grated lemon zest

5 tablespoons extra virgin olive oil

FOR THE CORN RELISH AND TOMATOES

5 fresh ears corn, shucked

½ cup lightly packed, thinly sliced basil leaves (see page 76)

About 2 pounds tomatoes, preferably heirlooms or ripe
    garden tomatoes, cut into wedges

A STEP AHEAD Make the lemon vinaigrette up to a day ahead and store it covered and refrigerated. Make the basil vinaigrette a few hours ahead and store it covered and refrigerated.

You can grill the corn an hour or two ahead, cut the kernels off the cobs, and leave the corn at room temperature. But don't slice the basil for the corn salad or pour the vinaigrettes over the corn or the tomatoes until you are ready to serve.

To make the basil vinaigrette, combine the basil, olive oil, lemon juice, and garlic in a blender. Puree until smooth, then pour the mixture through a fine-mesh strainer set over a bowl, pressing on the solids with a rubber spatula to extract as much of the vinai-

To chiffonade means to cut into very thin strips. The easiest way to cut basil leaves (or spinach or any other leaf) is to stack several leaves in a pile, then roll the pile of leaves up. Use a sharp knife to cut the roll of leaves crosswise into very thin strips. Because basil will discolor, it's best to slice it right before you plan to use it.

grette as possible. Discard the solid remains. Season to taste with salt and pepper and set aside.

To make the lemon vinaigrette, combine the lemon juice, shallot, and zest in a small bowl. Gradually add the oil, whisking until emulsified. Season to taste with salt and pepper and set aside.

Fire up the grill. Grill the corn over direct heat, uncovered, turning as needed, until done, about 8 minutes. The corn should be charred in places. Remove from the grill.

When the corn is cool enough to handle, use a knife to cut the kernels from the cobs and put them in a bowl. You should have about 4 cups. Add the lemon vinaigrette and the sliced basil to the corn and stir to combine. Season to taste with salt and pepper.

Mound the corn relish in the center of a large platter. Arrange the tomato wedges around the corn and season the tomatoes with salt and pepper. Drizzle the basil vinaigrette over the tomatoes.

VINE-ROASTED SQUAB WITH SYRAH JAM

MAKES 6 SERVINGS

Jackie enjoys eating little birds like squab and quail. Squab is a young domesticated pigeon, usually weighing one pound or less. Squabs are available fresh in the summer months in gourmet markets and frozen year-round. If you can't get squab, substitute small Cornish game hens, but try to find squab, because the richly flavored, moist, dark meat is special. Be careful not to overcook squab, because the meat can taste livery.

For the Syrah jam, I like to use Columbia Crest Syrah, one of the few Washington wines available around the country. This is not a jam that you spread on toast, but a syrupy sweet-and-savory sauce that matches the gamy flavor of the squab or can be served as an accompaniment to a grilled steak or roast lamb.

The little bacon-wrapped grilled skewers of innards make an extra treat. I grill the gizzards, but if you find it too difficult to remove the tough membrane around them, toss them and simply grill the livers and hearts.

If you have access to dried grapevines, throw some on your fire. They are aromatic, like wood chips.

FOR THE SYRAH JAM

1 bottle Syrah
1 cup sugar
1 cup finely chopped onion
¼ cup freshly squeezed lemon juice
1 tablespoon freshly grated lemon zest

FOR THE SQUABS

6 squabs (about ¾ to 1 pound each)
Kosher salt and freshly ground black pepper
Six 4-inch bamboo skewers and 6 sturdy toothpicks
Six 4-inch-long bacon strips
A handful of dried grapevines, soaked for at least 1 hour and
 drained

A STEP AHEAD Make the jam several days ahead and store it covered and refrigerated. Bring the jam to room temperature before serving. You can hasten this process by setting the jam over a bowl of hot water and stirring until it comes to room temperature.

To make the Syrah jam, put the wine into a heavy saucepan and add the sugar, onion, lemon juice, and zest. Bring to a boil over high heat and boil until reduced and thickened, about 30 minutes to an hour, depending on the surface area of your pan and the heat of your burner (see page 79). As the wine reduces, lower the heat a bit and stir occasionally. You should have 1¼ cups jam. The jam will still be pretty loose at this point but will thicken a bit more as it cools. Set the jam aside to cool at room temperature, about ½ hour, or you can set it over an ice bath to cool more quickly.

Remove the innards from the cavities of the squabs, setting aside the livers, gizzards, and hearts. Cut the gizzards in half, scraping them away from their tough outer coat with your knife. Remove and discard the neck bones from the squabs and cut off any excess neck skin. Trim any excess fat from the squabs. Cut out

the backbones, cutting through the hip joint on both sides. Split the squabs in half through the breastbones, being sure to cut off the breastbone from both sides. Cut off the wings at the first joint so the squabs will sit flatter on the grill and cook more evenly. You can discard the wing joints or grill them as a "chef's treat."

To grill the squabs, fire up your grill for direct heat. I don't brush the squabs with oil, because there is plenty of fat in the skin. Season the squabs generously with salt and pepper and set them aside on a platter. Using the bamboo skewers, skewer the livers, gizzards, and hearts, dividing them up evenly. Wrap each skewer with a strip of bacon, fastening the bacon with the toothpicks. Set the skewers aside with the squabs. When your coals are hot, lay the grapevines on top of them. As soon as the grapevines start to smoke, put the squabs on the grill, skin side down. Put the skewers on the grill as well. Grill the squabs over a hot direct fire, lid off, with the vents open, turning them when the skin is nicely browned, after about 5 minutes. Continue cooking the squabs, turning them as needed and turning the skewers as needed to cook them evenly, until an instant-read meat thermometer in the thickest part of the thigh reads 125°F, about 12 minutes total. Remove the squabs and the skewers from the grill.

Transfer the squabs and the skewers to a platter. Put the jam in a serving bowl and pass with the squabs.

HOW TO MAKE REDUCTIONS

Almost every fine restaurant has a huge pot of chicken or veal stock boiling away on the back of the stove until it's reduced to a few quarts of the thick, intensely flavored demiglace that's so highly prized for sauce making. Although I do make chicken stock at home on a regular basis, and freeze it, I only occasionally bother to make demiglace. On the other hand, I often find myself boiling several cups of wine until I have a small amount of intensely flavored syrup, also called a *reduction,* for the depth of flavor it will add to a sauce or stew. I also boil down the pan liquids from roasted meats to make gravy because I like the intensity of flavor and I don't like to add a lot of flour for thickness.

In a recipe involving a reduction, I often tell you how much liquid you should end up with—for example, "you should have ¼ cup reduced wine." It's best to keep a heatproof glass measuring cup near the stove and, when you think you're close, pour the liquid from your pan into the measuring cup to check that you have reduced it enough.

It can take a long time to reduce a bottle of wine or a quart or more of stock, and it's hard to tell you exactly how long because it depends on the surface of your pan and the heat of your burner. But keep in mind that liquid will boil down a lot faster as the volume decreases. It's amazingly easy to spend 45 minutes reducing something, only to take it too far and burn it or reduce it to nothing. Remember to keep a watchful eye on your reduction. Turn the heat down a bit and pay more attention as the volume decreases.

DUCK-FRIED JO JOS

MAKES 6 TO 8 SERVINGS

"Jo jos" is a somewhat old-fashioned name for thick-cut, oven-roasted, seasoned potato wedges, most often seen on casual and chain restaurant menus. These potatoes aren't deep-fried or pan-fried, but coated with flavorful fat and roasted until golden in a hot oven so they're "oven-fried."

Anytime you roast a duck, save all the delicious fat that is rendered out for frying potatoes and other foods. For example, our Roast Duck with Riesling, Black Pepper, and Thyme (page 238) yields plenty of fat. Duck fat keeps for a long time in the refrigerator and even longer in the freezer. You can also get mail-order duck fat (see Sources, page 265). If you don't have any duck fat, substitute a combination of butter and olive oil.

To get these potato wedges golden and crusty, it's important to spread them out; otherwise they steam. Divide this quantity of potatoes between two baking sheets.

4 large russet potatoes (about 3 pounds), peeled
6 tablespoons rendered duck fat, melted, or ¼ cup olive oil plus
    2 tablespoons unsalted butter, melted
Kosher salt and freshly ground black pepper

A STEP AHEAD Roast the potatoes a few hours ahead and leave them at room temperature, combining them into one pan to save room in the oven when you reheat them. Reheat at 400°F until hot, 8 to 10 minutes. If you are making the whole menu, you can roast the potatoes a few hours ahead in this manner and reheat them at 400°F while the tian is in the oven.

Preheat the oven to 450°F. Cut each potato lengthwise into 8 wedges. Put the potatoes in a bowl and toss them with the fat. Season generously with salt and pepper. Divide the potatoes between 2 metal baking sheets, spreading them out in a single layer with one of the flat sides of each wedge facing down. Use a rubber spatula to scrape all the fat out of the bowl and onto the potatoes. Put the pans in the oven, one on each oven rack.

When the potatoes are golden brown on the side facing the pan, after 15 to 20 minutes, use a metal spatula to turn each potato over to the other flat side. Don't turn them until they're browned and be sure to use the spatula to get all the crusty golden part as you turn. Also, for even cooking, turn the pans around and rotate them between the racks once in a while during the roasting time. Continue to roast until the second side is golden brown, 10 to 12 minutes more, then use a spatula to turn each potato so it's sitting on the rounded side (or bottom) of the wedge. You can use tongs to position them leaning against each other so they stand up. Roast until the rounded side of the wedge is browned, 5 to 8 minutes more. (Total roasting time is 35 to 40 minutes.) Remove the potatoes from the oven and season to taste with more salt and pepper. Pile the potatoes on a platter and serve immediately.

SUMMER SQUASH AND EGGPLANT TIAN

MAKES 6 SERVINGS

Tian is the French word for a shallow earthenware casserole or the food that gets baked in one. Any attractive oval earthenware baking dish will be perfect for this bread-crumb-topped vegetable casserole, which is served directly from the pan.

¼ cup olive oil, plus more for brushing the pan

⅓ cup dried bread crumbs

1 tablespoon minced garlic

2 tablespoons chopped fresh thyme

3 tablespoons chopped fresh flat-leaf parsley

½ cup freshly grated Parmesan cheese

Kosher salt and freshly ground black pepper

1 pound eggplant (about 1 medium globe eggplant)

½ pound zucchini (1 or 2 small to medium zucchini)

½ pound yellow summer squash, such as pattypan or yellow zucchini (1 or 2 small to medium squash)

2 tablespoons unsalted butter

2 medium onions, cut in half and thinly sliced (about 6 cups)

A STEP AHEAD Caramelize the onion and toast and season the bread crumbs early in the day and leave them at room temperature. Assemble the vegetables in the baking dish a few hours ahead and allow the dish to sit out at room temperature before baking.

Preheat the oven to 400°F. Brush a baking dish, such as a 9 by 13-inch baking pan or a shallow earthenware casserole, with olive oil.

To toast the bread crumbs, heat 1 tablespoon of the olive oil over medium-high heat in a small sauté pan. Add the dried bread crumbs and stir until the crumbs begin to brown and get crunchy, about 2 minutes. Remove from the heat and let cool slightly. Put the bread crumbs in a small bowl and stir in the garlic, thyme, parsley, and Parmesan. Season the bread crumbs to taste with salt and pepper. Set aside.

Cut the stem off the eggplant, then slice into ¼-inch rounds. Cut the stems off the squash and slice them into ¼-inch rounds, slightly on the bias for zucchini-type or slender squash. Set aside.

Melt the butter in a sauté pan over medium heat. Cook the onions, stirring frequently, until soft, golden, and caramelized, about 15 minutes. Season to taste with salt and pepper.

Spread the onions in the bottom of the baking dish. Layer the eggplant and squash, in alternate rows, overlapping the vegetables and pushing the rows together a bit as you work to make more room. You may have a few slices left over, depending on the shape of your baking dish. Season the vegetables with salt and pepper and drizzle with the remaining 3 tablespoons olive oil.

Bake, uncovered, until the vegetables are almost tender, about 45 minutes. Remove the pan from the oven and sprinkle the prepared bread crumbs evenly over the top. Return the pan to the oven and bake until the crumbs are golden and the vegetables are completely tender, about 25 minutes more. Serve immediately, directly from the baking dish.

DRIED BREAD CRUMBS

A HALF LOAF EUROPEAN-STYLE WHITE BREAD (ABOUT 12 OUNCES OR ABOUT 8 SLICES)
YIELDS 2½ CUPS BREAD CRUMBS

Homemade bread crumbs are a world apart from the kind you get at the supermarket. If you go to the trouble of making your own, you can keep some in the freezer and use them whenever you want to add a crisp, crunchy touch to a pasta dish, a casserole, or a pan of roasted vegetables.

A STEP AHEAD Dried bread crumbs will keep for a week or more at room temperature in a tightly sealed container. Or seal them in plastic bags and freeze them for a month or more.

Preheat the oven to 325°F. Cut the crusts off the bread and discard, then slice the bread ½ inch thick. Place the slices in a single layer on an ungreased baking sheet. Put the baking sheet in the oven and bake until the bread feels dried out in the center, about 40 minutes. Turn the bread over from time to time so it dries out evenly. Remove the bread from the oven and allow to cool. Tear the bread into pieces and place in a food processor. Pulse until the crumbs are very fine.

CHOCOLATE CRÊPES WITH GEWÜRZTRAMINER SYRUP

MAKES 6 SERVINGS

Our daughter, Loretta, is the crêpe maker of the house. It is her favorite food, and she has often stated that when she moves out on her own she's going to open a crêperie. I sure hope crêpes become really popular in America so she makes a lot of money and can take care of her poor mom and dad.

Jackie garnishes these dessert crêpes with fresh raspberries, but try blackberries or sweet cherries. A scoop of vanilla ice cream or a dollop of lightly sweetened whipped cream cuts the richness of the chocolate, and a drizzle of fragrant, golden Gewürztraminer syrup accentuates our wine dinner theme.

The flavor of these crêpes is as good as the chocolate they are made from. Try to find a premium dark unsweetened cocoa, such as Valrhona, and top-quality bitter or semisweet chocolate such as Valrhona or Scharffen Berger (see Sources, page 265).

This recipe provides enough batter to make 16 crêpes, if you don't mess any up, but you need only 12 perfect ones.

FOR THE CHOCOLATE CRÊPES

2 large eggs
⅓ cup sugar
1 cup milk
1 cup all-purpose flour
2 tablespoons unsalted butter, melted, plus more for cooking the crêpes
1 tablespoon plus 2 teaspoons unsweetened cocoa powder
1 teaspoon pure vanilla extract
Pinch of kosher salt

FOR THE GANACHE

¾ cup heavy cream
6 ounces semisweet or bittersweet chocolate, chopped

FOR THE GEWÜRZTRAMINER SYRUP

2½ cups Gewürztraminer wine, a medium-sweet style such as Ste. Michelle Columbia Valley Gewürztraminer
½ cup sugar

TO FINISH AND GARNISH THE CRÊPES

1 tablespoon unsalted butter, melted, plus more for buttering the pan
2 teaspoons sugar
Vanilla ice cream or Sweetened Whipped Cream (page 69)
1 pint fresh raspberries

A STEP AHEAD Crêpe batter keeps for a day or two, covered, in the refrigerator. You can wrap the stack of cooked crêpes in plastic wrap with wax paper in between and store them in the refrigerator for a day or two, or longer in the freezer.

The syrup can be made a week ahead and stored covered in the refrigerator. You might need to warm it over a bowl of hot water if it gets too thick to drizzle. You can whisk in a little water a teaspoon at a time to thin it as well.

Assemble the crêpes and place them in the prepared baking dish several hours ahead and leave at room temperature. Drizzle the crêpes with butter and sprinkle with the sugar before baking.

To make the crêpes, combine the eggs, sugar, milk, flour, butter, cocoa, vanilla, and salt in a food processor or a blender and process until smooth. Transfer the crêpe batter to a container and refrigerate, covered, for an hour or more before cooking the crêpes.

To cook the crêpes, heat a 7- or 8-inch nonstick crêpe or sauté pan over medium-high heat. Brush the pan with melted butter. Ladle 2 to 3 tablespoons batter into the pan as you tilt the pan so the batter completely coats the bottom. Cook each crêpe until lightly browned on one side, about 30 seconds, then flip to cook the other side, about 30 seconds or less. If your pan gets too hot while you are cooking the crêpes, reduce the heat to medium. Repeat until you have 12 crêpes. Set the cooked crêpes aside with wax paper in between.

To make the ganache, bring the cream to a boil in a small saucepan over medium-high heat. Put the chocolate in a heat-proof bowl. Pour the cream over the chocolate, let sit for 2 minutes, then whisk until very smooth. Allow the ganache to stand at room temperature for about 10 minutes to firm up a bit.

To make the Gewürztraminer syrup, combine the wine and the sugar in a heavy saucepan over high heat. Bring to a boil, stirring until the sugar is dissolved, and boil until reduced and syrupy. You should have about ½ cup syrup, which will be slightly golden and about as thick as honey. Set aside.

Preheat the oven to 400°F.

To assemble the crêpes, lay out a crêpe, prettiest side down. Put a heaping tablespoon of ganache in the center of the crêpe and spread with a butter knife or metal icing spatula to within ½ to 1 inch of the edges. Fold the crêpe in half, then in half again to form a triangle. Repeat until all the crêpes are filled. Butter a baking dish, such as a 9 by 13-inch pan. Place the filled crêpes in the baking dish in a single layer. Drizzle the melted butter over the top and sprinkle with the sugar. Bake until the crêpes are hot, about 12 minutes. Remove the pan from the oven.

Using a spatula, put 2 crêpes on each dessert plate. Drizzle some syrup around the crêpes. Top each serving with a scoop of ice cream or a dollop of whipped cream and garnish with the raspberries.

THE WASHINGTON WINE INDUSTRY

Of the 100,000 bottles of wine we sell in our restaurants every year, fully half are from our home state. The first commercial Washington winery started producing wine in 1977, just five years before my first head chef job at Café Sport. In fact, our restaurants and the wineries here have grown up together, and we treasure the organic relationship that exists between us and the winemakers. Many of the winemakers here have become close friends, so it brings us particular pleasure when we turn our customers and the world on to the joys of wines from this region.

Washington state is now the fastest-growing wine-producing region in the country. The majority of grapes are grown on the east side of the Cascade Mountains, where summers are sunny, hot, and dry, but believe it or not, some grapes actually are grown on the cooler, western side of the state. As a matter of fact, Puget Sound is one of the five current Washington appellations, along with the Yakima Valley, Columbia Valley, Walla Walla, and the Red Mountain areas. Like other wine regions, the range of varietals is expanding rapidly. Reisling, Muller-Thurgau, and Concord grapes have largely been replaced with Chardonnay, Sauvignon Blanc, Syrah, Cabernet, Merlot, Sangiovese, and Cabernet Franc.

There still are not many Washington wines available nationwide, but in almost every market you can find some wines from the premier wineries like Columbia Crest, Hogue, Ste. Michelle, Woodward Canyon, and L'Ecole. When I travel around the country doing my chefy things, I always take Washington wines with me. But if you have the chance, you should come see for yourself what all the hubbub is about by visiting Washington wine country.

DELICIOUS AND AFFORDABLE WASHINGTON WINES YOU CAN FIND AROUND THE COUNTRY

❖ Arbor Crest Sauvignon Blanc

❖ Columbia Crest Grand Estates Chardonnay

❖ Hogue Cabernet Sauvignon

❖ Woodward Canyon Cabernet

❖ L'Ecole Merlot

❖ Quilceda Creek red table wine

❖ Columbia Syrah

❖ Domaine Ste. Michelle sparkling wine (Chardonnay blend)

❖ Chaleur Estates D2 (Bordeaux blend)

DINNER WITH DALE CHIHULY

Jackie and I often visit local galleries, and our house and restaurants are filled with the work of local artists. So needless to say we were thrilled when famed Seattle glass artist Dale Chihuly came into the Palace Kitchen shortly after it opened. In fact, at one point early on Dale wanted to trade food and wine at the Dahlia for one of his chandeliers, which I am crazy about. I was very excited about the whole idea until I found out how much a Chihuly chandelier goes for.

Dale has stamped his imprimatur on the Seattle-Tacoma area in the same way Antonio Gaudi stamped his on the Barcelona cityscape. In fact, Dale and Gaudi share a penchant for sensuous, curving, almost surreal design. Further, I would say they have impacted their respective cities in equally big ways. Gaudi's work has come to symbolize Barcelona in the same way that Dale Chihuly's has come to symbolize Seattle.

When you visit Seattle, you can and should take a self-guided Chihuly glass tour. There are larger-than-life Chihuly installations sprinkled throughout this area that you can stare at for hours because you can't believe they're quite real: the three-story-high pearl white chandeliers at Benaroya Symphony Hall, the all-the colors of the-rainbow sea forms installation at Pacific Place that anchors my favorite public glass-art display in the city. A thirty-minute drive down I-5 to Dale's hometown of Tacoma will get you to the newly renovated Union Station. There, hanging from a ninety foot tall dome, hangs a twenty-foot-high, nine-foot-around cobalt blue chandelier, made with two thousand hand-blown pieces of glass. From there you walk across the Chihuly Bridge of Glass, with its spectacular crystallized forms, to the Museum of Glass, where blowers are working feverishly in front of the sixteen-hundred-degree ovens.

When Jackie and I had the opportunity to have dinner with

MENU

SPAGHETTI AGLIO E OLIO
WITH BROILED LOBSTER AND
CRUSTY BREAD CRUMBS

LAGEDER PINOT GRIGIO

OLIVE-STUFFED FLANK STEAK

CHERRY TOMATO CONFIT

WILTED ESCAROLE AND
GARLIC-FRIED GARBANZO
BEANS

PRODUTTORI BARBARESCO

RATTI BAROLO MARCENASCO

NEBBIOLO-POACHED FIGS
WITH SWEET GORGONZOLA
AND MOSCATO D'ASTI
"GLASS"

PINE NUT MARZIPAN TART

MOSCATO SARACCO

Dale, he gave us the option of cooking in the big kitchen of his Lake Union boathouse studio. Duh! Of course we jumped at the chance. Chihuly's legendary eighty-foot-long, six-inch-thick single-slab Douglas Fir dining room table could be the ultimate Big Dinner table in the world. What does he love to eat? I wondered. Turns out Dale loves lush foods with big flavors: lobster, red meats, and huge red wines. So we designed this menu of big juicy broiled lobsters, cut in half and served over olive oil–drenched thin spaghetti topped with garlicky, crunchy bread crumbs. And that was just the starter! We popped open some luscious Barbarescos to accompany one of my favorite family recipes for roasted flank steak stuffed with olives, herbs, pine nuts, and currants. As a tribute to Dale's art, we garnished the Nebbiolo-poached Black Mission figs with shards of Moscato "glass," or Moscato d'Asti set up with a little gelatin.

There is much I admire about Dale Chihuly. He took one simple idea, glass, and through sheer talent and chutzpah made it into a cultural phenomenon. I respect the audacity of his vision. One of these days, if I sell enough books and spice rub, I may finally be able to afford my own cherished Chihuly original . . . ooh, that's a lot of books and spice rub—I better get busy.

SPAGHETTI AGLIO E OLIO WITH BROILED LOBSTER AND CRUSTY BREAD CRUMBS

MAKES 6 SERVINGS

If you're in the mood to fire up the grill, these lobsters will be even more delicious charcoal broiled. It takes about the same time to grill them over a direct, hot fire as broiling does.

If you can't find live lobsters, substitute frozen and thawed lobster tails. Or you could omit the lobster and just serve the aglio e olio with freshly grated Parmigiano-Reggiano.

7 tablespoons extra virgin olive oil

1/2 cup Dried Bread Crumbs (page 83)

Kosher salt and freshly ground black pepper

2 tablespoons unsalted butter, softened

1 tablespoon plus 1 teaspoon minced garlic

1/4 teaspoon hot red pepper flakes or to taste

1 tablespoon anchovy paste

3 whole lobsters, 1 to 1 1/4 pounds each, or 3 thawed frozen lobster tails, 6 to 8 ounces each

3/4 pound spaghetti

1/4 cup chopped fresh flat-leaf parsley

1/2 lemon

A STEP AHEAD Toast the bread crumbs several hours ahead and leave them at room temperature.

To toast the bread crumbs, heat 1 tablespoon of the olive oil in a sauté pan over medium-high heat. Add the crumbs and stir for a few minutes, until browned and crunchy. Season to taste with salt and pepper. Set aside to cool.

Bring a large pot of salted water to a boil.

Put 4 tablespoons of the oil and the butter in a large sauté pan over medium heat. When the butter melts, add the garlic and red pepper flakes and heat gently for a few minutes, until aromatic and the garlic is just starting to turn golden. Remove the pan from the heat, stir in the anchovy paste, and set aside.

Shell sides up and starting at the heads, quickly split the lobsters in half with a large sharp knife. Drizzle each lobster, on both sides, with about 1 tablespoon of the remaining oil and season with salt and pepper. Remove the bands from the lobster claws. If using lobster tails, split them in half lengthwise, through the shell, then drizzle them on both sides with oil and season with salt and pepper. Turn the broiler on high and place the lobsters, meat side up,

on a broiler pan. Broil about 3 inches from the heat, rotating the pan occasionally and turning them over halfway, until the lobsters are done, about 10 minutes total time for whole lobsters. Lobster tails may take a few minutes less. The shells should be bright red. Remove the lobsters from the broiler and use the side of a heavy knife to crack the claws.

While the lobsters are broiling, cook the spaghetti in the boiling water until al dente. Drain. Add the spaghetti to the sauté pan. Add the parsley and toss. Season with salt and pepper, but taste first, because the anchovy paste is salty.

Divide the pasta among 6 large plates and top each portion with ½ lobster or ½ lobster tail. Squeeze some lemon juice over the top and sprinkle both the lobster and the pasta with the bread crumbs.

NOTE: If you're making the whole menu, preheat the oven to 400°F and pan-sear the olive-stuffed flank steaks right before your guests arrive. Leave the seared steaks at room temperature and start heating your pot of water for the pasta. When you are ready to serve the pasta course, turn the broiler on, broil the lobsters, make the spaghetti aglio e olio, and serve. Meanwhile, reheat the oven to 400°F and roast the steaks while you are eating the pasta course.

OLIVE-STUFFED FLANK STEAK

MAKES 6 TO 8 SERVINGS

My Grandma Fogarty made a real dinner *every* night, *from scratch*. When it came time to serve the meal, she would pop off her apron, looking pretty as a picture, fix a highball, light a candle, and pull one tasty treat after another out of the kitchen. Her meals were well thought out, wines were paired with the main course, and there was always a homemade dessert to finish, from apple brown betty to butterscotch meringue pie.

This flank steak and her boeuf bourguignonne were my favorites of her beef dishes. Grandma Louise used bread in her flank steak stuffing, but I've lightened it up a little bit, keeping all the ingredients except the bread.

This is a great company dish because it's easy to make but looks fancy and complicated due to the spiral filling inside each slice.

2 tablespoons olive oil, plus about 2 tablespoons for cooking the steaks

1 cup finely chopped onion

1 teaspoon minced garlic

1 cup chopped pitted Kalamata olives

¼ cup finely chopped fresh flat-leaf parsley

1 tablespoon finely chopped fresh thyme

½ cup toasted pine nuts (see page 24)

¼ cup currants

2 flank steaks, about 1¼ to 1½ pounds each

Kosher salt and freshly ground black pepper

Cherry Tomato Confit

A STEP AHEAD Make the olive stuffing a day or two ahead and store it, covered, in the refrigerator. Stuff and tie the steaks early in the day and store them, covered, in the refrigerator. Bring the steaks to room temperature about ½ hour before cooking.

To make the stuffing, heat the 2 tablespoons oil in a sauté pan over medium heat. Add the onion and cook until soft and caramelized, stirring occasionally, about 10 minutes. Add the garlic and cook until aromatic, a few minutes more. Remove from the heat and transfer to a bowl. Stir in the olives, herbs, pine nuts, and currants. Set aside to cool.

To prepare the flank steaks for stuffing, place one of the steaks on a work surface, cover it loosely with a piece of plastic wrap, and use a meat pounder to pound the steak until about ⅓ inch thick. The surface area of the steak should increase by only about 25 percent. Then, use your knife to score the steak in a crisscross pattern, making 3 or 4 shallow cuts in each direction, not cutting all the way through. Turn the steak over to the unscored side and spread half the stuffing evenly over the surface of the steak, then roll it up the long way, like a jelly roll. Using kitchen twine, tightly tie the steak in 5 or 6 places to keep it securely rolled up. Season the out-

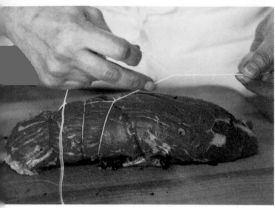

side of the steak with salt and pepper. Repeat with the other steak and the other half of the stuffing.

To pan-sear and roast the steaks, preheat the oven to 400°F. Pour about 2 tablespoons of olive oil into a roasting pan and place the pan over two burners over medium-high heat. When the oil is hot, put the steaks in the pan and sear them well on all sides, turning with tongs, until nicely browned, 6 to 8 minutes. Remove the pan from the heat and transfer the steaks to a plate. Discard any fat in the pan and scrape out and discard any burned bits that may have escaped from the stuffing. Put the steaks back in the roasting pan, put the pan in the oven, and roast, uncovered, for 7 to 8 minutes. Turn the steaks over and continue to roast until the internal temperature of the steaks reads between 120°F and 130°F on an instant-read meat thermometer, after 7 to 8 minutes more. Remove the pan from the oven and allow the steaks to rest for 5 to 8 minutes. Cut and remove the kitchen string, transfer the steaks to a cutting board, and use a sharp knife (a serrated knife works well) to cut them into slices ½ to ¾ inch thick. Arrange the slices on a platter and pour any pan juices that have collected over the top. Serve the steak with the cherry tomato confit.

CHERRY TOMATO CONFIT

MAKES 2½ CUPS

Classically, a confit is a duck cooked slowly in its own fat, but the word has taken on the meaning of almost any food cooked slowly in fat or oil. The tomatoes need to roast in a low oven for a long time, but they can be made well ahead.

These tomatoes, drained of most of the oil, would also be delicious tossed with pasta and some chunks of fresh goat cheese. Save the oil that you drain from the tomatoes and use it to make vinaigrettes or drizzle it over roasted or grilled vegetables or fish.

1½ pounds (3 half-pint baskets) cherry tomatoes, such as Sweet 100,
   stems removed
1 cup olive oil
Three 3-inch fresh rosemary sprigs
6 fresh thyme sprigs
6 garlic cloves, peeled
Kosher salt and freshly ground black pepper
2 teaspoons red wine vinegar
1 teaspoon chopped fresh thyme

A STEP AHEAD Make the confit up to 5 days ahead and store, with the oil, covered and refrigerated. The flavor improves significantly after 1 day. When you are ready to serve the confit, bring it back to room temperature, drain off the oil, and season as described.

Preheat the oven to 225°F.

Put the tomatoes in a baking pan large enough to hold them in a single layer. Pour the oil over the tomatoes, add the herb sprigs and garlic cloves, and season generously with salt and pepper. Roast, uncovered, until the tomatoes are swollen and the skins are wrinkled, about 3 hours.

Remove the tomatoes from the oven, allow to cool, then pour into a small bowl. For the best flavor, cover and refrigerate overnight, bringing the confit back to room temperature when you are ready to serve.

When you are ready to serve, pour the tomatoes into a strainer set over a bowl, reserving both the tomatoes and the oil. Place the drained tomatoes in a small bowl, discarding the herb sprigs and garlic cloves. Add the vinegar, chopped thyme, and 1 tablespoon of the reserved oil (reserving the remaining oil for another use). Mix gently, being careful not to break up the tomatoes. Season to taste with salt and pepper.

WILTED ESCAROLE AND GARLIC-FRIED GARBANZO BEANS

MAKES 6 SERVINGS

Typically, escarole is available year-round. The heads look a lot like butter or Bibb lettuce. There is a certain bitterness to escarole, but braising mellows out the flavor.

Use pure olive oil for frying, not extra virgin, because it has a higher smoke point. If you don't feel like frying the garlic and garbanzo beans, the wilted escarole makes an appealing side dish all by itself.

Pure olive oil as needed for frying

8 garlic cloves, peeled and sliced about $\frac{1}{8}$ inch thick ($\frac{1}{4}$ cup)

Kosher salt and freshly ground black pepper

2 cups cooked garbanzo beans (chickpeas)

2 heads escarole (about $2\frac{1}{2}$ pounds), cored and roughly chopped

$\frac{1}{2}$ lemon plus lemon wedges for garnish

A STEP AHEAD Fry the garbanzos and the garlic early in the day and keep them at room temperature. When you are ready to serve, heat the garbanzos in a 400°F oven until hot, about 5 minutes. The garlic can be served at room temperature.

Preheat the oven to 200°F.

To fry the garlic, fill a heavy saucepan with oil to a depth of about 1 inch. Heat the oil to 325°F, checking the temperature on a deep-frying thermometer (see page 14). Add the sliced garlic to the oil and scoop it out with a skimmer or slotted spoon as soon as it starts to turn golden, after about 10 seconds. Drain the garlic on paper towels and leave at room temperature. Season the garlic with salt and pepper.

Start adding the garbanzos to the oil, a small handful at a time, and fry until golden and crusty, 2 to 3 minutes. (If you add too many garbanzos at once, they will lower the temperature of the oil and won't fry properly.) As you are frying, keep checking the temperature of the oil with a deep-frying thermometer and adjust the heat as necessary to keep it between 325°F and 350°F. Using a skimmer or slotted spoon, scoop the garbanzos out as they are done and drain on paper towels. Season the fried garbanzos with salt and pepper, transfer them to a baking sheet, and keep them warm in the oven.

Remove the pan of oil from the heat and set it aside.

To wilt the escarole, put about 3 tablespoons of the reserved frying oil (discard the remaining oil when cool) in a large deep skillet or Dutch oven over medium high heat. Add as much escarole as will comfortably fit into your pan and toss with tongs until wilted. Then start adding the remaining escarole a handful at a time and keep tossing until all the escarole is wilted. Reduce the heat to medium, cover the pan, and cook for a few minutes more, until the escarole is tender, 8 to 10 minutes altogether. Season with salt and pepper to taste.

Arrange the escarole on a platter and squeeze the ½ lemon over it. Scatter the fried garbanzos over the surface of the escarole and scatter the fried garlic on top. Garnish the platter with lemon wedges.

NOTE: You can cook dried garbanzo beans for this recipe or use canned beans, drained well and patted dry with paper towels. To cook dried garbanzos, cover them with cold water and soak overnight. Drain the soaked beans, cover them with plenty of cold water, cook for an hour or more until tender, and drain well. One cup of raw garbanzos yields a little more than 2 cups of cooked beans.

NEBBIOLO-POACHED FIGS WITH SWEET GORGONZOLA AND MOSCATO D'ASTI "GLASS"

MAKES 6 SERVINGS

Warm figs and melted sweet, or dolce, Gorgonzola drizzled with a lustrous wine syrup functions as both a cheese and a dessert course. As a tribute to Dale, we surround the figs with a Moscato gelatin, cut up to resemble shards of glass.

Moscato d'Asti is a sweet sparkling Italian wine. The gelatin, which tastes just like a glass of Moscato, would be a nice little dessert by itself, cut into cubes and piled into a pretty glass with some fresh berries. Or, simplify this dessert by serving the figs and Gorgonzola without the "glass."

1 tablespoon plus 1 teaspoon unflavored gelatin
(less than 2 full envelopes)
2⅓ cups Moscato d'Asti
12 ripe fresh figs such as Black Mission
2 cups Nebbiolo, Dolcetto, or Barbera dry red wine
⅔ cup honey
Two 4-inch fresh rosemary sprigs
Pinch of freshly ground black pepper
2½ ounces Gorgonzola dolce cheese, cut into 12 small chunks
about 1 inch by ½ inch

A STEP AHEAD Make the "glass" a day ahead and store it, covered, in the refrigerator. The delicate flavor of the wine deteriorates if stored longer. Cut the gelatin into chunks several hours ahead and put the chunks in a plastic-lined pan, covered with a sheet of plastic wrap.

Poach the figs early in the day, remove them from the poaching liquid, and cover and refrigerate them. Make the syrup and store it in the refrigerator as well. About an hour before you are ready to serve, bring the figs to room temperature, stuff them with the cheese, and heat them under the broiler. Also, bring the syrup to room temperature, over a bowl of hot water if desired.

To make the "glass," smoothly line the bottom and sides of an 8-inch-square baking dish with a piece of plastic wrap, pressing the plastic wrap directly against the sides of the pan. Set aside. Put ⅓ cup cold water in a large bowl, sprinkle the gelatin over it, and let it stand for 5 minutes to soften. Put 1 cup of the Moscato in a saucepan over high heat and bring it to a boil, then pour it over the gelatin. Stir well until the gelatin is dissolved. Add the rest of the Moscato, stirring to combine, then pour the mixture into the prepared pan. (Don't worry about bubbles; most will dissipate as the gelatin chills.) Cover the pan with a piece of plastic wrap (not directly touching the surface of the gelatin) and refrigerate until firm, about 6 hours or overnight.

Cut the stems off the figs and cut the figs open by cutting an X through the stem end, making each cut about 1 inch long or about halfway down the fig.

Put the Nebbiolo wine, honey, rosemary, and black pepper in a heavy saucepan over medium-high heat and bring to a simmer, stirring to dissolve the honey. Add the figs, reduce the heat slightly, and poach until the figs are soft and infused with wine but not falling apart, about 10 minutes. Remove from the heat and use a spoon to transfer the figs carefully to a plate. Reserve ½ cup of the poaching liquid and discard the rest or reserve for another use. Pour the reserved poaching liquid into a small saucepan and reduce over high heat until syrupy. You should have ¼ cup of syrup. Set aside.

Remove the pan of Moscato "glass" from the refrigerator and remove the plastic from the top of the pan. Place a cutting board over the baking dish and invert the gelatin onto the board. Carefully peel off the plastic wrap. Cut the gelatin into 1½-inch cubes or other decorative shapes.

Preheat the broiler.

Insert a chunk of cheese into each fig, pressing the cut edges of the fig over the cheese to enclose it as much as possible. Set each fig, stem end up, in a small broilerproof, nonreactive pan. Ideally, use a pan small enough so the figs sit shoulder to shoulder and hold each other up, such as a small sauté pan with a heatproof handle.

Broil the figs 3 inches from the heat just until the cheese is melted, 2 to 3 minutes, then remove from the broiler.

Using a spoon, transfer each fig to a platter. Drizzle the reserved syrup over and around the figs, then decorate the platter with the chunks of "glass."

GORGONZOLA

I love Gorgonzola cheese—crumbled into a salad, with ripe pears or figs and a glass of red wine, or melting on top of a steak. It's pungent, tangy, and downright delicious. Gorgonzola, which comes from Lombardy, Italy, is one of the great blue cheeses of the world. According to Steven Jenkins, author of the *Cheese Primer* (Workman Publishing Company, 1996), sweet Gorgonzola, known as *dolce,* is the definitive familiar Gorgonzola, a soft, mild, and smelly cheese. Aged Gorgonzola, known as *naturale,* is firmer and more assertive and aged a year or more. Which is better? It's simply a matter of taste. Frequent a cheesemonger who will let you sample both and let your taste buds decide. But remember that a blue cheese can be Gorgonzola only if it comes from the Lombardy region of Italy—not Wisconsin—just as sparkling wine can be Champagne only if it comes from Champagne, France.

FIGS

A perfectly ripe fresh fig needs no help from chefs like me. Simply cut it open and serve with a glass of red wine. A few of the figs most commonly available in this country are:

Mission (also known as Franciscana) figs are a deep purple-black outside and a brilliant red inside. Their texture is a little coarser than that of other figs, but they taste oh-so-sweet and good. We see these figs the most often in our produce market.

Kadota or Cadota figs, known in Italy as Dottatos, are yellow-green on the outside and amber or violet inside. These figs seem to be increasingly available here.

Brown Turkey figs are Turkish in origin, where they are known as Bardajic figs. They have reddish brown skin and amber-pink flesh. We have a Brown Turkey fig tree growing like a weed in our backyard, and we fight the birds for the sweet ripe figs every September.

Smyrna figs, called Calimyrna in the United States, are similar to the original fig that has been cultivated in Asia for thousands of years. Although Calimyrna figs, grown in California, are the variety most widely available in this country, most of them are dried. If you can find some fresh ones, these large, golden-skinned figs are said to have a deliciously nutty flavor.

PINE NUT MARZIPAN TART

MAKES ONE 9-INCH TART, SERVING 8 TO 12

A thin wedge of this sweet, buttery, double-crust tart is the perfect accompaniment to the wine-poached figs. If there are any leftovers, enjoy with coffee the next morning.

Instead of the figs, serve the tart with a scoop of vanilla ice cream or with a glass of Vin Santo.

FOR THE TART DOUGH

1⅔ cups all-purpose flour

¼ teaspoon baking powder

¼ teaspoon kosher salt

9 tablespoons unsalted butter, softened

½ cup confectioners' sugar

1 large egg plus 1 large yolk, lightly beaten together

FOR THE PINE NUT MARZIPAN

1 cup (about 4 ounces) pine nuts, toasted (see page 24)

½ cup granulated sugar

1 large egg, lightly beaten

4 tablespoons unsalted butter, softened

TO FINISH THE TART

1 large egg yolk

1 tablespoon heavy cream

About 2 teaspoons granulated sugar, as needed,
    for sprinkling

A STEP AHEAD Make the tart dough a few days ahead and keep it wrapped and refrigerated or freeze it even longer

You can make and bake the tart early in the day and leave it at room temperature. Leftovers can be wrapped in plastic wrap and left at room temperature for another day or so.

To make the tart dough, combine the flour, baking powder, and salt in a bowl and set aside. In the bowl of an electric mixer, using the paddle attachment, cream the butter and sugar together. Gradually beat in the eggs. It's OK if the mixture looks broken. Add the dry ingredients to the butter-egg mixture and mix just until the dough comes together. If you don't have a mixer, you can cream the butter and sugar by hand using a rubber spatula or a wooden spoon, then beat in the eggs using a whisk and mix in the dry ingredients using a rubber spatula. Scrape the dough out onto a work surface and divide into one-third and two-thirds portions, forming each portion into a flattened round. Wrap the rounds in plastic wrap and chill for at least 1 hour.

To make the pine nut marzipan, combine the toasted pine nuts and sugar in the bowl of a food processor and pulse until finely ground. Add the egg and process until smooth. Gradually add the butter, a small bit at a time, pulsing until each bit of butter is completely incorporated. When all the butter is incorporated, scrape the marzipan into a bowl.

Preheat the oven to 400°F.

Unwrap the larger round of dough and place it on a lightly floured work surface. Using a lightly floured rolling pin, roll the dough out to an 11- or 12-inch round about ⅛ inch thick. Use flour as needed to roll the dough and lift the dough occasionally with a pastry scraper as you are working to check that it's not sticking. Transfer the dough to a 9-inch tart pan with a removable rim. It's easiest to do this by folding the dough into quarters. Pick up the folded dough and place it in the pan, with the pointed tip of the dough in the center of the pan, then unfold gently.

Ease the dough gently into the pan, patting it up against the sides. Trim the overhanging dough to about ¼ inch. The dough is a bit fragile. If it tears while you are lining the pan, use the dough trimmings to patch any holes. Using a rubber spatula or an angled icing spatula, spread the marzipan evenly over the bottom of the tart. Unwrap the smaller round of dough and roll it out to a 9-inch round. Transfer the round of dough to cover the marzipan. It's easiest to fold the dough into quarters to transfer it. Use a small knife to trim the dough to fit inside the top of the tart.

In a small bowl, beat the egg yolk lightly with the heavy cream. Brush ¼ inch of overhanging dough with some egg wash, fold the overhang over the top of the tart, pressing gently with a fork to seal. Brush the top of the tart lightly with egg wash and sprinkle with sugar. Cut a few 1-inch slashes in the top of the tart. Place the tart pan on a baking sheet and bake until golden, about 30 minutes. Remove from the oven and allow the tart to cool on a rack for 15 minutes before removing the rim of the pan. Allow the tart to cool at least 15 minutes more before serving, then cut into thin wedges, and serve slightly warm or at room temperature.

MY SECOND-FAVORITE WINE REGION IN THE WORLD

When the big decade birthday comes along, or the big wedding anniversary, and we're figuring out where to go and spend that special moment, the dream place always seems to be in the Italian hills of Barbaresco and Barolo. I know for many people the Cinque Terre and Portofino, with their beaches and bikinis, are more popular destinations. But Jackie and I follow our hearts and our noses right to Alba, for white truffles, ripe Tomme cheese, and gorgeous Italian plums, cherries, and hazelnuts. On our first trip wo faithfully followed Faith Willinger's book *Eating in Italy* to find the best restaurants, butchers, gelaterias, shops, and markets. By the time we had made our fifth trip, people started asking us for our list of where to go when visiting the region.

These days we stay at our friend Juliana's bed-and-breakfast on the hillside below the peak of Barbaresco, overlooking lush valleys of apple orchards, olive trees, and row after row of grapevines. One of the real treats of staying at Juliana's is that she cooks dinner one night during our stay. We might be served sausage fonduta—boiled sausage with cheese sauce—or sweet red pepper rabbit, braised for hours until the juices are reduced to a caramel. If we're really lucky, we'll get a dish of impossibly small plin (sage ravioli in a delicate butter sauce), which she and her daughter have been producing over lively conversation all afternoon, fingers moving like concert pianists, making perfect little pouches.

The main draw in these towns, where the money really is, and what drives the tourism, is the wine. Angelo Gaja decided some thirty years ago that the wines of this area were undervalued and underappreciated and set about on a globe-trotting public relations journey to change things— and he sure has. Many of his wines now retail in the hundreds of dollars per bottle, and his fellow winemakers are following close behind. I can't afford his wines anymore, but there is plenty of good juice coming from the region that I can fill my home and restaurant wine cellars with. Here are some of my favorites:

Bartolo Mascarello: Barolo
Renato Ratti: Dolcetto, Barbera, Barolo
La Spinetta: Barbaresco
Bruno Giacosa: Nebbiolo
San Drone: Barolo, Nebbiolo
Paolo Scavino: Barolo
Produttori Barbaresco, a cooperative: Barbaresco, Nebbiolo
Saracco: Moscato d'Asti
Romano Levi: the best grappa I've ever tasted
Gaja: Barbaresco, Cabernet Sauvignon

So, what's my number-one favorite wine region in the world? It has to be Washington's Yakima Valley (see page 87).

PUGET SOUND CRAB FEED

In our neighborhood the tide decides when we're having a picnic on nearby Blue Ridge Beach. If the tide is up, the rocky sand disappears and our parties are limited to the cabana on the grassy knoll. But when the tide is down, the beach extends out for three hundred yards of wet gray sand, and you'll see all kinds of cool things: the shells, moon snail nests, giant clams squirting like fountains, starfish, barnacles—all the typical saltwater tide pool stuff. It's great fun watching the blue herons chase the little sand darters. Even Ruby, our dog, has had to dodge bald eagles and sea lions at the beach. Ruby will swim way out into Puget Sound chasing ducks, and I half expect her to be dragged under by an outlaw sea lion.

Sometimes we borrow our neighbor's rowboat and set crab traps just five hundred yards from shore. If we're lucky, in a few hours we reap four or five large Dungies, perfect for steaming.

Whether I buy crabs at Shoreline Central Market or from Harry at Mutual Fish or catch them myself at the beach, I cook them in Jackie's canning pot—a gargantuan speckled black enameled thirty-three-quart pot. Even her rubber-edged canning tongs are perfect for handling the crabs.

I've served crab feeds on both the East and West Coasts with different kinds of crabs. East Coast blue crabs are small and sold by the bushel. West Coast Dungeness get as big as 4 pounds, although we look for 2½ pounders. Either way, spread a good layer of newspapers on the picnic table and provide plenty of cracking hammers and picks.

I boil blue crabs with loads of spice. When you serve them (plan a half dozen per person), you don't need butter or cocktail sauce. On the other hand, I serve one 2½-pound Dungeness crab per person, and this is truly a feast. The flavor of Dungeness is lighter than blue crab, so you want to stay away from heavy Old Bay–style seasoning. Go for citrus and aromatics, like lemons and bay leaves,

MENU

SAUVIGNON BLANC PEACH
SANGRIA

CHARRED SQUID SKEWERS ON
GARLIC TOAST WITH ARUGULA

CHILLED CRACKED
DUNGENESS CRAB WITH SEA
SALT BUTTER AND GINGER
MAYONNAISE

CHOP SALAD WITH CORN,
SNAP PEAS, AND BACON

MAC AND CHEESE SALAD
WITH BUTTERMILK DRESSING

BLUE MOUNTAIN OKANAGAN
VALLEY PINOT GRIS

BLUEBERRY CORNMEAL
CROSTATA

BARNARD GRIFFIN SYRAH,
WASHINGTON

oranges and fennel. Sea salt butter and ginger mayonnaise are delicate accompaniments, elevating and enhancing the essential sweetness of the crab.

From our little beach we love to watch the sun set behind the Olympic Mountains. Our fabulous beach picnic can mostly be made ahead of time at the house, except for the squid we grill on the hibachi we carry to the beach. We take a blanket with us, set the hibachi in the sand, and pull up a couple of driftwood logs for chairs. Eating cracked crab and drinking peach sangria as we stare at and stoke a bonfire on the beach is as pleasant a way to spend a summer or early fall evening, as we know.

SAUVIGNON BLANC PEACH SANGRIA

This unconventional version of sangria is infused with subtle peach flavor, but you can still appreciate the fresh, crisp characteristics of the Sauvignon Blanc. Fragrant, ripe, tasty peaches are essential. Many recipes for sangria advise you to let it sit for four hours or overnight, but we think this version tastes best after just two hours.

Double the recipe to serve more than one glass of sangria to each of your guests

3 peaches (1 to 1½ pounds), peeled (see page 66), pitted, and sliced
1 lime, sliced
¼ cup sugar
1 bottle Sauvignon Blanc

Put the peaches, lime, and sugar in a large pitcher and pour in the wine. Stir gently with a long spoon to help dissolve the sugar. Cover the pitcher with plastic wrap and refrigerate for 2 hours. Remove the pitcher from the refrigerator, uncover, and stir again. Then pour through a fine-mesh strainer or a cheesecloth-lined strainer into a large bowl or pitcher. Save 6 each of the nicest-looking peach and lime slices for garnish and discard the rest.

Pour the sangria into ice-filled glasses. Garnish each glass with a peach and a lime slice.

CHARRED SQUID SKEWERS ON GARLIC TOAST WITH ARUGULA

MAKES 6 SERVINGS

Often squid is deep-fried, so it's fun to grill it for a change. For tender, lightly charred squid, cook the skewers quickly over a direct fire, with the coals as close as possible to the grate. A small hibachi that you can carry down to the beach will work very well (and, if you're making this whole menu, you can also use the hibachi to keep your Sea Salt Butter warm). The spiced and charred squid skewers are served over a little bed of lemony arugula, with garlic toast underneath to catch all the vinaigrette and juices. Grill the toasts before you grill the squid and set them aside in a warm place.

Chermoula is a slightly spicy Moroccan sauce made with cilantro and garlic. Also try this marinade on grilled shrimp, scallop skewers, or chicken breasts.

Not in the mood for squid? The Grilled Oysters with Horseradish Butter (page 148) also make a great start for this menu.

2 pounds cleaned squid bodies, with or without tentacles

12 or more 10-inch bamboo skewers, soaked in water for 30 minutes and drained

FOR THE CHERMOULA MARINADE

3 tablespoons finely chopped fresh flat-leaf parsley

2 tablespoons finely chopped fresh cilantro

2 tablespoons freshly squeezed lemon juice

2 teaspoons minced garlic

2 teaspoons paprika

2 teaspoons sambal oelek (see page 265) or $\frac{1}{4}$ teaspoon cayenne pepper

2 teaspoons freshly grated lemon zest

$\frac{3}{4}$ teaspoon kosher salt

$\frac{1}{2}$ teaspoon freshly ground black pepper

$\frac{1}{2}$ cup extra virgin olive oil

FOR THE LEMON VINAIGRETTE

1 tablespoon freshly squeezed lemon juice

2 teaspoons minced shallot

2 tablespoons extra virgin olive oil

Kosher salt and freshly ground black pepper

5 cups loosely packed arugula, stems trimmed, washed and dried

6 Garlic Toasts (page 55), made on the grill

Lemon wedges for garnish

A STEP AHEAD Cut the squid and assemble the skewers up to a day ahead and store, covered with plastic wrap, in the refrigerator. Make the chermoula marinade and the lemon vinaigrette up to a day ahead and store, covered, in the refrigerator. Marinate the skewers 30 minutes before you plan to grill them.

If your squid bodies have fins (thin flaps) attached to them, slice off and discard them. Put the blade of your knife inside a squid body and carefully slice it open, cutting away from you, so you have one flat piece. Cut this piece in half lengthwise. You will have two squid pieces, shaped like two long, tapered rectangles. Using your knife, lightly score the inside of each rectangle in a crosshatch pattern, not cutting all the way through. Repeat this procedure with all the squid bodies. To skewer the squid, thread one rectangle, lengthwise, onto a bamboo skewer, followed by two tentacles (if using), then another rectangle. Pick up another skewer and continue until all the squid bodies are used. (You may have some tentacles left over; you can thread them together on a skewer.) Place the skewers in a nonreactive pan.

To make the marinade, combine the parsley, cilantro, lemon juice, garlic, paprika, sambal oelek, lemon zest, salt, and pepper in a bowl and whisk in the oil. Pour the marinade over the squid, cover with plastic wrap, and refrigerate for 30 minutes.

To make the lemon vinaigrette, combine the lemon juice and shallot in a small bowl and whisk in the olive oil. Season to taste with salt and pepper. Set aside.

Fire up your grill. Remove the skewers from the refrigerator and allow the squid to come to room temperature. Shake off the excess marinade, then grill the skewers over a hot fire, direct heat, with the lid off. Turn the skewers several times as needed, until the squid is cooked through, opaque, and charred in a few places, about 1 to 3 minutes, depending on the heat of your fire. Do not overcook, or the squid will be tough. Remove the skewers from the grill.

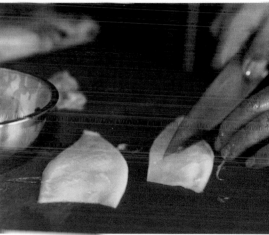

Put the arugula in a bowl and toss it with about 2 tablespoons of the lemon vinaigrette. Arrange the garlic toasts on a platter. Top each toast with some arugula salad. Put two squid skewers on top of each toast and drizzle the remaining vinaigrette over the skewers. Garnish with the lemon wedges.

HOW TO CLEAN SQUID

If you buy whole squid instead of cleaned squid bodies, they will have to be cleaned. Place the whole squid on a cutting board and grasp the head and tentacles with one hand and the body with the other. Pull your hands apart. The head and tentacles will separate from the body.

Take the head and tentacle piece and, with a knife, slice off the tentacles just past the eyes. Squeeze out the hard beak and discard. Reserve the tentacles. Holding the body piece, pull out and discard the transparent quill. Use your finger to reach inside the body and pull out any remaining guts. Peel off the skin and rinse the inside of the body under running water.

CHILLED CRACKED DUNGENESS CRAB WITH SEA SALT BUTTER AND GINGER MAYONNAISE

MAKES 6 SERVINGS

At the fish market, choose crabs that are large, heavy, and lively. While preparing the pot, keep the crabs on their backs so they won't be able to scurry away. A 2½-pound crab might seem large, but after it's shelled, there's less than 8 ounces of crabmeat. One crab per person is the norm in our household.

As with all of our recipes, it's more important to use local fresh ingredients than to try to find crabs from across the country. So use whatever crab is freshest in your area and adjust the cooking times as needed. If you can't get live crabs, you can serve chilled cooked crabs or thawed frozen king crab legs, accompanied by the butter and mayonnaise.

Eating steamed crabs is delightfully messy. Provide crab crackers or crab hammers, cocktail forks, bowls for the shells, a big stack of napkins, and lemon water for cleaning your hands. Plastic bibs keep your clothes tidy and are often sold at fish markets.

2 lemons, cut in half lengthwise and thickly sliced

5 bay leaves, crushed with your hands

2 tablespoons sea salt

6 live Dungeness crabs (about 2½ pounds each)

FOR THE SEA SALT BUTTER

½ pound (2 sticks) unsalted butter, melted

1 tablespoon plus 1 teaspoon freshly squeezed lemon juice

Sea salt

FOR THE GINGER MAYONNAISE

1 cup mayonnaise, homemade (page 13), or good-quality store-bought

1 teaspoon peeled and grated fresh ginger

2 tablespoons thinly sliced fresh chives

Sea salt and freshly ground black pepper

Lemon wedges for garnish

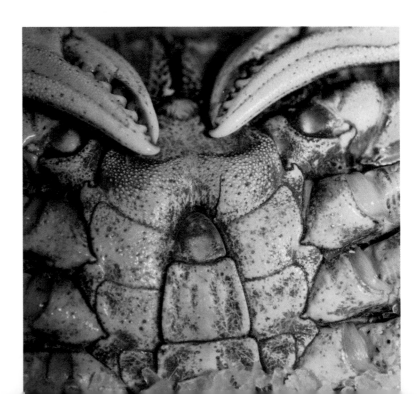

Put 2 gallons water, the lemons, bay leaves, and sea salt in a very large pot and bring to a boil over high heat. Add the crabs to the pot and cover with a lid. Boil the crabs until they are cooked through, 11 to 15 minutes. The crabs will turn red and will be covered with some of the coagulated crab juices, which look like cooked egg white. If you're not sure whether the crabs are done, pull one out, pull off the top shell, and look at the meat. The crabmeat should be white and opaque, not translucent.

When the crabs are cooked, pull them out of the pot and place them in the sink. Quickly rinse the crabs with cold water, then allow them to cool in the sink. Don't cover the crabs with cold water or ice water, because you will rinse away the flavor.

To clean the crabs, pick up a crab and pry the top shell (carapace) from the body. Gently rinse the gunklike "mustard" from the crab and remove and discard the gills. Some people like to eat the "mustard," which consists of fat and edible organs. If you do, you don't need to rinse it off. Break the crab body in half, removing the tablike apron (tail) from the bottom shell. Continue until all the crabs are cleaned, reserving a few of the top shells for garnish. If you are not serving the crabs right away, refrigerate them.

To make the sea salt butter, combine the butter and lemon juice in a small bowl and season to taste with sea salt. To make the ginger mayonnaise, combine the mayonnaise, ginger, and chives in another small bowl and season to taste with salt and pepper.

Pile the crabs on a large platter and garnish the platter with a few of the top shells and the lemon wedges. Serve with the butter and mayonnaise.

NOTE: If you are making the whole menu, double the mayonnaise recipe to yield 1½ cups. Use 1 cup of the mayonnaise here and the remaining ½ cup for the Mac and Cheese Salad.

CHOP SALAD WITH CORN, SNAP PEAS, AND BACON

MAKES 6 TO 8 SERVINGS

I love chop salads because you can change them to suit your whim or the season. Substitute diced salami for the bacon or diced Gouda for the Parmesan. Add a handful of diced celery or some cooked garbanzo beans. Just keep in mind that everything should be cut into small pieces and there should be more vegetables than lettuce.

FOR THE MUSTARD VINAIGRETTE

2 tablespoons red wine vinegar

1 tablespoon freshly squeezed lemon juice

1 tablespoon Dijon mustard

2 teaspoons minced garlic

$\frac{1}{2}$ cup plus 1 tablespoon olive oil

Kosher salt and freshly ground black pepper

FOR THE SALAD

$\frac{1}{2}$ pound sliced bacon

6 ounces sugar snap peas ($1\frac{1}{2}$ cups), strings removed, cut in half on a diagonal

$1\frac{1}{2}$ cups fresh corn kernels (about 2 ears)

$\frac{1}{2}$ head romaine

1 medium cucumber, peeled, seeded, and cut into $\frac{1}{4}$-inch dice

1 medium carrot, peeled and grated

$\frac{1}{2}$ medium red bell pepper, cut into $\frac{1}{4}$-inch dice

$\frac{1}{2}$ bunch radishes, thinly sliced (about $\frac{1}{2}$ cup)

$\frac{1}{2}$ bunch scallions, thinly sliced (about $\frac{3}{4}$ cup)

$\frac{1}{2}$ pint cherry tomatoes, stemmed, cut in half

1 cup fresh basil leaves (about 1 ounce), cut into thin strips

$\frac{1}{2}$ cup freshly grated Parmesan cheese

A STEP AHEAD Fry and chop the bacon early in the day and store it in the refrigerator. Reheat it for a few minutes in a 400°F oven until warm. Make the vinaigrette a few days ahead and store it, covered, in the refrigerator. Prepare all the vegetables several hours ahead and keep them covered and refrigerated. Chop the lettuce, slice the basil, and toss the salad at the last minute.

To make the mustard vinaigrette, combine the vinegar, lemon juice, mustard, and garlic in a bowl. Gradually whisk in the oil until emulsified. Season to taste with salt and pepper.

In a skillet over medium heat, fry the bacon until crisp and drain on paper towels, discarding the fat. Chop the bacon and set aside.

Bring a saucepan of lightly salted water to a boil and set up a bowl of ice water. Set a strainer filled with the snap peas into the saucepan and cook for a minute or two. Remove the snap peas and immediately plunge them into the bowl of ice water. Put the corn in the strainer and put it into the saucepan of boiling water for a minute or two. Remove the corn and plunge it into the ice water with the peas. Drain the corn and peas and set aside.

Chop the romaine leaves and place them in a large bowl. You should have about 4 cups chopped leaves. Add the peas, corn, cucumber, carrot, red pepper, radishes, scallions, tomatoes, and basil to the bowl, then toss with enough vinaigrette to coat everything lightly. Add the Parmesan, toss again, and season to taste with salt and pepper.

Mound the salad on a large platter and sprinkle the bacon over the top.

MAC AND CHEESE SALAD WITH BUTTERMILK DRESSING

MAKES 6 SERVINGS

My take on mac and cheese is a chilled pasta salad with creamy buttermilk dressing and ricotta salata. In the spring, toss in some blanched and sliced asparagus or blanched fresh peas. The buttermilk dressing would also be tasty on a salad of poached shrimp, cucumbers, and Bibb lettuce or mixed into a bowl of steamed and chilled baby red potatoes.

Ricotta salata is a slightly tangy Italian sheep's milk cheese. Grate it on the finest holes of a box grater. If you can't find ricotta salata, substitute pecorino, another Italian sheep's milk cheese.

Mâche, sometimes called *corn salad* or *lamb's lettuce,* has small dark green leaves with a mild nutty flavor. Tender young pea sprouts would also be nice here. Baby spinach or small arugula leaves will do the trick, too.

FOR THE BUTTERMILK DRESSING

½ cup mayonnaise, homemade (page 13), or good-quality store-bought
½ cup sour cream
½ cup buttermilk
1 tablespoon chopped fresh dill
¼ cup thinly sliced fresh chives
2 teaspoons minced garlic
2 teaspoons minced shallot
2 teaspoons freshly squeezed lemon juice
Kosher salt and freshly ground black pepper

FOR THE SALAD

1 pound shaped pasta such as fusilli, farfalle, or cavatappi
¼ cup thinly sliced scallion
3 ounces ricotta salata, grated (about ¾ cup)
5 cups loosely packed mâche or baby spinach leaves

A STEP AHEAD Cook the pasta a few hours ahead, run cold water over it, and drain. Spread the pasta in a single layer over a lightly oiled baking sheet. Cover the pasta with plastic wrap and refrigerate. Make the dressing early in the day, but toss the pasta salad with the dressing only when you are ready to serve.

To make the buttermilk dressing, whisk together the mayonnaise, sour cream, and buttermilk in a bowl. Add the dill, chives, garlic, shallot, and lemon juice and whisk again. Season to taste with salt and pepper.

Bring a large pot of salted water to a boil, add the pasta, and cook until al dente. Drain the pasta and immediately run under cold water until it is completely cool. Drain well.

Put the pasta in a large bowl and, using a rubber spatula, fold in enough dressing to coat it generously. Fold in the scallion, cheese, and mâche. Mound the salad on a large platter and serve.

BLUEBERRY CORNMEAL CROSTATA

MAKES ONE 9-INCH TART, SERVING 8

This gorgeous tart with its golden-yellow crust and deep purple filling is adapted from one of my favorite cookbooks, Michele Scicolone's *La Dolce Vita* (William Morrow, 1993).

Garnish the tart with whipped cream, vanilla ice cream, or vanilla mascarpone. To make vanilla mascarpone, scrape the seeds from a vanilla bean into a tub of mascarpone and beat in a little sugar.

FOR THE BLUEBERRY JAM
4 cups blueberries

1 cup sugar

1/8 teaspoon ground cinnamon

FOR THE CORNMEAL CRUST
1¾ cups all-purpose flour

½ cup medium-ground yellow cornmeal

½ cup sugar

1 teaspoon baking powder

1 teaspoon freshly grated lemon zest

½ teaspoon kosher salt

12 tablespoons (1½ sticks) cold unsalted butter, diced

1 large egg plus 1 large yolk, whisked together

TO FINISH THE TART
Sweetened Whipped Cream (page 69)

A STEP AHEAD The jam can be made a few days ahead and refrigerated. The dough can also be made a few days ahead and refrigerated or frozen for a few weeks.

Make the tart early in the day and leave it at room temperature.

To make the blueberry jam, combine the blueberries, sugar, and cinnamon in a heavy saucepan over medium-high heat. Cover the pan and cook until the blueberries begin to release some liquid, about 5 minutes. Remove the cover, stir to dissolve the sugar, and continue to cook, stirring occasionally, until the mixture is reduced and thickened, about 15 minutes. Turn the heat down a bit as the jam thickens. Remove the jam from the heat, allow to cool, then cover and chill. (You should have about 2 cups jam.) The jam will continue to thicken as it cools.

To make the cornmeal crust, combine the flour, cornmeal, sugar, baking powder, lemon zest, and salt in the bowl of an elec-

tric mixer with the paddle attachment. Add the cold butter and mix until the butter forms small crumbs. Add the egg mixture and mix briefly. Add up to 2 tablespoons water, a few teaspoons at a time, mixing briefly each time, adding only enough water until the dough is moist enough to just hold together. You can also make the dough by hand by cutting the butter into the dry ingredients with a pastry blender, then mixing in the eggs and the water using a rubber spatula. Pat the dough into a rough round, wrap it in plastic wrap, and chill for about an hour.

Preheat the oven to 350°F. To roll out the dough, unwrap the dough and divide it into two unequal portions, about two-thirds and one-third of the total. Place the larger piece on a lightly floured work surface and, using a lightly floured rolling pin, roll it out into an 11- to 12-inch circle about ⅛ inch thick. Transfer the dough to a 9-inch tart pan with a removable rim. (It's easiest to fold the dough in half, transfer it, and then unfold it into the pan.) Ease the dough loosely and gently into the pan. This dough is soft and fragile, so if it starts tearing or falling apart as you transfer it, just pat it into the pan, pressing it into the bottom of the pan and up the sides. Roll your rolling pin back and forth over the top of the tart pan to cut off excess dough or remove the excess dough by pressing it against the sharp rim of the tart pan with your finger-tips. Fill the dough-lined pan with the chilled blueberry jam and smooth the top.

Place the remaining third of the dough on the lightly floured work surface and roll it out into a 9- or 10-inch circle about ⅛ inch thick. Using a knife or a pastry wheel, cut the circle into strips ¾ inch wide. Lightly brush the pastry along the rim of the tart pan with a pastry brush dipped in water. Lay half the strips diagonally across the top of the tart. Lay the remaining strips diagonally in the opposite direction across the top of the tart. You don't need to use up all the strips; be sure to leave plenty of jam showing. Use the rolling pin or your fingers to trim the overhanging strips by pressing against the sharp edge of the tart pan. Place the tart on a baking sheet lined with parchment or foil to catch any drips.

Bake the tart until the crust is golden brown, 35 to 40 minutes. Remove from the oven and allow to cool on a rack for about 15 minutes before removing the rim of the pan. Allow the tart to cool completely before serving, 1½ to 2 hours.

Cut the tart into wedges and serve with dollops of whipped cream.

SAUVIGNON BLANC

While many specific wines go with specific foods, we have found that when somebody wants a white wine with dinner, and not just with one course, the safest bet is Sauvignon Blanc. Normally there's enough acid to cut through any heavy sauce or fish flavor, enough fruit to complement aromatics like lemon and ginger in the food. Sauvignon Blanc is usually not overly oaked, so it doesn't drag down your palate. There are some very distinct styles of Sauvignon Blanc that tend to be representative within a region. These are all general descriptions, for certainly, within these large areas, individual wines can have other characteristics:

❖ Washington: ripe fruit of fig or pineapple, often softened with a little oak aging.

❖ New Zealand: exuberant fruit, bone-dry, but not very minerally. Rarely oaked.

❖ Loire: Green grass, minerally, highest acidity, somewhat stony, rarely if ever oaked.

❖ California: ripe fruit, lower acidity in general, often blended with Semillon, which adds a round quality. Often considered a sweet hay taste. Often slightly oaked.

GRANDPA LOUIE'S
DREAM GREEK VACATION

Jackie and I have several "new restaurant" fantasies, and one idea that we have been discussing for years is opening a Greek restaurant in Seattle. Maybe it's because Jackie is half-Greek, and maybe it's because I love the Platonic ideal of Greek food: impeccably fresh, simply grilled fish and shellfish, meze (starters) like stuffed grape leaves and anything made with the excellent Greek feta cheese, succulent charcoal-grilled lamb, and tangy, creamy Greek-style yogurt that is lip-smackingly tart. I've never been to Greece, but in my mind's eye I see Jackie, Loretta, and me sitting on a gorgeous Greek beach eating grilled just-caught-that-morning fish.

Seattle's small Greek-American population holds a fun Greek festival every year in September, the Festival of St. Demetrios Greek Orthodox Church. The festival reminds Jackie of her grandpa Louis Kakaris, who came to America when he was eighteen and settled in eastern Washington to work on the railroads. So in Uncle Louis's honor Jackie, Loretta, and I eat, dance, and sing up a storm at St. Demetrios every year.

A few years ago Jackie, her mom, Rodothea (Dot), her sister, Jeri, and our daughter, Loretta, representing three generations of Cross women, took a cruise through the Greek islands. They had been setting some money aside for ten years to take a vacation together, and they decided this was the perfect way to spend it. Loretta was ten at the time, so after visiting yet another ancient Greek ruin she asked, "Do we have to go see any more old rocks?"

Dot's mom, Lola, was a mail-order bride from Kentucky who cared much more about starting a family and a new life in eastern Washington than she did about her husband's Greek heritage. As with many immigrants, ethnicity was put into the closet so they could better fit into America. Grandpa Louie always wanted to revisit his homeland, but he could never talk Lola into making the trip. The closest to Greece that Dot ever came in her lifetime,

MENU

SANTORINI-TINIS

GRAPE LEAVES STUFFED WITH LEMONY RICE AND MINT

GREEN BEAN SALAD WITH TINY CHERRY TOMATOES AND FETA

GRILLED LAMB SKEWERS WITH RED WINE AND HONEY GLAZE

GRILLED SHRIMP AND GARLIC-STUFFED BLACK OLIVE SKEWERS

PARSLEY SALAD

COOL CUCUMBER YOGURT

SMASHED GREEK POTATOES

FFUDI DI SAN GREGORIU/FIANO DI AVELLINIO

TAURINO SALICE SALENTINO

SWEET GOAT CHEESE TURNOVERS WITH PISTACHIOS AND HONEY

A NOTE ON GREEK WINES: GREEK WINE IS OFTEN HARD TO FIND. BY ALL MEANS SUBSTITUTE GREEK WINES HERE IF THEY ARE AVAILABLE.

before "The Cruise," was the Cross Saturday night supper of Greek spaghetti: piles of pasta drenched in seriously blackened butter, smothered in grated mizithra cheese, always accompanied by a crisp green salad, Kalamata olives, and crunchy cucumbers dressed with lemon and olive oil.

We haven't yet turned our Greek restaurant into a reality, but we do love to set out a huge spread of Greek food for our family and friends. Thank goodness somebody's importing more varietals of Greek wine like Mandelari and Kotsifali, so I don't have to suffer through any more rounds of turpentine—I mean Retsina. Make sure you have plenty of grilled pita bread for spreads and dips, big bottles of Greek olive oil, loads of lemons, and bunches of Greek oregano, without which you can't have a Greek dinner.

SANTORINI-TINIS

MAKES 2 SERVINGS

Greeks are crazy about the anise-flavored liqueur called ouzo. Splash some water into a glass of ouzo and the clear liquid turns cloudy and opaque.

2 narrow strips lemon zest, about 2 inches long

6 espresso beans

2 small lemon wedges (¼ lemon)

4 ounces vodka (½ cup)

½ ounce ouzo (1 tablespoon)

Chill 2 martini glasses. Rub the rim of the glasses with the strips of lemon zest, then drop 1 zest and 3 espresso beans into each glass.

Put the lemon wedges in a cocktail shaker and muddle them with a bar stick. Add enough crushed ice or broken-up ice cubes to fill the shaker halfway. Add the vodka and ouzo. Shake, then strain into the chilled martini glasses and serve.

GRAPE LEAVES STUFFED WITH LEMONY RICE AND MINT

This is the perfect cocktail snack—salty, lemony, light, and easy to eat with your fingers. Even better, if you have grapevines in your yard, simply pick some leaves in the late spring to summer, and briefly blanch them in boiling water, shocking them in ice water to retain their beautiful green color. This works best with grape leaves about the size of your hand.

5 tablespoons olive oil, plus more for brushing the baking dish

1½ cups chopped onion

1 tablespoon minced garlic

⅓ cup currants

⅓ cup pine nuts, toasted (see page 24)

½ teaspoon ground cinnamon

⅛ teaspoon cayenne pepper

1 cup long-grain white rice

¼ cup chopped fresh mint

¼ cup chopped fresh flat-leaf parsley

3 tablespoons chopped fresh dill

3 tablespoons freshly squeezed lemon juice

1 teaspoon freshly grated lemon zest

Kosher salt and freshly ground black pepper

26 to 28 grape leaves, from a jar of brine-packed grape leaves, rinsed in cold water and patted dry

Lemon wedges for garnish

A STEP AHEAD Make up to 1 day ahead and store, covered, in the refrigerator.

Preheat the oven to 350°F. Brush a baking dish (such as a 9 by 13-inch pan) with oil. Heat 3 tablespoons of the olive oil in a sauté pan over medium-high heat and add the onions. Sauté, stirring occasionally, until the onions are translucent, about 5 minutes. Add the garlic and sauté for a few minutes more. Stir in the currants, pine nuts, cinnamon, cayenne, rice, and 1 cup water. Reduce the heat to medium-low and cover the pan. Simmer until the rice is partially cooked, about 10 minutes. Remove from the heat, transfer the rice mixture to a bowl, and mix in the fresh herbs, lemon juice, and zest. Season to taste with salt and pepper and allow the mixture to cool to lukewarm.

Place a grape leaf, shiny side down, on a work surface and trim off the stem. Spoon about 2 scant tablespoons of the rice mixture into the center of the leaf at the widest part. Fold the bottom of the leaf up, fold the sides in, and roll up tightly. Place the stuffed grape leaf seam side down in the prepared dish. Repeat until all the rice and leaves are used, placing the stuffed leaves close together. If there's an empty space left in the pan, you can fill it with a few leftover or damaged grape leaves. Pour ¾ cup water and the remaining 2 tablespoons olive oil into the pan and cover tightly with foil. Bake until the rice is cooked through and the liquids in the pan have been absorbed, about 45 minutes. Remove the grape leaves from the oven, allow to cool, then chill for several hours or overnight. Pile the grape leaves on a platter and serve them cold with lemon wedges to squeeze over them.

GREEN BEAN SALAD WITH TINY CHERRY TOMATOES AND FETA

MAKES 6 SERVINGS

This simple salad is a pleasing mix of colors—red, green, and white—and flavors: sweet, salty, and tangy. Buy the smallest cherry tomatoes you can find, such as Currant tomatoes, Sweet 100, or Sugar Plums. Search out dried Greek oregano, which is more fragrant and floral than regular dried oregano. It's often sold on the stem, so strip the leaves and blossoms off the stems before using. Sheep's milk feta has the most flavor, though cow's milk feta is much easier to find in supermarkets.

1 pound green beans, stem ends trimmed, cut in half if long

2 tablespoons freshly squeezed lemon juice

2 teaspoons freshly grated lemon zest

2 teaspoons minced shallot

1 teaspoon chopped garlic

½ teaspoon dried Greek oregano or other fragrant dried oregano

5 tablespoons extra virgin olive oil

Kosher salt and freshly ground black pepper

1 half-pint basket cherry tomatoes (8 ounces), the smallest you can find, cut in half unless they're really tiny

One 3-ounce block feta cheese, thinly sliced crosswise into shards (about ¾ cup)

A STEP AHEAD Make the vinaigrette a few days ahead and store it, covered, in the refrigerator. Blanch and shock the beans early in the day and refrigerate them, covered with plastic wrap. Cut the cherry tomatoes in half and slice the feta a few hours ahead, but don't dress the salad until you are ready to serve.

Bring a large pot of lightly salted water to a boil and set out a bowl of ice water. Add the green beans to the pot and cook until they are just tender, 5 to 8 minutes. Drain the beans and immediately plunge them into a bowl of ice water. Drain the beans again and spread them out on paper towels to dry.

To make the vinaigrette, whisk together the lemon juice and zest, shallot, garlic, and oregano in a small bowl. Whisk in the olive oil until emulsified. Season to taste with salt and pepper.

Put the green beans in a large bowl and toss them with about ¼ cup of the vinaigrette or enough to coat them. Transfer the beans to a platter. Put the tomatoes in the same bowl and toss them with about 2 tablespoons of the vinaigrette or enough to coat them. Using a slotted spoon, transfer the tomatoes to the platter and arrange them in a circle around the beans. Arrange the shards of feta over the beans and drizzle them with about 1 tablespoon of the remaining vinaigrette. Grind black pepper over the salad and serve.

GRILLED LAMB SKEWERS WITH RED WINE AND HONEY GLAZE

I like the flavor of red wine with lamb, but a long marinade in red wine breaks down the texture of the meat and makes it a little mealy. So, to give the lamb a good hit of rich wine flavor, I make a red wine and honey glaze and brush it on the meat as it grills. Try this glaze on lamb T-bone chops or even a grilled steak.

The lamb skewers marinate several hours or a day ahead, so plan accordingly.

2 pounds boneless leg of lamb, cut into 1-inch chunks

Six 10-inch bamboo skewers, soaked in water for 30 minutes and drained

½ recipe Greek Marinade

1 tablespoon unsalted butter

2 tablespoons minced shallot

2 cups dry red wine, such as Cabernet Sauvignon

2 tablespoons honey

Kosher salt and freshly ground black pepper

½ recipe Parsley Salad (page 136)

A STEP AHEAD Marinate the lamb skewers up to a day ahead. You can make the glaze a day or two ahead and store, covered, in the refrigerator. Allow the glaze to come to room temperature before using.

Thread the lamb chunks on the bamboo skewers and place them in a nonreactive pan. Pour the Greek marinade over the lamb, turning the skewers to coat. Cover the pan with plastic wrap and allow to marinate in the refrigerator for 6 hours or overnight.

To make the red wine and honey glaze, melt the butter in a saucepan over medium-high heat and sauté the shallot for a few minutes, until lightly browned. Add the red wine, increase the heat to high, and boil until the wine is syrupy and reduced. You should have about ⅓ cup reduced wine. Whisk in the honey, season to taste with salt and pepper, and cook the glaze for another minute. Then remove from the heat and allow the glaze to cool.

When you are ready to grill the lamb, fire up the grill. Remove the lamb from the refrigerator and allow the meat to come to room temperature. Remove the skewers from the marinade, shaking off the excess marinade. Season the skewers on both sides with salt and pepper. Grill the lamb over direct heat, with the lid off, turning frequently with the tongs. Brush with the glaze as you turn them the first time and keep brushing as you turn them,

using up all the glaze, until the lamb is done to your liking. The skewers will take / to 8 minutes for medium-rare, depending on how hot your fire is. Pile the skewers on a platter and top with the parsley salad.

GRILLED SHRIMP AND GARLIC-STUFFED BLACK OLIVE SKEWERS

MAKES 6 SERVINGS

Your seafood shop will sell shrimp anywhere from "5 and unders" all the way to "50 and ups." This refers to the average number of shrimp per pound. The most common size I use are 16/20s with an average of 18 shrimp per pound. This is an easy way to figure out how many shrimp to buy per person.

Don't throw away the garlic-flavored oil left after cooking the garlic cloves. Use part of it as the olive oil called for in the Smashed Greek Potatoes or save it for another use.

Also try serving these skewers on top of a platter of Greek salad for lunch or a light supper.

18 garlic cloves, peeled

¼ cup olive oil, plus oil for the grill

18 large black olives, such as Kalamata, pitted

18 large shrimp, about 1 pound, shelled and deveined, tails on (see page 33)

Six 10-inch bamboo skewers, soaked in cold water for 30 minutes and drained

½ recipe Greek Marinade

Kosher salt and freshly ground black pepper

½ lemon

½ recipe Parsley Salad (page 136)

A STEP AHEAD Prepare the garlic-stuffed olives and skewer them with the shrimp a day ahead. Store the skewers, covered with plastic wrap, in the refrigerator. But don't marinate them for more than 15 to 30 minutes before grilling.

Put the garlic cloves in a small saucepan, cover with ¼ cup olive oil, and bring to a simmer over medium heat. As soon as the oil comes to a simmer, turn the heat to very low and cook the garlic, stirring occasionally, until soft and very lightly browned, 10 to 12 minutes. Drain the garlic cloves and set aside. Reserve the garlic oil for another use. Stuff each olive with a garlic clove, cutting the olive open a little if necessary. Nestle a stuffed olive into the curve of each shrimp. Thread 3 olive-stuffed shrimp onto each skewer. Be sure to pass the skewer first through the tail of the shrimp, then through the garlic-stuffed olive, then through the head of the shrimp so everything is securely skewered.

Fire up the grill.

Place the skewers in a nonreactive pan and cover them with the marinade. Marinate the skewers for 15 to 30 minutes. Remove the skewers from the pan, shaking off the excess marinade, and season them on both sides with salt and pepper. Brush the grill with oil.

Grill the skewers over direct heat, with the lid off, turning them as needed, until cooked through, about 4 minutes. If you're not sure whether they're cooked through, take a skewer off the grill and cut into the thickest part of a shrimp with a small knife—it should be opaque all the way through. Squeeze the lemon over the skewers right before you take them from the grill. Pile the skewers on a platter and top with the parsley salad.

GREEK MARINADE

Metaxa is a sweet, dark Greek brandy. You can buy three-, five-, or seven-star Metaxa, the number of stars indicating the number of years the brandy has been aged. The seven-star version works just fine here, and it's good for sipping, too. Any brandy will work in this marinade, but when Zorba the Greek is singing on the CD player, there's nothing quite like a tall splash of Metaxa for the cook.

1 tablespoon plus 1 teaspoon minced garlic

1 tablespoon plus 1 teaspoon dried Greek oregano or other fragrant dried oregano

2 teaspoons freshly grated lemon zest

3 tablespoons Metaxa brandy

1 teaspoon kosher salt

1 teaspoon freshly ground black pepper

⅔ cup extra virgin olive oil

A STEP AHEAD Make the marinade a day or two ahead and store it, covered, in the refrigerator.

In a bowl, whisk together the garlic, oregano, zest, brandy, salt, and pepper. Gradually whisk in the olive oil.

PARSLEY SALAD

Think of parsley as a vegetable, not just a limp garnish on the side of your plate. This bright green, lemony salad gives a fresh-tasting lift to the grilled lamb and shrimp skewers.

1 large bunch fresh flat-leaf parsley, leaves picked from the stems, washed and dried well (about 3 cups picked leaves)

½ lemon

1 tablespoon extra virgin olive oil

Kosher salt and freshly ground black pepper

A STEP AHEAD You can wash and pick the leaves off the parsley a day ahead and store, covered with a damp kitchen towel, refrigerated. Toss the salad right before you serve it.

Put the parsley leaves in a bowl. Squeeze the lemon over the parsley and toss. Drizzle the oil over the parsley and toss again. Season to taste with salt and freshly ground black pepper.

COOL CUCUMBER YOGURT

MAKES ABOUT 3½ CUPS

This cucumber yogurt, which the Greeks call *tzatziki,* is similar to the one from my first book, *Tom Douglas' Seattle Kitchen,* and it's the perfect accompaniment to a Greek dinner. Try to find rich, creamy, full-flavored whole-milk yogurt.

1 cucumber (about 14 ounces)

Kosher salt

3 cups plain yogurt, preferably whole-milk yogurt

¼ cup chopped fresh flat-leaf parsley

¼ cup chopped fresh mint

2 tablespoons freshly squeezed lemon juice

Freshly ground black pepper

A STEP AHEAD You can make this up to a day ahead and store it, covered, in the refrigerator.

Peel and seed the cucumber. Grate the cucumber and place it in a strainer set over a bowl. Generously salt the cucumber and let drain for half an hour, then squeeze the liquid out. In a bowl, combine the cucumber, yogurt, parsley, mint, and lemon juice. Season to taste with salt and pepper.

SMASHED GREEK POTATOES

MAKES 6 TO 8 SERVINGS

The tastiest version of this recipe I ever had was when Jackie dug some red spuds out of her garden. The potatoes are roasted until tender in the oven, then smashed and roasted with olive oil until crispy. Use any kind of small thin-skinned potatoes, about the size of a golf ball or a little smaller.

3 pounds small red potatoes, washed and dried but not peeled
½ cup plus 1 tablespoon extra virgin olive oil
Kosher salt and freshly ground black pepper
1 tablespoon dried Greek oregano or other fragrant dried oregano
1 tablespoon minced garlic

Preheat the oven to 450°F.

Put the potatoes in a roasting pan large enough to hold them in a single layer and roast them until they are just tender, about 40 to 45 minutes, depending on their size. When the potatoes feel tender, remove the roasting pan from the oven and place it on top of the stove or on another heatproof surface. Using the flat bottom of a sturdy china mug, press down on and flatten each potato, one at a time, right in the roasting pan. A smashed potato should be about ½ inch thick. The potato skin will break, showing some of the white flesh, but the potato should still more or less retain its round shape. Don't worry if a few of the potatoes break up and fall apart. Repeat until all the potatoes have been smashed. Drizzle ¼ cup of the oil over the potatoes, season generously with salt and pepper, and return them to the oven. Roast the potatoes until they are browned on the bottom, about 25 minutes, then remove them from the oven and turn them over with a large spatula. Drizzle another ¼ cup oil over the potatoes and return them to the oven. Roast the potatoes until they are browned on the second side, about 25 minutes more, then remove the pan from the oven. Scatter the oregano and garlic over the surface, season again with salt and pepper, and drizzle them with the remaining 1 tablespoon oil. Toss the potatoes with the spatula to distribute the seasonings evenly, then return them to the oven for 5 more minutes. Roasting time after the potatoes are smashed is about 55 minutes; total time is about 1 hour plus 35 minutes.

Use a spatula to transfer the potatoes to a large platter. Serve immediately.

SWEET GOAT CHEESE TURNOVERS
WITH PISTACHIOS AND HONEY

MAKES 6 SERVINGS

My friend Steven Steinbock makes fresh chèvre for our restaurants every week with goat's milk from Bainbridge Island. He learned the craft from our friends Jacques and Marie Joubert, who passed on both the mother (culture) and their technique when they retired. We miss the Jouberts terribly, but Steven does a most admirable job.

Frying these turnovers in olive oil makes them especially delicious — and very Greek. Use pure olive oil, not extra virgin, because it has a higher smoke point.

8 ounces soft fresh goat cheese

1 tablespoon heavy cream

5 tablespoons sugar

2 teaspoons freshly grated lemon zest

1 large egg yolk

18 to 20 circles Turnover Pastry Dough

Pure olive oil as needed for frying

⅓ cup flavorful honey, as needed

½ cup chopped toasted pistachios (see page 24)

½ cup fresh mint leaves

A STEP AHEAD Assemble the turnovers a day ahead and place them, uncooked, on vegetable oil–sprayed, parchment-lined baking sheets. Cover them with plastic wrap and refrigerate until you are ready to fry them.

Fry the turnovers several hours ahead and set them aside at room temperature. Reheat them in a 400°F oven until they're hot, about 5 minutes.

To make the goat cheese filling, put the goat cheese, cream, sugar, and lemon zest in a bowl and beat with a rubber spatula or wooden spoon until combined.

To make the egg wash, beat the egg yolk and 1 tablespoon water together with a fork in a small bowl until just combined.

Lay the pastry circles out on a lightly floured work surface. Put a heaping teaspoon (about 2 level teaspoons) of filling in the center of a circle. Using a pastry brush, brush egg wash all around the edge of each circle, then fold over to form a half-moon turnover, pressing with a fork to seal. Continue to fill and shape all the turnovers in the same manner. Set the turnovers aside on parchment-lined baking pans sprayed with vegetable oil spray to prevent sticking. Or use a flexible nonstick baking sheet, such as Silpat, and you won't need to spray it.

To fry the turnovers, fill a heavy saucepan with oil to a depth of at least 1 inch. Heat the oil to 325°F to 350°F, checking the temper-

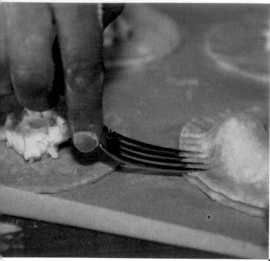

ature on a deep-frying thermometer (see page 14). Fry the turn-overs, in batches as necessary, turning to brown both sides. If your oil is too hot, the turnovers may brown before the dough is cooked through. It should take at least 3 minutes to brown a turnover on both sides. You may want to cut a turnover open and check that the dough is thoroughly cooked by the time it is browned. If the turnovers are browning too fast, turn the heat down a little. As the turnovers are browned, remove them with a slotted spoon or skimmer and drain on paper towels.

Arrange the turnovers on a large platter. Drizzle them with honey and sprinkle with the pistachios. Tear the mint leaves into pieces and scatter them over the top. Serve immediately.

TURNOVER PASTRY DOUGH

MAKES ABOUT 20 PASTRY CIRCLES

2½ cups all-purpose flour

2 tablespoons sugar

1 teaspoon kosher salt

½ pound (2 sticks) cold unsalted butter, cut into pieces

A STEP AHEAD Make the pastry dough a day or two ahead and keep it wrapped and refrigerated or freeze the dough for a few weeks. Thaw frozen dough several hours or overnight before using.

Roll the dough out and cut it into circles several hours ahead. Put the pastry circles on a parchment-lined baking sheet, cover them loosely with a piece of plastic wrap, and refrigerate until you are ready to use them.

Place the flour, sugar, and salt in the bowl of a food processor and pulse to mix. Add the cold butter all at once and pulse a few times until the butter and flour form crumbs. Transfer the butter-flour mixture to a bowl and start adding 6 to 8 tablespoons ice water, 1 or 2 tablespoons at a time, mixing with a fork or rubber spatula. Add only as much water as needed for the dough to hold together when a clump is gently pressed between your fingers (see page 142). Dump the dough out onto a large piece of plastic wrap. Use the plastic wrap to gather the dough together and force it into a flattened round. Chill the plastic-wrapped dough for an hour or longer before rolling it out.

When you are ready to roll out the dough, unwrap it, place it on a lightly floured work surface, and cut it in half. With a lightly floured rolling pin, roll half of the dough out into a rough circle about ⅛ inch thick. Use a 4-inch biscuit cutter to cut the dough into 9 or 10 circles, setting them aside on a piece of parchment or wax paper. Repeat with the rest of the dough for a total of 18 to 20 circles.

HOW TO MAKE PASTRY

When I was growing up, my mom baked a pie at least once a week, but today many folks don't want to bother making their own pastry dough. It's worth going the extra mile, because the flakiness and buttery taste of a homemade pie or tart crust beats anything available in the freezer section of your supermarket.

You can cut the butter into the flour the old-fashioned way, using two forks or a handheld pastry blender. I prefer to cut the butter in using a food processor, because it's quick, the butter stays cold, and the pastry turns out light and flaky. You can finish making the pastry dough in the processor, carefully adding the water a tablespoon at a time and briefly pulsing, but it's safer to dump the butter-flour mixture into a bowl and add the water by hand, stirring with a fork or rubber spatula, because you're less likely to add too much water or overprocess the dough.

Flaky pastry is made with cold butter. Cut the butter into small pieces, then put it in the freezer for 10 minutes before making the dough.

The amount of water needed varies with the humidity in the air and the moisture in the flour, so always add the water gradually, a tablespoon at a time. Gather up a piece of dough; if it holds together, it's done. If not, add another tablespoon of water, mix, and see if it holds together.

Always chill your dough before rolling it out and try to handle it as little as possible. When you're ready to roll, lightly flour your board, your rolling pin, and your hands. Use just enough flour to keep things from sticking. While you're rolling, lift the dough occasionally with a plastic or metal pastry scraper to check that it's not sticking, adding more flour as needed.

The easiest way to transfer a round of dough to a tart or pie pan is to fold it into quarters and place it in the pan with the pointed end touching the center of the pan, then unfold the dough. Always ease the dough gently into the pan. Never stretch the dough when you're fitting it into a pan or it may shrink as it bakes.

OUZO

Ouzo is the licorice-flavored national drink of Greece. A combination of pressed grapes, herbs, spices, nuts, berries, blossoms, and roots is added to an alcohol base, and the mixture may or may not be distilled before being bottled. The island of Lesbos is known for the best ouzo. The secret to drinking ouzo, without being overwhelmed by the high alcohol content, is to sip it slowly while munching on plenty of snacks, or mezedes, preferably in a charming café in a sunny Greek village. Another trick is to keep splashing a little water into your glass as you sip, turning the ouzo milky white and diluting the alcohol a little.

SPECIALTY GREEK PRODUCTS FROM NEW YORK

Making phyllo dough by hand is a lost art, but the folks at the Poseidon Bakery in New York have been doing it for seventy years. They'll ship it next-day air (5-pound minimum): 629 Ninth Avenue, New York, NY 10036; (212) 757-6173.

SCREEN DOOR **BARBECUE**

Barbecue has long been one of my passions. For my fortieth birthday Jackie took Loretta and me to Kansas City, where we spent seventy-two food-filled hours eating barbecue at legendary joints such as Arthur Bryant's, Gates, and LC's. Barbecue styles vary all over the country, and KC's barbecue is as much about the sauce and the fries as it is about the meat. I reckon that if your sauce and your fries aren't up to snuff in KC, you'd be closed down. I can still taste those crunchy, greasy, perfect fries at LC's, made extra-delicious by double-dipping them in lard.

Two years ago I used the excuse of promoting my line of rubs in Texas to tour some of central Texas's justly famous barbecue joints. It was there that I had the brisket of my dreams at Black's in Lockhart. Black's brisket had this blackened, caramelized crust that kept the outside crunchy and the inside meat tender and moist, so the meat literally crackles in your mouth. I figure the folks at Black's got that crust by using a sweet spray of some combination of vinegar and sugar, but my plea to learn their secret has always fallen on deaf ears.

In fact, for some years our retirement dream has been for us to open a barbecue joint in Seattle, which we would call Screen Door Barbecue. I should say "my" dream, because I think Jackie would prefer to retire to a life of relative leisure in Provence, rather than cook whole hogs over hardwood charcoal. In my mind's eye, I'd be tending the meat in a T-shirt two sizes too small watching a thirteen-inch black-and-white TV with foil on the antenna. Jackie would of course be wearing curlers and fluffy slippers, and when someone would drive up and ring the bell, I'd yell out, "Answer the damned door."

What do I love about barbecue? Everything. I love just-smoky-enough ribs with a little chew and a little crunch. I love the slow burn of just-hot-enough barbecue sauce. I love the slow-cooked collard greens flavored with some big ol' ham hocks. I love singing

and dancing along with Aretha and Reverend Al Green as I stoke the fire and keep a watchful eye on the slow-cooking meat.

Patience is a virtue when it comes to making great barbecue. Brisket is an all-day affair, and if you find yourself unwilling or unable to spend the time, you can always get Black's to ship you a whole brisket (see page 153). But even the ribs you'll find on page 150 take six hours cooked low and slow. That's okay, because we have a blast showing Loretta how to get our ribs nice and brown in the course of half a day. In the end, surrounded by people you enjoy hanging out with, you will, like us, find out that good things do indeed come to those who wait.

BARBECUE JOINTS IN SEATTLE NOT TO MISS

❖ Jones Barbecue at Martin Luther King Way and Hudson, for ribs
3216 S. Hudson
(206) 725-2728

❖ Frontier Room, First and Lenora, for brisket
2203 1st Ave.
(206) 956-RIBS

❖ Kings Barbecue House, for Chinese-style duck and classic Cantonese barbecue
518 6th Ave. S.
(206) 622-2828

❖ Secret Garden Restaurant, in Lynnwood, for kalbi short ribs and Korean barbecue
21025 Hwy. 99
Lynnwood
(425) 771-5546

❖ Willie's Taste of Soul BBQ and Custom Smoke House, especially for the sweet potato pie
6305 Beacon Ave. S.
(206) 722-3229

HARD WATERMELON LEMONADE

MAKES 6 SERVINGS

If you're gonna eat barbecue, you gotta have lemonade, especially this version with its sweet tang and rosy hue. Tequila makes the lemonade hard. You can add the tequila for your guests or leave the tequila bottle out for everyone to add to taste. Substitute lime juice for the lemon juice and you will have an equally delicious watermelon limeade or watermelon margarita.

¾ cup sugar
3 pounds watermelon
1½ cups freshly squeezed lemon juice
6 shots tequila (7½ ounces)
6 lemon or lime wedges

A STEP AHEAD You can make the simple syrup a few days ahead, and you can make the watermelon juice early in the day. Store both covered and refrigerated. For the freshest-tasting lemonade, mix everything together no more than a few hours ahead. Keep the lemonade chilled and add the tequila when you're ready to drink it.

To make the simple syrup, combine the sugar and ¾ cup water in a saucepan over high heat. Bring to a boil and cook, stirring, until the sugar is completely dissolved. Remove from the heat and allow to cool.

Slice off and discard the rind from the watermelon. Cut the flesh into chunks, removing as many of the seeds as you can. Liquefy the watermelon in a food processor or a blender, in batches as necessary, then pour the juice through a strainer set over a bowl. You should have about 3 cups of watermelon juice. Add the lemon juice and simple syrup and stir. Pour into a pitcher and chill until ready to serve. Stir before serving.

For each serving, fill a tall ice-filled glass with lemonade. Add a shot of tequila and stir with a long spoon. Garnish each glass with a lemon or lime wedge.

GRILLED OYSTERS WITH HORSERADISH BUTTER

Grilled oysters are a tradition in Jackie's family. Jackie's dad would gently grill the oysters over hot coals until the shells popped, then slip in a little pat of butter to melt and pool around each oyster.

To keep the oysters upright so their liquor and the melted butter stay in the shell, I put a bed of rock salt, raw rice, or dried beans on a rimmed baking pan and set the shucked oysters on top. Then I set the pan on a cooler part of the grill and let guests help themselves. The thyme sprigs are just for garnish; remove them before you eat the oysters. And be sure to have a bucket filled with ice and beer bottles nearby.

FOR THE HORSERADISH BUTTER

8 tablespoons (1 stick) unsalted butter, softened
2 teaspoons freshly squeezed lemon juice
1½ teaspoons freshly grated lemon zest
1 teaspoon chopped fresh thyme
1 teaspoon prepared horseradish
Pinch of cayenne pepper
Kosher salt and freshly ground black pepper

FOR THE OYSTERS

18 to 24 oysters, scrubbed and rinsed
3 cups rock salt, raw rice, or dried beans
Fresh thyme sprigs for garnish if desired
Lemon wedges for serving

A STEP AHEAD The seasoned butter can be made up to 3 days ahead and stored, covered, in the refrigerator. Allow the butter to come to room temperature before using it.

To make the horseradish butter, combine the butter, lemon juice and zest, thyme, horseradish, and cayenne until smooth in a food processor, with an electric mixer, or by hand. Season to taste with salt and pepper.

Fire up the grill.

Grill the oysters over high heat for about 5 minutes until they "pop" open, being sure to put them on the grill flat side up and cupped side down so that when they open the oyster liquor isn't lost in the fire. Remove the oysters from the grill as they pop open. After 10 minutes, remove all of them from the grill, whether they've opened or not, and place them on a folded towel. Using a towel or an oven mitt to protect your hands, shuck the oysters with an oyster knife, discarding the top shells, and be sure to pick out any pieces of shell or dirt (see following page). Also use the oyster knife to scoop under the oyster and cut the bottom muscle. Put about 1 teaspoon of the butter on top of each oyster. Return the oysters to the grill for another minute or so until the butter begins to melt, then remove them from the grill.

Pour the rock salt onto a rimmed baking sheet, set the oysters on top, and set the pan on a cooler part of the grill. Garnish each oyster with a small thyme sprig and set a plate of lemon wedges nearby.

NOTE: If you are making the whole menu, remove the ribs from the grill, wrap them in foil, and let them rest for 15 minutes. Meanwhile, clean the grill with a grill brush, add charcoal to get a hot fire going, then put the oysters on to grill.

HOW TO SHUCK OYSTERS

Stick the oyster knife in at the hinge while holding the oyster down on the counter with your other hand, protecting your hand with a towel, then twist the knife.

Pull back the knife and clean the dirt and broken shell.

Return the knife to the oyster and, with the blade angled toward the top of the shell, slice through the length of the oyster.

Remove the top shell.

Clean away any dirt or bits of shell on the oyster.

Scoop under the oyster and cut the bottom muscle.

Last, place the oyster on a bed of crushed ice or a bed of rock salt.

PIT-ROASTED PORK SPARERIBS

MAKES 6 SERVINGS

Grilling is an art; barbecue is a religion. While it takes time to learn how to grill and to get a feel for when a piece of fish or meat is done, you can also just stick a thermometer in your steak and you'll know when to grab it off the grill, perfectly cooked. But with barbecue, you've got to have faith—letting the smoke do the work, managing the fire to the perfect temperature for 5 to 6 hours, and having the patience not to lift the lid every 10 minutes. You have to learn to regulate the heat of the fire for an hour at a time just by adjusting the dampers up and down. Temperature is so important. The slow cooking allows you to render fat without losing all the moisture, and the fat literally bastes the meat as it drips away. On the other hand, if you stoke your fire and let it get up to 400°F, you will ruin the texture and moisture of your barbecue. To barbecue like the pros just plain takes practice, like learning how to play the piano or tap-dance. With barbecue, you're better off finishing a couple hours early than being a couple hours tardy. Your barbecue will sit and rest beautifully, but it can't be hurried to a finish.

FOR THE PORK SPICE RUB

3 tablespoons firmly packed light brown sugar

1 tablespoon plus 1 teaspoon paprika

1 tablespoon plus 1 teaspoon cumin seeds, toasted and ground (see page 24)

1 tablespoon plus 1 teaspoon coriander seeds, toasted and ground

1 tablespoon plus 1 teaspoon kosher salt

2 teaspoons pure ancho chile powder or regular chili powder

$1\frac{1}{2}$ teaspoons freshly ground black pepper

$\frac{1}{2}$ teaspoon cayenne pepper or more to taste

2 full racks pork spareribs (about 3 pounds each)

FOR THE RIB SPRAY

$\frac{1}{4}$ cup cider vinegar

2 tablespoons honey

Burn-Yer-Lips BBQ Sauce

A STEP AHEAD Make the spice rub up to a week ahead and keep it in a jar at room temperature.

Combine all the spice rub ingredients in a bowl.

Trim any large globs of fat from the spareribs. Remove the tough membrane that runs along the bony side of the racks (see page 42). Generously rub the racks on both sides with the spice rub.

Set up your charcoal for slow indirect heat. Make a fire on one side of your grill, then set the racks of ribs opposite the fire and put the lid on. Partially close the vents and keep the temperature of the grill between 175°F and 225°F, adding more charcoal and more hardwood chunks as needed.

The ribs will take 5 to 6 hours to smoke. Rotate the positions of the ribs 2 or 3 times during the cooking time so both racks cook evenly.

My Weber grill has two handy charcoal baskets, and I move these around where I need them. For barbecue, I fill just one of the baskets with charcoal. If you don't have baskets, move the coals, about ½ gallon's worth, to one side of the grill and start your fire. Then, to create the smoke, set a few chunks of alderwood, oak, mesquite, or hickory to smolder on top of the charcoal. If you don't have chunks of hardwood, you can wrap wet hardwood chips in heavy-duty foil, poke a few holes in the foil, and set that on top of the charcoal. Then position the two full racks of spice-rubbed spareribs on the grill, on the side opposite the burning charcoal. Finally, put on the lid, rotating it so the vent is on the side opposite the fire, to help draw the smoke over the ribs. Adjust your dampers and keep your eye on your grill thermometer; ideally, it should read between 175°F and 225°F the whole time. You will need to add charcoal from time to time, and more hardwood chunks if they burn away, and you will need to keep adjusting the vents to keep the fire at this temperature. Spraying the ribs with a vinegar-honey mixture toward the end of the smoking time helps to form a delicious crust on the surface of the ribs.

To make the rib spray, mix ⅔ cup water, the vinegar, and the honey together and pour this mixture into a clean spray bottle. During the last hour of the cooking time, spray the ribs twice.

When the ribs are done, the meat will be very tender and starting to pull away from the bone. Remove the ribs from the grill, wrap them in heavy-duty foil, and allow to rest for 15 minutes. Then transfer the ribs to a cutting board and cut between the bones.

Pile the ribs on a large platter and pass a bowl of barbecue sauce on the side.

BURN-YER-LIPS BBQ SAUCE

This sweet and hot sauce, with its complex flavor of chiles and toasted spices, is very close to the Redhook Brewery Blackhook Porter Sauce that I bottle and sell.

Chipotle chiles are smoked ripe jalapeños. You can find small cans of chipotle peppers in adobo sauce in the Mexican food aisle of many supermarkets. Dump the contents of the can into your food processor and puree until smooth. It's a great spicy-hot seasoning to have handy in your refrigerator to season bean dishes, salsas, or scrambled eggs. The recipe calls for enough chipotle puree to make the barbecue sauce pleasantly hot, but if you really want to burn your lips, feel free to add more.

If you find pure chipotle chile powder, use it instead of the chipotle puree. It's quite hot, so start with about $\frac{1}{2}$ teaspoon and taste. Try to find pure ancho chile powder because the flavor is sweet, well rounded, and almost fruity.

I like to toast and grind whole spices for the best flavor. Mix the coriander, cumin, and fennel seeds together so you can toast and grind them at the same time.

2 tablespoons vegetable oil

$\frac{3}{4}$ cup finely chopped onion

$1\frac{1}{2}$ teaspoons minced garlic

$1\frac{1}{2}$ teaspoons cumin seeds, toasted and ground (see page 24)

$1\frac{1}{2}$ teaspoons fennel seeds, toasted and ground

1 teaspoon coriander seeds, toasted and ground

2 cups ketchup

$\frac{1}{2}$ cup firmly packed light brown sugar

$\frac{1}{2}$ cup molasses

$\frac{1}{2}$ cup cider vinegar

$\frac{1}{2}$ cup Redhook Blackhook Porter or water

$\frac{1}{3}$ cup drained and finely chopped canned green chiles

1 tablespoon plus 2 teaspoons pure ancho chile powder

1 tablespoon pureed chipotle, from a can of chipotles in adobo sauce, or to taste

Kosher salt and freshly ground black pepper

1 lemon, cut in half

A STEP AHEAD The sauce can be made up to a week ahead and stored, covered, in the refrigerator.

Heat the oil in a saucepan over medium heat. Add the onion and cook slowly, stirring, until soft and golden, 10 to 15 minutes. Add the garlic and the ground seeds and sauté for a few minutes. Add the ketchup, brown sugar, molasses, vinegar, porter, green chiles, chile powder, and chipotle. Season to taste with salt and pepper. Simmer gently to combine the flavors and thicken the sauce, about 25 minutes. Squeeze in the lemon halves, catching the seeds in your hand or a small strainer, and throw the squeezed-out rinds into the pot. Continue to simmer the sauce for 10 minutes. Remove from the heat and remove and discard the lemon rinds.

FIVE GREAT PLACES FOR MAIL-ORDER BARBECUE

In many parts of the country, including my beloved Seattle, it's hard to find great barbecue at restaurants. Thankfully, I've found a few great barbecue joints from around the country that will ship anywhere. Ordering the brisket from Black's is an especially attractive proposition, because smoking a whole brisket is incredibly time-consuming and difficult to pull off. So, if you don't want to slow-roast and smoke your own meat, you can make the other items on this menu and just order the meat from any of the following sources:

Black's, for whole brisket
215 N. Main St.
Lockhart, TX 78644
(512) 398-2712
blacksbbq@austinweb.com

Armstrong's Pit Barbecue, for
whole pork shoulder and ribs
303 Valley Dr.
Helena, AR 72342
(870) 338-7746

Mitchell's, for chopped pork
6228 S. Ward Blvd.
Wilson, NC 27893
(252) 291-9189

Charlie Vergos' Rendezvous
Room, for dry-rub ribs
52 S. Second St.
Memphis TN 38103
(901) 523-2746

Moonlight Barbecue, for lamb
2840 W. Parrish Ave.
Owensboro, KY 42301
(800) 322-8989

MOLASSES BAKED BEANS

MAKES 6 TO 8 SERVINGS

Go ahead, impress your friends and make your own baked beans from scratch. It seems a shame to spend six hours smoking ribs, only to open a can of baked beans. These are simple and delicious, and you'll be happy you stepped up to the plate. And tomorrow if you have any leftovers, cut up a few franks into your bean pot and transport yourself back to preteenhood. Your own version of Velvet Elvis.

1 pound dried navy beans

12 slices bacon

1½ cups coarsely chopped onion

½ cup molasses

½ cup firmly packed light brown sugar

¼ cup cider vinegar

2 tablespoons tomato paste

2 tablespoons Dijon mustard

⅛ teaspoon ground cloves

Kosher salt and freshly ground black pepper

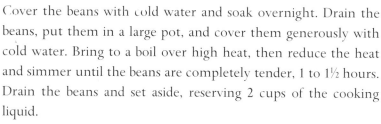

A STEP AHEAD Cook the navy beans a few days ahead and store them, covered, in the refrigerator.

Cover the beans with cold water and soak overnight. Drain the beans, put them in a large pot, and cover them generously with cold water. Bring to a boil over high heat, then reduce the heat and simmer until the beans are completely tender, 1 to 1½ hours. Drain the beans and set aside, reserving 2 cups of the cooking liquid.

Preheat the oven to 375°F.

Set aside 6 whole strips of bacon and dice the remaining 6. In a large pot, sauté the diced bacon over medium-high heat. Add the onion as soon as the bacon has rendered some fat and sauté until softened, stirring occasionally, about 7 minutes. Add the molasses, brown sugar, vinegar, tomato paste, mustard, cloves, and reserved cooking liquid. Stir to combine, bring to a simmer, and simmer for a few minutes. Add the cooked beans and season generously with salt and pepper. Bring the beans to a simmer, then pour them into a baking dish, such as a 2½- to 3-quart ceramic or earthenware pot. Lay the reserved slices of bacon on top. Bake until the beans are bubbling and the bacon slices are cooked, about 1 hour. Serve the beans directly from the baking dish.

DOWN-HOME COLLARD GREENS

MAKES 6 SERVINGS

Collard greens are delicious and molt-in-your-mouth tender when cooked correctly, and they're good for you too! I was on such a collard green kick I asked Jackie to grow them in her garden. It was amazing how little cooking time the first harvest of tender leaves took—they were actually a little sweet. By late August, their cooking time had quadrupled and their bitterness level easily doubled. If your collards are too bitter for you, add a little molasses or brown sugar for balance.

To prepare the collard greens, tear the leaves away from the stems; don't just cut off the stem. You need to remove the entire stem, because it's tough.

When the collards are finished simmering, there will be some liquid, or "pot liquor," in your pot. Don't discard it. Serve it with the greens and sop it up with corn bread or drain the greens and save the pot liquor for making soup.

2 large bunches collard greens (2 to 2½ pounds total)
2 tablespoons olive oil
2 teaspoons chopped garlic
½ teaspoon hot red pepper flakes or to taste
4 cups Ham Hock Stock, made with water instead of
    chicken stock
1 to 1½ cups ham hock meat
2 tablespoons apple cider vinegar or to taste
1½ cups canned whole tomatoes and their juice
Kosher salt and freshly ground black pepper
Molasses or brown sugar to taste

A STEP AHEAD Cook the collard greens a day or two ahead and store them, covered, in the refrigerator. Reheat to a simmer before serving.

Wash the collard greens well, discarding any discolored or bruised leaves. Remove the stems and roughly chop the greens. Set aside.

In a large pot, heat the olive oil over medium-high heat. Add the garlic and red pepper flakes and sauté for about 1 minute, until the garlic is fragrant. Add the ham hock stock, ham hock meat, collard greens, and vinegar. Pour the tomatoes into a bowl and crush them by squeezing them with your hands or remove them from the can with a slotted spoon and chop them roughly on a cutting board with a knife. Add the tomatoes and their juice to the pot. The greens won't be covered with the liquid. Cover the pot and simmer, checking every 5 or 10 minutes, pushing the greens down into the liquid as they wilt. When the greens are mostly submerged in liquid, remove the cover and adjust the heat to keep them at a simmer. Simmer, stirring occasionally, until the greens are very tender, about an hour. Season to taste with salt and pepper and add more vinegar and red pepper flakes plus a little molasses or brown sugar if desired. Pour the collard greens into a serving bowl and serve hot.

HAM HOCK STOCK

MAKES ABOUT 5 CUPS STOCK AND 1 TO 2 CUPS SHREDDED HAM HOCK MEAT

Ham hock stock is a bonus for making perfect southern-style collard greens. Although it's not necessary, it certainly adds a delicious element or, as we often say, great depth of flavor. I also use it in my seafood chowder (page 175). If you're making this stock for the collard greens, use water instead of chicken stock. But use chicken stock for richer flavor if you're making the seafood chowder. Try using this stock the next time you make black bean or split pea soup.

Depending on the meatiness of your ham hock, you may end up with more ham hock meat than you need for a recipe. Leftover meat can be saved in the freezer, or just use it up the next morning in your scrambled eggs.

1 teaspoon olive oil

2 celery ribs, coarsely chopped

1 medium carrot, coarsely chopped

1 medium onion, coarsely chopped

1 bay leaf

¼ teaspoon black peppercorns

1 smoked ham hock (1 to 1½ pounds)

2 quarts Chicken Stock (page 8) or water

A STEP AHEAD Make the stock a few days ahead. Store both the stock and the shredded ham hock meat, covered, in the refrigerator or freeze for several weeks.

Heat the oil in a large saucepan over medium-high heat. Add the celery, carrot, and onion and sauté until lightly browned, stirring occasionally, about 5 minutes. Add the bay leaf, peppercorns, ham hock, and chicken stock and bring to a boil. Turn the heat down to keep the stock at a simmer, partially cover the pan with a lid, and cook for about 2 hours, until the ham hock meat is very tender and almost falling off the bone. If the ham hock isn't completely submerged in the stock, use a large spoon or tongs to turn it over a few times as it cooks. Pull out the ham hock and set aside. Pour the stock through a strainer, pressing lightly on the solids. Let the stock sit for 10 minutes, then skim off any fat. Or, if you refrigerate the stock overnight, it's easiest to remove the fat the next day. When the ham hock is cool enough to handle, remove all the meat from the bone, discarding the bone and any bits of tough rind, gristle, and fat. Use your hands to pull the meat into shreds or chop it.

GREEN CHILE AND FRESH-CORN CORN BREAD

MAKES ONE 9 BY 13-INCH PAN, SERVING 6 TO 12
12 SQUARES OF CORN BREAD, ABOUT 3 INCHES SQUARE

A pan of corn bread is compulsory at any barbecue. Jackie bakes corn bread in our big 10-inch-wide, 3-inch-deep cast-iron pan. The black iron pan helps brown the outside of the corn bread and looks great on the table. The real difference between the baking pan and the cast-iron pan is that you get a thicker, crunchier crust. And since the level of batter is deeper in the cast-iron pan, it takes a little longer to cook through, so it's a little bit drier. If you have a similar pan, you can put 2 tablespoons of bacon fat in the bottom, then get the pan hot in the oven or on top of a burner. Pour in the corn bread batter; it should sizzle when you add it to the preheated pan. Then bake at 375°F until golden, 45 to 50 minutes.

1½ cups fresh corn kernels (about 3 ears)

2 cups medium-ground yellow cornmeal

2 cups all-purpose flour

1 tablespoon plus 1½ teaspoons baking powder

1 tablespoon kosher salt

4 large eggs

1 cup milk

1 cup sour cream

⅓ cup honey

8 tablespoons (1 stick) unsalted butter, melted, plus more for buttering the pan

1½ cups grated Cheddar cheese

3 tablespoons seeded and minced poblano or Anaheim pepper

1 tablespoon plus 1 teaspoon seeded and minced jalapeño pepper

Sweet BBQ Butter or unsalted butter, softened

A STEP AHEAD Make the corn bread early in the day and serve it at room temperature. Or you can cut the corn bread into squares, wrap it in foil, and reheat in a 400°F oven for 5 to 10 minutes, until warm.

Preheat the oven to 375°F. Butter a 9 by 13-inch pan. Bring a saucepan of lightly salted water to the boil and set up a bowl of ice water. Add the corn to the saucepan and cook for a minute or two. Strain the corn and immediately plunge it into the bowl of ice water. Drain the corn and set aside.

Combine the cornmeal, flour, baking powder, and salt in a large bowl. Put the eggs in another bowl and whisk them just to blend, then whisk in the milk, sour cream, and honey until everything is well combined. Add the egg mixture to the dry ingredients and whisk until smooth. Whisk in the melted butter. Using a rubber spatula, fold in the corn, cheese, and peppers. Scrape the batter into the prepared pan. Bake until the corn bread is golden brown and a skewer inserted in the center of the pan comes out clean, 35 to 40 minutes. Remove the corn bread from the oven and allow to cool slightly.

Cut the corn bread into 12 squares and, using an angled spatula, transfer the squares to a platter. Serve the corn bread with the butter.

SWEET BBQ BUTTER

Serve a small bowl of this flavored butter with Green Chile and Fresh-Corn Corn Bread or slather it on corn on the cob, grilled vegetables, or grilled fish.

Ancho chile powder, made from ground dried ancho chiles, has a sweet and slightly smoky taste. You can find it in spice markets, Mexican specialty stores, or by mail order (see Sources, page 265). Chili powders from the supermarket are mixtures of ground dried chiles with other spices, such as cumin, oregano, and sometimes garlic and onion powder. If you use a regular chili powder, try adding just a teaspoon to the butter and taste before you add more.

12 tablespoons (1½ sticks) unsalted butter, softened

2 tablespoons honey

1 tablespoon pure ancho chile powder or regular chili powder to taste

¼ teaspoon cayenne pepper or to taste

A STEP AHEAD Make this up to a week ahead and store it, tightly wrapped, in the refrigerator. Allow the butter to come to room temperature before serving.

In a food processor, with an electric mixer, or by hand, combine the butter, honey, chile powder, and cayenne until smooth. Scrape into a small bowl.

ORANGE-GLAZED STRAWBERRY TART

Do you remember when you were a kid and you walked by the bakery and saw those strawberry pies with the strawberries piled as high as Mount Rainier? Inevitably, there was thick gooey candy-apple-red glaze dripping like lava in between the berries, studded with cumulus clouds of whipped cream. Those strawberry volcanoes were serious pies that no kid could resist. I've taken that memory and updated the ingredient list a little bit with ripe local strawberries to make my version of a treasured childhood memory, a beautiful strawberry tart. It might not be as dramatic, but it tastes a heck of a lot better.

Instead of strawberries, try piling fresh raspberries or blackberries on top of the pastry cream and omit the glaze.

FOR THE ORANGE PASTRY CREAM

1¼ cups half-and-half

Zest from 1 orange, removed in 1-inch strips with a
    vegetable peeler

½ cup sugar

3 tablespoons all-purpose flour

4 large egg yolks

Pinch of kosher salt

2 tablespoons unsalted butter, softened

1 tablespoon orange liqueur, such as Cointreau

2 to 3 pints strawberries, hulled

1 prebaked 9-inch tart shell

FOR THE ORANGE GLAZE

1 tablespoon sugar

½ cup orange marmalade

1 teaspoon orange liqueur, such as Cointreau

Sweetened Whipped Cream (page 69), if desired

A STEP AHEAD The pastry cream can be made a day ahead and stored chilled in the refrigerator, covered with plastic wrap as described. Make the glaze several days ahead and store, covered, in the refrigerator. Melt the glaze over a pan of simmering water before using. Slice the strawberries several hours ahead, cover them with a piece of plastic wrap, and keep them refrigerated.

The tart is best served as soon as possible after it is assembled. If you have ready the tart shell, the pastry cream, the sliced strawberries, and the glaze set over a pan of hot water, it will take less then 10 minutes to assemble the finished tart. Keep the tart refrigerated for an hour or two until you are ready to serve it.

To make the pastry cream, combine the half-and-half and the zest in a saucepan over medium-high heat and stir occasionally until

the mixture almost comes to a boil. Remove the pan from the heat and allow to steep for 15 minutes. Strain out and discard the zest, then return the half-and-half to the pan and reheat it to just under the boiling point. In a bowl, whisk together the sugar, flour, yolks, and salt. The mixture will be thick. To keep the yolks from scrambling, pour a ladle (about ⅓ cup) of the scalded half-and-half into the yolk mixture while whisking. Then add the warmed yolk mixture back to the saucepan. Cook over medium-high heat, whisking constantly, until starting to bubble. Then reduce the heat to medium and continue to whisk until the pastry cream is very thick and smooth, about 3 minutes more. Remove from the heat and whisk in the butter, then the liqueur. Transfer the pastry cream to a small bowl and chill over a larger bowl of ice water, stirring occasionally, until it is cool. Place a piece of plastic wrap directly over the surface of the pastry cream to prevent a skin from forming, then refrigerate until cold, a few hours or longer.

To make the glaze, put 3 tablespoons water and the sugar in a small saucepan and stir over medium heat until the mixture simmers and the sugar is completely dissolved. Add the orange marmalade and heat, stirring occasionally, until melted and smooth. Remove from the heat and stir in the liqueur. Strain the glaze through a fine strainer set over a small bowl. If the glaze cools and thickens before you're ready to use it, set the bowl over a saucepan of simmering water for a few minutes.

Set a strawberry, stem side down, on a work surface and use a small paring knife to cut the berry vertically into 4 or 5 slices, holding the slices together with your other hand to keep them stacked together like a whole berry. Carefully place the sliced berry on a large platter or baking sheet and continue until all the berries are sliced. Set aside.

When the pastry cream is cold, scrape it into the tart shell and smooth the surface with a rubber spatula. Set the berries on top of the pastry cream, fanning them open slightly and arranging them in a circular pattern, starting on the outside and working your way in, using as many strawberries as you can to completely cover the top of the tart. Using a pastry brush, brush the berries with the glaze.

Remove the sides from the tart pan by pushing up on the bottom of the pan with your fingers and allowing the ring to fall away. Use a large spatula to slide the tart off the tart pan bottom onto a large platter.

Use a long serrated knife to cut the tart into wedges, using a sawing motion as you cut through the edge of the pastry. Use an angled spatula to transfer each wedge to a dessert plate. Serve with dollops of whipped cream, if desired.

PREBAKED TART SHELL

MAKES ONE 9-INCH TART SHELL

Blind-baking a tart shell means baking an unfilled pastry-lined pan. Use dried beans to weigh down the crust and keep the bottom from puffing up during baking. The beans can be stored in a jar and used over and over.

Be sure your tart shell is thoroughly baked or the final result will be soggy or tough rather than crisp. There should be a few light brown patches on the bottom crust. Cool the shell completely before using.

1¼ cups all-purpose flour

2 teaspoons sugar

½ teaspoon kosher salt

8 tablespoons (1 stick) cold unsalted butter, diced

A STEP AHEAD The dough can be made a day or two ahead, wrapped in plastic, and refrigerated or frozen for a few weeks. Before using, thaw frozen dough in the refrigerator for several hours or overnight. The dough can be rolled out and fitted into the tart shell, then refrigerated or frozen for the same amounts of time. Frozen tart shells can be baked directly out of the freezer without thawing. The baking time will be just a little bit longer. The baked tart shell, in its pan, can be left at room temperature for several hours before filling.

Place the flour, sugar, and salt in the bowl of a food processor. Pulse to mix. Add the cold butter all at once and pulse a few times until the butter and flour form crumbs. Transfer the butter-flour mixture to a bowl and start adding 4 to 6 tablespoons of ice water, 1 or 2 tablespoons at a time, mixing with a fork or a rubber spatula. Add only as much water as needed to make the dough moist enough to hold together when a clump is gently pressed between your fingers (see page 142). Dump the dough out onto a large piece of plastic wrap and use the wrap to gather the dough together and force it into a flattened round. Chill the plastic-wrapped dough for at least an hour before rolling it out.

When you are ready to roll out the dough, unwrap it and place the round of dough on a lightly floured work surface. Lightly flour the rolling pin. Roll the dough out into a circle about ⅛ inch thick. Occasionally lift the dough with a scraper to check that it is not sticking and add more flour if needed.

Transfer the circle of dough to a 9-inch tart pan with a removable rim. Ease the dough loosely and gently into the pan, pushing the dough against the sides of the pan. Don't stretch the dough or it will shrink as it bakes. Trim the excess dough to about a ½-inch overhang. Fold the excess dough inward and press it against the sides of the tart pan. Chill the unbaked tart shell for at least an hour before baking to prevent the dough from shrinking in the oven.

To blind-bake the tart shell, preheat the oven to 400°F. Place a piece of aluminum foil (lightly buttered on the side facing the pastry) or parchment paper in the tart shell and fill with dried beans. Bake the tart shell until the pastry rim looks set, about 20 minutes. Remove the pan from the oven. Remove the foil and beans, prick the bottom of the shell in several places with a fork, and return the tart shell to the oven. Bake until the pastry rim is golden brown and the bottom crust has a few golden-brown patches, 12 to 15 minutes. Remove the tart shell from the oven and allow to cool in the pan before filling.

TOM'S 'CUE TIPS

HARDWARE
Fancy, expensive grills have become the latest in household status symbols, but I've gotten great results using indirect heat on inexpensive Weber-type kettles.

FIRESTARTERS
I don't much care for gas grills, but I have no problem using a grill with a gas starter. It's hard to beat the simple chimney starters in which you place balls of newspaper in the bottom and charcoal in the top. My dad used to make a chimney starter out of a big metal can that he would pry holes into with a can opener, but given how inexpensive chimneys are, I don't think that's really necessary.

FUEL
I prefer cooking with hardwood itself (like oak or cherry), because I think the sap seeping out of the wood adds great flavor to the meat. But it is hard to control the temperature of the fire using only wood, so I often find myself buying the all-natural hardwood charcoal that is now widely available. I try to avoid using the pressed-charcoal briquettes and/or starter fluid because I don't like the flavor they impart to the meat.

TAKIN' YOUR TEMPERATURE
Finally, it is imperative to know how hot your fire is at any time when you're making barbecue, so some kind of grill thermometer is an absolute necessity. If your kettle grill doesn't have one, you can drill a small hole in the lid and insert your own thermometer. Be sure to get one that reads up to 600°F or better (see Sources, page 265).

POP POP'S
WINTER SOLSTICE

Jackie's dad, Jim (Pop Pop), a retired marketing executive and life-long poet, is well read and a very fine writer. I treasure the influence he's had on my daughter, Loretta, a budding poet in her own right.

Eagerly awaiting the return of the sun every year, Dad celebrates the shortest day of winter and the start of the longer daylight hours with a party that's come to be known as Pop Pop's Winter Solstice. Since Jim enjoys a martini every day, it's no surprise that the menu for his party starts with the recipe for the perfect martini. His wife, Sharon, has now taken over bartender duties, and Dad has taught her well. Unlike most bartenders who now wave the bottle of vermouth over a martini glass instead of actually pouring some, Sharon knows the difference between a real martini and a glass of gin.

Pop Pop says that the solstice represents the moment of faith when we can say that tomorrow the earth will return to its Northern Hemisphere tilt toward the sun—or, to quote Shelley, "If winter comes, can spring be far behind?" When we sit down to our solstice chowder, Pop Pop reads his favorite paragraph from Dylan Thomas's "Note" to the 1952 anthology of his "Collected Poems": "I read somewhere of a shepherd, who, when asked why he made, from within fairy rings, ritual observances to the moon to protect his flocks, replied, 'I'd be a damn fool if I didn't!' These poems are . . . written for the love of man and in praise of God and I'd be a damn fool if they weren't."

I've had Pop Pop's creamy seafood chowder every winter solstice for the past ten years, and it just gets better with time. He never cooks with a recipe, but I can remember the smells and flavors as if the pot were sitting in front of me—smoked pork, celery, mussels and sweet clams popped open. The soup warms you up like a thick, comfy sweater. It's a perfect party dish, especially at this time of year.

MENU

POP POP'S PERFECT MARTINI

CARAMELIZED FENNEL TART

CREAMY SEAFOOD CHOWDER

SMOKED PAPRIKA ROUILLE

PARSLEY SCONES

HENRI BOURGEOIS SANCERRE

**CORNMEAL ROSEMARY CAKE
WITH LEMON GLAZE**

**TAYLOR FLADGATE 10 YEAR
TAWNY PORT**

POP POP'S PERFECT MARTINI

MAKES 2 SERVINGS

A real martini is made with gin *and* vermouth. Pop Pop doesn't believe in the superdry-martini obsession, because a martini is not just a cold glass of gin. If you've been adding vermouth with an eyedropper, try making a martini the old-fashioned way, and you may find that you prefer it. The best martinis are made in small quantities, not by the pitcher.

I love the little slivers of ice you get in the glass when you shake the cocktail shaker hard. This happens best with ice from a home ice maker, because the ice is so cold it shatters when you shake it vigorously.

4 ounces or ½ cup gin
⅔ ounce dry vermouth
4 olives divided between 2 cocktail picks

Chill 2 martini glasses. Pour the gin and vermouth into a cocktail shaker half filled with ice cubes. Shake, then strain into the chilled glasses. Garnish with the olives.

CARAMELIZED FENNEL TART

MAKES 6 SERVINGS AS AN APPETIZER

My friend Ana Sortun has a restaurant in Boston called Oleana, where she offers zesty North African-, Turkish-, and Mediterranean-inspired food. This fennel tart was inspired by one of the dishes I had in her restaurant.

The golden, caramelized fennel covering the top of the tart is a lovely, appetizing sight. For color and contrast, mound a bit of bright red radicchio salad in the center. Save some of the fennel fronds for the salad when you trim your fennel bulbs.

To get your fennel nice and caramelized, use a heavy 10-inch sauté pan or a cast-iron skillet, but not a nonstick pan.

2 large fennel bulbs (about 1 pound each before trimming), trimmed of feathery greens and stalks
1 tablespoon plus 2 teaspoons unsalted butter
1 teaspoon olive oil
1 tablespoon sugar
1½ teaspoons chopped fresh thyme
Kosher salt and freshly ground black pepper
Pastry Dough

FOR THE RADICCHIO SALAD

1 cup finely julienned radicchio (about ½ small head)
¼ cup feathery fennel fronds, reserved from trimming the fennel bulbs
1 teaspoon olive oil, as needed
1 lemon wedge

A STEP AHEAD Caramelize the fennel and leave it in the sauté pan at room temperature for a few hours. Roll out the round of dough, place it on a parchment-lined baking sheet, cover it with plastic wrap, and refrigerate it several hours ahead. The tart should be baked right before you plan to serve it. Dress the radicchio salad right before you mound it on the tart.

Preheat the oven to 425°F.

Cut the fennel bulbs in half and cut out the cores, then cut each half into wedges ¾ inch thick. You should have at least 12 wedges.

Heat the 2 teaspoons and the olive oil in a 10-inch sauté pan over medium heat until the butter is melted. Remove the pan from the heat and sprinkle the sugar evenly over the bottom of the pan. Arrange the fennel wedges in the pan, placing them side by side, with the cut sides down. Use as many wedges as will fit in the pan in a single layer, trimming some to fill in any empty spaces. Place the pan over medium heat and cook, covered, until the fennel begins to soften, about 5 minutes. Remove the cover,

raise the heat to medium-high, and cook until the fennel is golden-brown and caramelized, about 5 more minutes. Don't move the fennel or turn it over while it is cooking—only one side of the fennel will be browned. Use a small spatula to gently lift a piece of fennel occasionally to check the color. Remove the pan from the heat. Sprinkle the thyme over the fennel and season generously with salt and pepper. Dot the top of the fennel with the 1 tablespoon butter.

On a lightly floured work surface, roll the pastry dough into a circle about ⅛ inch thick and trim it to a 10-inch round. Cover the fennel in the sauté pan with the pastry round. The easiest way to transfer the round of dough is to fold it in half and in half again. Then pick it up, place it on top of the fennel with the point in the center of the pan, and gently unfold it. Any excess dough that doesn't fit snugly over the fennel can be folded back on itself to form a little collar around the circumference of the pastry circle. Bake the tart until the crust is golden brown, about 25 minutes.

Remove the pan from the oven. The tart should be unmolded as soon as possible, while it is still hot. Cover the pan with a large inverted plate, then, protecting your hands with a kitchen towel, invert the whole thing. The tart should slide right out onto the plate. If any fennel remains stuck to the pan, use a small spatula to remove it and place it on the tart.

To make the salad, combine the radicchio and fennel fronds in a small bowl. Toss them with enough olive oil to lightly coat the leaves. Squeeze the lemon wedge over, season to taste with salt and pepper, and toss again.

Mound the radicchio salad in the center of the tart and present it at the table before you cut it into 6 wedges for serving.

PASTRY DOUGH

MAKES ONE 10-INCH ROUND

1 cup all-purpose flour

$^1/_2$ teaspoon kosher salt

6 tablespoons cold unsalted butter, diced

A STEP AHEAD Make the pastry dough up to a day ahead and keep it wrapped and refrigerated. Or the dough can be frozen for several weeks. Thaw the frozen dough in the refrigerator for several hours or overnight before using it.

Put the flour and salt in the bowl of a food processor and pulse to mix. Add the cold butter and pulse a few times until the butter and flour form crumbs. Transfer the butter-flour mixture to a bowl and start adding 3 to 4 tablespoons ice water, 1 or 2 tablespoons at a time, mixing with a fork or rubber spatula. Add only as much water as needed for the dough to hold together when a clump is gently pressed between your fingers (see page 142). Dump the dough out onto a large piece of plastic wrap and use the plastic wrap to gather the dough together and force it into a flattened round. Chill the plastic-wrapped dough for at least an hour before rolling it out.

CREAMY SEAFOOD CHOWDER

MAKES 6 SERVINGS

Certain foods and cocktails, like hot toddies and coffee nudges, and slow-braised short ribs, are meant for cold, harsh winter days. Pop Pop's creamy seafood chowder is perfect.

Vary the fish and seafood, keeping the total quantity roughly similar to the amounts specified. Instead of king crab legs, substitute one cooked and cleaned Dungeness crab, cut into sections and cracked. You could use more clams or shrimp and omit the mussels or scallops. You need a pot, with a lid, that will be large enough to hold the chowder base and the seafood. The king crab legs you buy will most likely be frozen. Defrost them slowly in the refrigerator to preserve their quality, *not* at room temperature under running water.

Be sure your soup bowls are warm before you fill them. Since these are big, generous bowls of chowder, consider making a double batch of the scones, for dunking in the broth.

This chowder has a lot of ingredients, but if you make the chowder base ahead, and have all your seafood scrubbed, debearded, sliced, and otherwise prepped, you can bring it to the table in about 15 minutes.

2 tablespoons plus 2 teaspoons olive oil

1 leek, white and light green parts only, split in half lengthwise, washed, and finely chopped

1 medium onion, finely chopped

1 celery rib, finely chopped

1 carrot, peeled and finely chopped

1 tablespoon plus 2 teaspoons minced garlic

1 cup ham hock meat (see page 157)

2 cups dry white wine

2 cups canned tomato puree

5 cups Ham Hock Stock (page 157), hot, made with Chicken Stock (page 8)

2 medium thin-skinned potatoes (about ¾ pound), such as Yukon Gold, cut into ½-inch dice

1 cup heavy cream

¼ cup finely chopped fresh flat-leaf parsley

1 tablespoon finely chopped fresh thyme

Kosher salt and freshly ground black pepper

½ teaspoon Tabasco sauce or to taste

1 pound small steamer or baby clams, scrubbed and rinsed

1 pound mussels, scrubbed, debearded, and rinsed (see page 177)

½ pound large sea scallops, sliced in half horizontally

12 large shrimp (about ½ pound), shelled and deveined, with tails on (see page 33)

½ pound white fish fillets such as halibut, cod, or yellow eye rockfish, cut into 1½-inch pieces

8 cups loosely packed spinach leaves (1 large bunch, about 12 ounces, or 4 ounces bagged ready-to-eat spinach leaves)

3 cooked king crab legs (1 to 1½ pounds), thawed if frozen, each leg cut into 3 sections crosswise and split in half lengthwise

½ **lemon**

12 Parsley Scones and unsalted butter, softened, for serving
Smoked Paprika Rouille

A STEP AHEAD Make the chowder base, but without adding any of the
fish or shellfish, or the spinach up to 2 days ahead, and store, covered, in the
refrigerator. Bring to a boil, reduce the heat to simmer, add the clams and
mussels, and continue as described.

Heat the oil in a large pot over medium-high heat. Add the leek,
onion, celery, and carrot and sauté until the vegetables are starting
to brown, about 6 minutes. Add the garlic and the ham hock meat
and sauté for a few more minutes. Stir in the wine and tomato
puree and bring to a simmer. Stir in the ham hock stock and the
potatoes, adjusting the heat to keep the mixture at a simmer.
Cover the pot and cook until the potatoes are just tender, about 12
minutes. Stir in the cream and herbs, season to taste with salt and
pepper, and add the Tabasco.

Add the clams and mussels, cover the pot, and cook until they
open, about 4 minutes. Season the scallops, shrimps, and fish with
salt and pepper, then add them to the pot, using a big spoon to
submerge everything as much as possible in the simmering liquid.
Cover and simmer for 2 more minutes. Open the lid, stir in the
spinach, then put the crab legs on top of the chowder split sides up
so the crabmeat doesn't fall out. Cover and continue to simmer for
1 minute. Turn off the heat and let the pot sit, covered, for 5 minutes. Remove the lid and check that the scallops, shrimp, and fish
are cooked through and that the crab is warm. Squeeze the lemon
into the pot and season to taste with salt, pepper, and Tabasco.
Using a slotted spoon and ladle, divide all the fish, shellfish, and
chowder among 6 large shallow soup plates, discarding any clams
or mussels that have not opened.

Split 6 of the parsley scones in half, dollop the cut side of each
half with rouille, and balance 2 halves on the rim of each soup
bowl. Scrape the rest of the rouille into a pretty dish and pass with
the chowder, also passing the remaining 6 scones, split, and spread
with butter.

NOTE: If you prefer, you can substitute chicken stock for the ham hock stock, omitting the ham hock meat.

HOW TO DEBEARD MUSSELS

Rinse the mussels and scrub them with a stiff brush. Grasp the beard—the rough, scrubby threads that the mussel uses to attach itself to a surface—of each mussel firmly between your thumb and forefinger and pull it off with a hard yank.

SMOKED PAPRIKA ROUILLE

MAKES ABOUT 1 CUP

I tried Spanish smoked paprika after being told about it by the owner of The Spanish Table, a Spanish import store here in Seattle. Often, smoked products can be too smoky, but when you add this paprika to a dish, the smoke becomes an accent to flavor rather than overwhelming everything else. Here, smoked paprika (see Sources, page 265) adds a little smoky flavor and sweetness to a lemony rouille sauce.

When you shop for Spanish paprika, the sweet (dulce) and the hot (picante) versions are usually packed in similar-looking cans with just one small word on the label describing the difference. Ask, if you need to, to make sure you end up with a can of sweet smoked paprika. If you can't find smoked paprika, use the most flavorful kind you can, such as a good sweet Hungarian paprika.

¾ cup mayonnaise, homemade (page 13), or good-quality store-bought
2 teaspoons chopped garlic
2 tablespoons plus 1 teaspoon freshly squeezed lemon juice
1 teaspoon freshly grated lemon zest
1 tablespoon smoked or regular paprika
Kosher salt and freshly ground black pepper

A STEP AHEAD Make the rouille a few hours ahead and store it, covered, in the refrigerator.

Put the mayonnaise in a bowl and whisk in the garlic, lemon juice and zest, and paprika. Season to taste with salt and pepper.

PARSLEY SCONES

MAKES 12 SCONES

Scones are best eaten warm from the oven, split and buttered, but you can make the scones ahead, freeze them unbaked, and pop them into the oven at the last minute. Also try these for breakfast with scrambled eggs and bacon.

The bottoms of these scones should turn a nice golden brown, but if they seem to be browning too fast, double-pan them by sliding another baking sheet underneath.

An inexpensive pastry blender, a tool consisting of several thick parallel wires attached on both ends to a wooden handle, is a nice, low-tech device for cutting butter into flour by hand.

2½ cups all-purpose flour

2 tablespoons sugar

1½ teaspoons kosher salt

½ teaspoon freshly ground black pepper

2½ teaspoons baking powder

½ teaspoon baking soda

10 tablespoons cold butter, diced

1 teaspoon freshly grated lemon zest

2 tablespoons thinly sliced chives

⅓ cup finely chopped fresh flat-leaf parsley

¾ to 1 cup buttermilk, as needed

A STEP AHEAD The unbaked scones can be frozen for 2 weeks or more. Place the baking sheet of scones in the freezer. When they are frozen hard, you can remove them from the baking sheet and seal them in a plastic bag. Bake the scones directly from the freezer as directed. Because these scones are quite flat, the baking time doesn't change.

Preheat the oven to 400°F. Combine the flour, sugar, salt, pepper, baking powder, and baking soda in a large bowl. Using a pastry blender or your fingertips, cut the butter into the dry ingredients until the mixture resembles coarse bread crumbs. Stir in the lemon zest, chives, and parsley using a wooden spoon or a rubber spatula. Gradually add the buttermilk, stirring, until the dough just comes together into a soft, slightly moist dough. Gently knead the dough with your hands for a minute or two to help it cohere, but do not overmix. Turn the dough out onto a lightly floured work surface and divide it into 2 equal pieces. Pat each piece with your hands into a flat round about ½ inch thick. Cut each round into 6 wedges with a floured knife or metal scraper. Place the scones on a parchment-lined baking sheet and bake until golden, 20 to 25 minutes. Remove the scones from the oven and allow to cool slightly before serving.

CORNMEAL ROSEMARY CAKE WITH LEMON GLAZE

MAKES ONE 9-INCH CAKE, SERVING 8 TO 10

When we told Pop Pop we were putting a cornmeal cake in the book to finish his menu, he rolled his eyes and let out an awful grunt. Growing up dirt poor in an Italian family meant polenta, or cornmeal mush, was a staple. Once he made his way to a more prosperous life, he swore he would never eat cornmeal again. The first time we made this cake for him we didn't tell him what it was, but Jackie and I exchanged a sly grin at the pleasure he took in consuming the entire piece.

Creamy, buttery mascarpone, an Italian triple-cream cheese, is worth seeking out because it adds something very special to the texture and moistness of this cake. Leftover mascarpone is good with fresh berries and some cookies.

The icing for this cake is an almost-transparent powdered sugar glaze flecked with rosemary leaves and lemon zest. The rosemary is blanched first to remove some of its pungency. For a less dressy cake, omit the glaze. Simply brush the cake with the lemon syrup and serve with sliced fresh figs or small bunches of grapes.

1½ cups all-purpose flour

¾ cup medium-ground yellow cornmeal

1 tablespoon finely chopped fresh rosemary

1 tablespoon freshly grated lemon zest

1 teaspoon baking powder

¼ teaspoon kosher salt

⅔ cup mascarpone

4 large eggs

1⅓ cups granulated sugar

8 tablespoons (1 stick) unsalted butter, melted, plus more for buttering the pan

FOR THE LEMON SYRUP

½ cup freshly squeezed lemon juice

⅓ cup granulated sugar

FOR THE LEMON GLAZE

1 tablespoon rosemary leaves (stripped from the stem, not chopped)

1½ cups confectioners' sugar, sifted

¼ cup heavy cream

2 tablespoons freshly squeezed lemon juice

1 teaspoon freshly grated lemon zest

A STEP AHEAD Because this cake is quite moist, you can make it a day ahead. After the cake is brushed with the syrup, allow it to cool completely, then wrap it tightly in plastic wrap and leave it at room temperature. A few hours before you're ready to serve the cake, make the glaze and glaze the cake.

Preheat the oven to 350°F. Butter a 9-inch cake pan, line it with a circle of parchment paper, and butter the paper.

In a bowl, combine the flour, cornmeal, finely chopped rosemary, zest, baking powder, and salt. In a large bowl, briefly whisk

A restaurant tip: Unmold your cake onto a circle of sturdy cardboard cut the same size as the cake pan. (See Sources, page 265, for cardboard cake circles, or you can easily cut one yourself.) Then you can move the cake to a rack for glazing and back to a cake plate for serving, without having to disturb the cake with a spatula. If the cardboard is cut to the same diameter as the cake, it won't be visible when you set the cake on a cake plate.

the mascarpone to loosen it. Add the eggs one at a time, whisking to combine. Add the sugar and whisk until smooth. Using a rubber spatula, fold the dry ingredients, in 2 batches, into the wet ingredients, mixing until smooth. Stir in the melted butter. Scrape the cake batter into the prepared pan and bake until a skewer comes out clean, about 40 minutes.

While the cake is baking, make the lemon syrup. Combine the lemon juice and sugar in a small saucepan over medium heat and

cook for a few minutes, stirring occasionally, until the sugar dissolves. Remove from the heat.

Allow the cake pan to cool on a rack for 5 minutes before unmolding. To unmold, run a small knife around the cake. Place an inverted plate over the cake pan and, protecting your hands with a kitchen towel, invert the whole thing. The cake should slide right out onto the plate. Peel off the parchment paper, then place a 9-inch cardboard circle or an inverted plate over the cake and invert the whole thing, again. Remove the top plate, and the cake will be right side up. With a wooden skewer, poke a few dozen holes all over the top of the cake. While the cake is still warm, brush the cake with the lemon syrup. Continue brushing for several minutes, giving the syrup time to sink into the cake, until you've used all or most of the syrup. Allow the cake to cool.

To make the lemon glaze, bring a small saucepan of water to a boil. Add the rosemary leaves and blanch them for 1 minute. Scoop out the rosemary leaves with a small strainer and drop them immediately into a small bowl of ice water. Drain and spread the rosemary leaves on a paper towel to dry. In a bowl, whisk the confectioners' sugar, cream, and lemon juice until smooth, then whisk in the blanched rosemary leaves and the zest. When the cake is completely cool, transfer it to a rack set over a baking sheet. If your cake is not on a cardboard circle, use a wide spatula to transfer it. Pour the glaze over the top of the cake and allow it to drip off the sides. You can gently tilt the cardboard circle or the wire rack back and forth to encourage the glaze to flow completely over the top of the cake.

While the glaze is still wet, transfer the cake to a cake plate. Allow the fondant to dry, an hour or more, before serving the cake. If you allow the glaze to dry before you transfer it, the glaze may crack a bit unless you are transferring it on a cardboard circle.

REMEMBERING LABUZNIK

Everyone needs a home-away-from-home restaurant, where the only difference between eating there and at home is you don't have to cook or do the dishes. For me it was Seattle's only Czech restaurant, Labuznik. There the waiters knew I liked my martini wet and my roast pork with extra gravy. They knew there wasn't a choice between soup and salad: I wanted both. They knew I always wanted a side order of sweet carrots and creamed spinach instead of dessert. In fact, Labuznik was the kind of restaurant we all dream about finding, where the waiter brings you what you want before you ask for it.

For me, chef and owner Peter Cipra was Labuznik. Peter fled Czechoslovakia during the Russian invasion in 1968. He opened his first restaurant, Prague, in the underground of Seattle's historic Pioneer Square, in 1972. Five years later he moved and opened Labuznik (Czech for *gourmand*) in the then-seedy First Avenue neighborhood, surrounded by sleazy bars and porno theaters. He turned out to be just a little bit ahead of his time, as the neighborhood has since become the trendy Belltown.

As a young chef I was simultaneously drawn to his restaurant by knowledgeable foodie friends and intimidated by his legendary temper and brusque demeanor exacerbated by his thick accent. And yet Labuznik quickly became my home-away-from-home restaurant. Watching Peter's wife, Susan, run the dining room was invaluable when it came to opening my own place. Her remarkable grace in the dining room, her diligent care of the customer, and her nurturing manner made her the best host in the city. Peter and Susan became trusted friends and mentors.

Labuznik was known for meat slowly roasted until it falls off the bone. Most dishes were accompanied by sauerkraut and dumplings. My meals there started with the ground veal soup that had just a little slick of oil on top of the bowl for extra flavor. My standard was the *vepro*, slow cooked pork roast studded with car-

MENU

FRIED JARLSBERG CHEESE
WITH TARTAR SAUCE

CHINON JOGUET—YOUNG
VINE RED WINE

ROMAINE SALAD WITH
PICKLED CUCUMBERS AND
RED CABBAGE

SLOW-ROASTED PORK WITH
CARAWAY ONION GRAVY

BREAD DUMPLINGS

SAUERKRAUT

SUGARED CARROTS

CREAMED SPINACH

LUNGAROTTI RUBESCO
RISERVA

CHATEAU 'D'FLEUZAC

PESSAC LEOGNAN BORDEAUX

BITTER ORANGE CHOCOLATE
MOUSSE

GRAHAM'S SIX GRAPE RUBY
PORT

away and drenched with gravy made from the caramelized chine bones and pan drippings. Jackie invariably ordered the roast duck, its skin crisped golden brown, the richness of the duck lightened by the zesty sauerkraut. And oh those dumplings! The best I've ever had. This was Czech soul food of the first order. Peter's wine list of amazing Bordeaux was better than at any restaurant in town; it complemented the meat-heavy menu perfectly.

In the end, Labuznik closed because Peter Cipra's unyielding vision for the restaurant meant he refused to be a slave to food fashion. When everyone else was doing Pacific Rim, Peter was still serving schnitzel, incredibly delicious schnitzel at that. When Peter wasn't in the kitchen, Labuznik wasn't open. So when he was ready to retire, there was really no way for my favorite restaurant to carry on. For us, Labuznik is all about indelibly etched food memories. In fact, the recipes that follow are a blend of those food memories, long phone conversations with Peter, and e-mails that never seemed to make it from his computer to mine. They are inspired by our memories of a spot we truly loved. We hope we do Labuznik's food justice, because if we don't, we'll hear about it— from Peter, of course.

FRIED JARLSBERG CHEESE WITH TARTAR SAUCE

MAKES 6 TO 8 SERVINGS

"Labuznik Fried Cheese with Imported Jarlsberg Cheese" was a classic on Peter Cipra's menu. The double coat of bread crumbs forms a nice golden crust, and the cheese doesn't leak out while it's being fried.

Peter always served his fried cheese with a tartar sauce heavy on the pickles, but try it with a fresh tomato salsa or a fresh fruit relish or chutney, such as the Sweet Cherry Chutney on page 205.

You can bread the cheese slices ahead, but it's best to fry the cheese right before you serve it, while your guests are enjoying a glass of wine.

Pâté was another Labuznik classic. If you prefer, you could start this dinner with the Chicken Liver Pâté on page 219.

1 cup all-purpose flour
2 teaspoons kosher salt
1 teaspoon freshly ground black pepper
4 large eggs
2 cups Dried Bread Crumbs (see page 83)
¾ pound Jarlsberg or Emmenthaler cheese, cut into about 18 slices, 1 inch wide, 2 inches long, and ¼ inch thick
Peanut or vegetable oil as needed for deep frying
Tartar Sauce

A STEP AHEAD Bread the cheese a few hours ahead and let it sit, uncovered, in the refrigerator.

Preheat the oven to 400°F.

Set out 3 bowls for breading the cheese. In the first bowl, combine the flour, 1 teaspoon of the salt, and ½ teaspoon of the pepper. In the second bowl, beat the eggs together. In the third bowl, combine the bread crumbs with the remaining teaspoon of salt and ½ teaspoon pepper. Dip a slice of cheese first into the flour, shaking off the excess, then into the eggs, shaking off the excess, and finally into the bread crumbs, shaking off the excess. Place the breaded cheese on a baking sheet lined with parchment or wax paper. Continue until all the cheese slices have been breaded. Allow the cheese slices to rest for about 5 minutes, uncovered, in the refrigerator, to set the crust, then give each slice a second coat by dredging first in egg, then in crumbs. (Don't dredge in the flour for the second coat.) Allow the breaded slices to rest again for 5 minutes, uncovered, in the refrigerator.

Meanwhile, fill a heavy straight-sided pan with at least an inch of oil and heat over medium-high heat until the temperature of the oil reads 350°F on a deep-frying thermometer (see page 14). Slip the cheese slices into the oil, in batches without crowding them, and fry until golden brown on one side, then turn gently

with a skimmer or a slotted spoon to brown the other side, about 2 minutes total. Gently scoop out the cheese slices with a skimmer as they are done and drain on paper towels.

Transfer the cheese slices to a parchment-lined baking sheet and bake for 5 minutes, until hot and the cheese is melted all the way through. Arrange the fried cheese on a platter and serve with small bowls of tartar sauce for dipping.

TARTAR SAUCE

MAKES ABOUT 1 CUP

Cornichons are very small, tart pickled gherkins. If you like dill pickles, substitute them for the cornichons.

¾ cup mayonnaise, homemade (page 13), or good-quality store-bought
1 tablespoon chopped drained capers
3 tablespoons finely chopped cornichons
1 tablespoon plus 1 teaspoon finely chopped red onion
1 tablespoon minced fresh flat-leaf parsley
2 teaspoons freshly squeezed lemon juice
2 teaspoons freshly grated lemon zest
1 teaspoon Worcestershire sauce
¼ teaspoon Tabasco sauce or to taste
Kosher salt and freshly ground black pepper

A STEP AHEAD Make this a day ahead and store it, covered, in the refrigerator.

Put the mayonnaise in a bowl and stir in the capers, pickles, onion, parsley, lemon juice and zest, Worcestershire, and Tabasco. Season to taste with salt and pepper.

ROMAINE SALAD WITH PICKLED CUCUMBERS AND RED CABBAGE

MAKES 6 SERVINGS

This dinner salad is the only one I ever ordered at Labuznik. The other salads on the menu might have been equally tasty, but I'll never know. I was so hooked on the perfectly pickled red cabbage and delicious vinaigrette with chunks of feta that I never needed anything else.

English cucumber has a thin, unwaxed skin and very small seeds. If you substitute another kind of cucumber, peel and seed it first.

FOR THE CARAWAY PICKLES

½ large English cucumber, sliced in half lengthwise and then crosswise, ⅛ inch thick (about 2 cups)

¼ medium red cabbage, cored and thinly sliced, preferably on a slicer or mandoline (about 2 cups)

1 cup white wine vinegar

½ cup sugar

1 tablespoon plus 1 teaspoon kosher salt

2 teaspoons coriander seeds

2 teaspoons caraway seeds

1 teaspoon black peppercorns

FOR THE WHITE WINE VINAIGRETTE

3 tablespoons white wine vinegar

2 teaspoons sugar

1 teaspoon Dijon mustard

6 tablespoons pure olive oil or vegetable oil

Kosher salt and freshly ground black pepper

FOR THE SALAD

1 large head romaine (about 1 pound), cored, tough outer leaves discarded

3½ ounces feta cheese, crumbled (about ½ cup)

A STEP AHEAD The caraway pickles can be made a day ahead and stored in the pickling brine, covered, in the refrigerator.

The vinaigrette can be made a week ahead and stored, covered, in the refrigerator.

To make the caraway pickles, set out 2 heatproof bowls and put the cucumber in one and the red cabbage in the other. Combine the vinegar, ½ cup water, sugar, and salt in a saucepan. Wrap up the spices in a small piece of cheesecloth and tie up the bundle with a piece of kitchen twine. Add the cheesecloth bundle to the saucepan and bring the pickling syrup to a boil, stirring to dissolve the salt and sugar. Immediately pour half the boiling brine over the cucumbers and the rest over the cabbage, placing the cheesecloth bundle in the bowl with the red cabbage. Cool to room temperature, then cover and refrigerate the bowls for at least 1 hour.

To make the vinaigrette, whisk together the vinegar, sugar, and mustard in a small bowl and slowly whisk in the oil. Season to taste with salt and pepper.

Drain the cucumber pickles and the red cabbage pickle, discarding the pickling liquid and the cheesecloth bundle.

Chop the romaine leaves into pieces about 1 inch square. You should have about 12 cups loosely packed chopped leaves. Place the romaine in a large bowl and toss with enough vinaigrette to coat the leaves lightly. Season the salad to taste with salt and pepper.

Divide the romaine salad among 6 plates, sprinkling some feta over each salad. Garnish each plate with a little mound of cucumber pickle and another little mound of red cabbage pickle.

SLOW-ROASTED PORK WITH CARAWAY ONION GRAVY

MAKES 6 TO 8 SERVINGS

My favorite entree at Labuznik was always the "Vepro Kneldo Zelo," slow-roasted pork served with dumplings and sauerkraut and drenched in gravy. Oh, that gravy—rich, silky, and fragrantly scented with caraway seeds. Peter always saves a cup or two of the gravy for making the next pork roast, just like a sourdough starter. Twenty-five years and thousands of pork loins later, his gravy has a history that could almost rival Prague's.

Peter prefers the blade end of a pork loin rib roast because it's more marbled with fat. Ask your butcher to remove the chine bone but reserve it for you, because it adds flavor to the gravy. You'll need a good heavy roasting pan for this recipe—one that you can put directly on the burner.

Allow a roast to rest before you carve it, to give the juices a chance to be redistributed in the meat. If you cut your meat immediately, all the juices will rush out and be lost. After you remove the pork from the roasting pan, it will take about 10 minutes to make your gravy—the perfect amount of time for the pork to rest.

One 6- to 7-pound bone-in pork loin rib roast, cut from the blade end, chine bone removed and reserved
Kosher salt and freshly ground black pepper
2 tablespoons caraway seeds
1 tablespoon bacon fat
1 medium onion, peeled, cut in half, and julienned
5 garlic cloves, peeled
3 tablespoons tomato paste
5 cups Chicken Stock (page 8), hot
1 tablespoon "quick mixing" flour, such as Wondra
Bread Dumplings, steamed

Preheat the oven to 300°F. Season the pork generously with salt and pepper and sprinkle with the caraway seeds. Melt the bacon fat over medium-high heat in a roasting pan placed over 2 burners. Add the pork and the chine bone and brown on all sides, about 10 minutes. Remove the pan from the heat. Place the onion in the pan and arrange the pork roast, bony side up, on top of the onions. Leave the chine bone in the pan and put the pan in the oven.

After 1½ hours, remove the pan from the oven. The onion should be browned and caramelized. Turn the roast over to the other side and add the garlic, tomato paste, and chicken stock. (Don't worry about stirring globs of tomato paste into the stock since you'll be whisking the gravy later.) Return the pan to the oven for another hour.

After 2½ hours of roasting, an instant-read thermometer inserted into the meat should read about 165°F. If the temperature is lower, continue to roast the pork until the thermometer reads 165°F, then remove the pan from the oven. Transfer the pork to a platter and set it in a warm spot, loosely covered with foil.

Place the roasting pan on 2 burners over medium-high heat and bring the liquid to a simmer. Gradually sprinkle in the flour, whisking constantly. Continue whisking for about 5 minutes, until the flour taste is cooked out, any lumps of tomato paste are smooth, and the gravy is barely thick enough to coat a spoon. Also whisk in any juices from the platter that have collected around the roast. You can strain the gravy if you prefer, but I like the texture of the chunks of onion and the rustic look of unstrained gravy here.

Transfer the pork to a cutting board and cut it into portions between the bones. Pile the pork on a platter and pour about a quarter of the gravy over the meat. Pour the rest of the gravy into a sauceboat and serve the pork accompanied by the gravy and dumplings.

BREAD DUMPLINGS

MAKES 6 TO 8 SERVINGS

I was thrilled that Peter Cipra was willing to share his secrets for Czechoslovakian-style bread dumplings. His are tender and almost fluffy, but with just enough breadlike structure to make them the perfect sponge for plenty of flavorful pork gravy. I discovered that Peter uses "instant" or "quick mixing" flour like Wondra instead of regular flour. For the bread croutons, he uses packaged croutons, often sold as dressing or stuffing mix, such as Pepperidge Farm. If you can't find unseasoned croutons, decrease the salt as instructed in the recipe.

The texture of these dumplings is best if you make them ahead, then slice and reheat them in a steamer when you are ready to serve. For steaming the dumplings, a multi-tiered Chinese bamboo steamer with two steaming baskets works perfectly. Set your bamboo steamer over a wok or a large saucepan partially filled with boiling water. If you don't have a multitiered bamboo steamer, divide the dumplings between two pots with steamer baskets.

A flexible plastic scraper is a great little tool for mixing the dough.

2 teaspoons active dry yeast

½ teaspoon sugar

1¾ cups "quick mixing" flour, such as Wondra

1 tablespoon kosher salt (decrease to 2 teaspoons salt if your croutons are already seasoned)

1 teaspoon baking powder

1 large egg plus 3 large yolks, lightly beaten together

1½ cups croutons from a box of packaged stuffing mix

A STEP AHEAD Make the dumplings, shape them into logs, and boil them up to 2 days ahead. Cool, then store them, wrapped in plastic, in the refrigerator. Or you can freeze them for a few weeks, tightly wrapped, then thaw for several hours or overnight in the refrigerator. When you are ready to serve the dumplings, slice and steam them as described.

Put ⅓ cup water in a small saucepan and gently heat to lukewarm, about 90°F to 100°F. Pour the lukewarm water into a large bowl and sprinkle the yeast and sugar over it. Set the bowl in a warm place until slightly foamy, about 10 minutes. In another bowl, mix together the flour, salt, and baking powder. Add the dry ingredients and the eggs to the yeast mixture, mixing with a rubber spatula or plastic scraper until a dough is formed. If the mixture seems too dry, add about a tablespoon more water, then mix in the croutons. Don't overwork the dough.

On a lightly floured surface, cut the dough into 3 equal pieces and roll each piece into a smooth log, about 5 inches long and 1½ inches wide.

Set a large pot filled with about 6 quarts of water over high heat and bring to a boil. Drop the logs into the pot (they should float to the surface) and boil them until cooked through, 12 to 14 minutes, using a large slotted spoon or a skimmer to gently turn them over a few times so they cook evenly. Use your slotted spoon or skimmer to remove the dumplings from the water and set them on a large plate. When the dumplings are cool, wrap each log tightly in plastic wrap and refrigerate.

When you are ready to serve the dumplings, unwrap them and use a serrated knife to slice them about ⅓ inch thick, at an angle, as if you were slicing a baguette. You should have 24 to 28 slices. Set up a 2-basket bamboo steamer over a pot of water and bring to a boil. Dampen 2 large clean cotton napkins or kitchen towels and lay them out on a work surface. Arrange half the dumpling slices in the center of each towel, placing the slices close together or slightly overlapping, in a single layer. Fold the edges of the napkins over to completely enclose the dumplings and lay each filled napkin in a steamer basket. Cover the top basket with the lid and steam over boiling water until the dumplings are hot, about 10 minutes. Remove the napkins from the steamers and unwrap the dumplings.

SAUERKRAUT

MAKES 6 SERVINGS

The secret to Peter's sauerkraut is grated potato; it mellows the flavor of the sauerkraut. Who knew?

I buy my sauerkraut from Bavarian Meats in the Pike Place Market, which has an impressive array of imported cans and jars of the stuff. But you can buy sauerkraut, in jars, cans, or refrigerated plastic bags, from almost any supermarket.

This is also delicious with grilled sausages and a pot of grainy mustard.

3 tablespoons vegetable oil

1 cup chopped onion

6 tablespoons white wine vinegar

6 tablespoons sugar

1 tablespoon caraway seeds

1 tablespoon kosher salt

2 pounds sauerkraut, drained

1 medium boiling potato (such as a thin-skinned red potato), peeled and grated (about 1 cup)

A STEP AHEAD Make the sauerkraut up to a week ahead and refrigerate, covered. Reheat in a covered saucepan, adding a little water if it seems dry.

Heat the oil in a large saucepan over medium heat. Add the onion and sauté, stirring occasionally, until transparent, about 5 minutes. Add the vinegar, sugar, caraway, salt, and 1½ cups of water. Bring to a boil, stirring to dissolve the sugar. Add the sauerkraut, bring to a simmer, cover, and simmer for about 10 minutes, stirring occasionally. Remove the cover and stir in the potato. Cover and simmer over medium-low heat, stirring occasionally and adding more water if the mixture seems dry, until the potato is completely cooked and almost dissolved into the sauerkraut, about 15 minutes. Taste and adjust the seasoning with more vinegar, sugar, and salt. Remove from the heat, transfer the sauerkraut to a platter, and serve immediately.

SUGARED CARROTS

MAKES 6 SERVINGS

The same vegetables were on the Labuznik menu from the day the restaurant opened until the day it closed. I always looked forward to Peter's sweet carrots, cooked to perfect tenderness, never al dente.

2 pounds medium carrots (10 to 12), peeled
4 tablespoons unsalted butter
3 tablespoons sugar
Kosher salt and freshly ground black pepper to taste

A STEP AHEAD Peel and cut the raw carrots a day ahead and refrigerate them, covered with plastic wrap.

Cut the carrots in half lengthwise, then slice them ¼ inch thick on the bias. Put the carrots in a heavy saucepan with the butter and 2 tablespoons water, then sprinkle the sugar over the top. Cover with the lid and cook slowly over medium-low heat until the carrots are very tender, 20 to 25 minutes. Remove the lid, raise the heat to high, and boil until the liquid is reduced to a glaze that just covers the carrots with a few tablespoons left in the bottom of the pan. Stir to combine everything well and season to taste with salt and pepper. Transfer the carrots to a platter and serve immediately.

CREAMED SPINACH

MAKES 6 SERVINGS

Peter Cipra would never, ever serve creamed spinach with this menu, because pork must be served with sauerkraut. At Labuznik, the creamed spinach came on the plate with Peter's Tournedos Rossini or Veal Orloff. But the sauerkraut, while delicious, didn't fill my need for vegetables. After ordering the roast pork, I always ordered a side of sweet carrots and creamed spinach, with Peter, I'm sure, shaking his head in bewilderment in the kitchen.

You may be tempted to cheat and use frozen spinach, but the taste of the fresh stuff really is better. If you can buy bagged prewashed ready-to-eat spinach leaves at the supermarket, you'll save yourself some of the work.

4 pounds spinach (about 5 bunches or 1½ pounds bagged ready-to-eat spinach leaves)

3 tablespoons unsalted butter

3 tablespoons all-purpose flour

1 cup milk, hot

½ cup heavy cream, or more as needed

Kosher salt and freshly ground black pepper

A STEP AHEAD You can blanch, shock, drain, and squeeze the spinach a few days ahead and store it, covered with plastic wrap, in the refrigerator.

Bring a large pot of salted water to a boil. Add the spinach leaves, in batches if necessary, and cook until wilted, which takes only a minute or less. As the spinach is cooked, scoop it out of the pot with a long-handled strainer and plunge it immediately into a large bowl of ice water. Drain the spinach in a colander, then, using your hands, squeeze out most of the water. Finely chop the spinach, by hand or by pulsing in a food processor, and set aside. You should have about 3 packed cups squeezed and chopped spinach.

To make the béchamel, melt the butter in a large sauté pan over medium heat. Whisk in the flour until the mixture is smooth and cook the roux for a few minutes. Gradually add the hot milk to the roux, whisking after each addition of milk until smooth, then reduce the heat to low and cook the béchamel for 4 to 5 minutes, whisking occasionally. Whisk in ¼ cup of the cream and season to taste with salt and pepper.

Add the spinach to the pan, stirring until well combined with the béchamel. Gradually stir in as much heavy cream as needed to get a slightly loose, creamy consistency. Continue to cook, stirring, until the mixture is simmering and hot. Season to taste with salt and pepper. Transfer the spinach to a platter and serve immediately.

BITTER ORANGE CHOCOLATE MOUSSE

MAKES 6 SERVINGS

I never had room for dessert at Labuznik, but Loretta always did. This classic chocolate mousse was her favorite, especially since it was served in a wineglass, which made her feel very grown up.

Candied orange zest has a hint of delicious bitterness that balances the mellow flavor of this smooth, creamy mousse. The candied zest will be the prettiest if you use a tool called a five-hole citrus zester (see page 265) to pull long thin strips from the oranges.

Semisweet chocolate is slighter sweeter than bittersweet, but either can be used here. The flavor of the mousse depends on the best-quality chocolate you can find. I prefer Callebaut, Valrhona, or Scharffen Berger (see Sources, page 265).

FOR THE CANDIED ZEST

4 thick-skinned oranges, such as navels

½ cup sugar

FOR THE CHOCOLATE MOUSSE

4 ounces semisweet or bittersweet chocolate, chopped

2 ounces unsweetened chocolate, chopped

¼ cup orange liqueur, such as Grand Marnier

4 large eggs, separated

2 tablespoons sugar

1 cup heavy cream

FOR THE ORANGE CREAM

¾ cup heavy cream

1 tablespoon orange liqueur, such as Grand Marnier

A STEP AHEAD The mousse can be made up to a day ahead and stored, covered with plastic wrap, in the refrigerator. The candied zest can be made up to 5 days ahead and stored, covered, in the refrigerator.

To make the candied zest, remove the zest from the oranges in long thin strips, using a 5-hole citrus zester. If you don't have a zester, you can remove the zest in long strips with a vegetable peeler. Be sure to scrape off any white pith from the undersides, then julienne it very finely with a sharp knife. Bring a small saucepan of water to a boil, add the zest, and boil for 1 minute. Drain off the water and reserve the zest. Return the empty saucepan to the stove, add the sugar and ½ cup water, and bring to a boil over medium-high heat, stirring occasionally to dissolve the sugar. Add the blanched zest to the syrup, reduce to a simmer, and cook until tender, about 5 minutes. Remove the saucepan from the heat and allow the zest to cool in the syrup, then strain, reserving both the candied zest and 1 tablespoon of the syrup.

To make the mousse, combine the chocolates, liqueur, and

3 tablespoons water in a heatproof bowl over a saucepan of very hot but not boiling water, stirring occasionally until the chocolate is melted and the mixture is smooth. Remove the bowl from the heat and allow the chocolate to cool slightly. In a large bowl, using a whisk, beat the egg yolks until well combined. Using a rubber spatula, blend a small amount of the warm chocolate into the yolks to temper them and prevent them from scrambling, then add the rest of the chocolate and mix with the spatula until smooth. In the bowl of an electric mixer with the whisk attachment, or in a bowl with a handheld electric mixer, combine the egg whites and the sugar and whip to soft peaks. Add about a quarter of the whites to the chocolate mixture and whisk them in to lighten the mixture. Then, using a rubber spatula, gently but thoroughly fold the rest of the whites, about a third at a time, into the chocolate mixture. Clean the mixer bowl and the whisk, then whip the cream to soft peaks. Fold the whipped cream, about a third at a time, into the mousse, folding until the mixture is smooth and there are no white streaks. Spoon the mousse into a glass serving bowl. Cover with plastic wrap and chill for at least 3 hours or overnight.

To make the orange cream, place the cream, liqueur, and reserved syrup in a bowl and whip to soft peaks with an electric mixer.

Pipe or spoon the orange cream decoratively over the mousse, then heap the candied zest over the cream.

KAY AND CLAY'S MERLOT RELEASE PICNIC

Many people who work in the restaurant business dream about opening their own restaurant, bed-and-breakfast, or winery some day. Typically it would be a small, personal endeavor way out in the country with a couple of employees at most. Whatever you produce, be it wine or cheese, could come only from your own two hands. It may not work out for whatever reason, either circumstances beyond anyone's control or market conditions. But sometimes it does work out, as it has for winemaker Kay Simon.

Kay and her husband, Clay Mackey, own the Chinook Winery, located in the tiny Yakima Valley town of Prosser. Passion and dreams have shaped their charming enterprise. What was once a cute little farmhouse is anchored by a wood-floored, china cabinet–filled tasting room that doubles as a twenty-seat dining room. There's also a forties-style kitchen (original equipment included), from which Kay turns out her remarkable grilled lamb, Merlot biscotti, and Bing cherry cobbler. The old back bedroom houses Kay's viticultural lab.

Kay's beautiful gardens— her perennials as well as her vegetables and herbs—surround the house. Prosser gets more sun than any other town in the state of Washington, and her garden is testament to that fact. Clay, the farmer half of the couple, is in charge of the immaculate barn that houses the winery, the barrel cellar, and the bottling machine, not to mention the surrounding vineyards and orchards. Backing up the winery are the sagebrush-laced Horseheaven Hills. Huge fruit-packing warehouses dot the landscape, served by mile-long trains taking the produce to market.

Kay and Clay give new meaning to the term *hands-on*. They not only make the wine, but they also drive the three and a half hours to our restaurants to deliver it. One of the ways we know the seasons are changing in Seattle is what Jackie and I call the Kay and Clay clock. April finds them at our door with not only our wine

MENU

RIPE CAMEMBERT GRILLED IN GRAPE LEAVES WITH SWEET CHERRY CHUTNEY

CHINOOK SAUVIGNON BLANC

GRILLED ASPARAGUS AND WALLA WALLA ONIONS WITH MERLOT BALSAMIC

LAMB CHOP T-BONES IN CRUSHED CHERRY MARINADE WITH TARRAGON MUSTARD

SEA SALT–ROASTED RED JACKET POTATOES

CHINOOK MERLOT

MERLOT-POACHED APRICOTS AND CHERRIES

KAY'S MERLOT BISCOTTI

MORE CHINOOK MERLOT

delivery but also the first asparagus of the season, grown by their neighbors. August brings sweet corn and Kay's home-grown tomatoes, and even in December, when very little is being harvested near Prosser, Kay shows up with both wine and her justly acclaimed Merlot biscotti.

Kay and Clay are sweet, passionate people who have taught me how to support Washington wine in an intensely personal fashion. Their patient approach to making and selling wine is exemplary. There are very few wineries, not only in Washington but anywhere, that wait an extra year to release their reds. That extra time gives their red wines character, maturity, and time for the bottling shock to wear off.

Father's Day marks the annual trek to Kay and Clay's Merlot Release lamb barbecue and the picking of the perfectly ripe Bing, Montmorency, and Lambert cherries from the orchard right outside their door.

The Merlot Release June picnic is held in Kay and Clay's garden, filled with pink peonies, black walnut trees, and fragrant lilies. As with all people who put their heart and soul into something, there's such a release of energy that comes with the success of the crop. Table talk naturally turns to the qualities of the current vintage, comparing it to past vintages, and thoughts of future vintages. The exchanges at the picnic table are passionate without ever getting heated. Kay's Merlot Biscotti add a lovely, sweet accent to the whole day. Sweet and passionate, like Kay and Clay.

RIPE CAMEMBERT GRILLED IN GRAPE LEAVES WITH SWEET CHERRY CHUTNEY

MAKES 6 SERVINGS

If you've ever grown your own grapes, you know that grapevines are so prolific, it seems a waste to prune them and throw all the leaves away. This recipe is just one of many ways to take advantage of these tasty treats of the vine. If you have access to fresh grape leaves, a quick blanch in boiling water followed by a dip in ice water gives you a fresh-tasting grape leaf—not briny like the grape leaves from a jar. If you're using brined grape leaves, be sure to rinse them well in cold water.

Pan-searing these leaf packets works just as well as grilling. Sear them in a hot pan with a little olive oil, turning once, until the cheese begins to melt, about 1½ minutes per side. You can substitute any sort of good melting cheese for the Camembert, such as chèvre, Brie, or Gorgonzola. Just use about a 1½-ounce portion of cheese per grape leaf.

Save the sweet, vinegary juice from the chutney for other uses. Drizzle a spoonful over ripe melon wedges dusted with freshly ground black pepper or flavor a mayonnaise for chicken salad.

1 cup champagne vinegar or other mild vinegar such as rice wine vinegar

½ cup sugar

6 peeled fresh ginger coins (see page 46)

1 cinnamon stick, about 2 inches long

¼ teaspoon toasted and ground coriander seeds (see page 24)

⅛ teaspoon freshly ground black pepper

1 pound sweet cherries, such as Bing or Rainier, pitted and halved (about 3 cups)

6 grape leaves, from a jar of brine-packed grape leaves, rinsed in cold water and patted dry

One 10-ounce wheel of Camembert, cut into 6 wedges

A STEP AHEAD Make grape leaf packets early in the day and store them, covered with plastic wrap, in the refrigerator. The cherry chutney can be made up to a day ahead and stored in its liquid, covered and refrigerated.

To make the cherry chutney, heat the vinegar, sugar, ginger, and spices in a small saucepan over medium-high heat. Bring the mixture to a boil and boil for 2 minutes. Add the cherries and bring back to a boil, then immediately pour the chutney into a bowl and let cool. To develop the flavor, allow the chutney to stand for at least ½ hour.

Fire up the grill.

To wrap the cheese, place a grape leaf, shiny side down, on a work surface and trim off the stem. Place a wedge of cheese toward the bottom of the leaf, with the tip of the wedge pointing toward the tip of the leaf. Fold the bottom of the leaf up, fold the sides in, and roll up, continuing to fold the sides in as you go, so the cheese is completely enclosed. If your leaf is large, trim it as needed to prevent the wrapping from becoming too thick. Repeat until all the cheese wedges and grape leaves are used.

Grill the packets over direct heat, lid off, turning as needed,

until the cheese is soft and just starting to ooze, 2 to 3 minutes total, depending on the heat of grill. Remove the packets from the grill.

Drain the chutney, discarding the liquid and the cinnamon stick (or save for another use). Mound the chutney in the center of a platter and arrange the grape leaf packets around it. Serve immediately, providing your guests with both forks and knives.

GRILLED ASPARAGUS AND WALLA WALLA ONIONS WITH MERLOT BALSAMIC

MAKES 6 SERVINGS

Walla Walla, Washington, is nestled at the foot of the Blue Mountains. The name, meaning "many waters," comes from the Nez Perce Indians. The Walla Walla Valley, rich with volcanic soil, grows wheat, peas, wine grapes, alfalfa hay, and, of course, the world-famous Walla Walla sweet onions. The earliest Walla Wallas of the season are small salad onions, sold on the stalk, like very bulbous scallions. They can be split in half and grilled, with the greens left on. As the season advances, the onions get bigger and aren't sold with their green stalks. You can substitute two or three of these larger sweet onions by slicing them thickly, brushing with oil, and grilling the slices on both sides.

The Merlot balsamic adds sweetness and depth, similar to the way a drizzle of aged balsamic vinegar would, but with the scarlet color and richness of a good Merlot. Try it with a grilled steak, instead of steak sauce.

FOR THE MERLOT BALSAMIC
1½ cups Merlot
1 tablespoon plus 2 teaspoons honey
1 tablespoon balsamic vinegar
⅛ teaspoon freshly ground black pepper

FOR THE LEMON VINAIGRETTE
1 tablespoon freshly squeezed lemon juice
1 teaspoon freshly grated lemon zest
2 tablespoons extra virgin olive oil
Kosher salt and freshly ground black pepper

6 Walla Walla salad onions, with 1- to 2-inch-diameter bulbs and the greens on (about 1½ pounds), or other salad onions of the same size
2 bunches asparagus (about 2 pounds), tough bottoms snapped off
Olive oil for brushing
1½ ounces Parmesan cheese in a chunk (about ¼ cup shaved)

A STEP AHEAD Make the Merlot balsamic and the lemon vinaigrette a day or two ahead and keep them covered and refrigerated. Bring back to room temperature before serving.

Grill the vegetables an hour ahead and keep them at room temperature. Dress them with the lemon vinaigrette and finish with the Merlot balsamic and Parmesan shavings when you are ready to serve.

To make the Merlot balsamic, put the wine in a saucepan, bring to a boil, and boil until reduced and syrupy. You should have ¼ cup reduced wine. Remove from the heat and stir in the honey, vinegar, and pepper. Return to the heat, bring back to a boil, and boil for a few minutes more, until the honey is dissolved and the mixture is

thick and syrupy. You should have about 3 tablespoons syrup. Remove from the heat, pour into a small bowl, and set aside.

To make the lemon vinaigrette, combine the lemon juice and zest in a small bowl. Slowly whisk in the oil. Season to taste with salt and pepper. Set aside.

Fire up the grill and preheat the oven to 400°F.

Trim the root end from the onions, discard any discolored leaves, and trim a few inches off the tops of the greens if they are scraggly. Cut the onions in half lengthwise, right through the greens. Brush the onions and the asparagus with olive oil and season them on both sides with salt and pepper. Lay the onions horizontally across the grill grates (to keep the greens from falling through the grates), cut sides down, and grill over direct medium heat with the lid off until you have nice grill marks, 2 to 4 minutes. Turn them to the other side and grill for another 2 to 4 minutes, then transfer them to a baking sheet and bake until tender, 8 to 10 minutes. The oven time will vary depending on the size of your onions and the heat of your grill. Cut a small slice out of the center of an onion bulb to see if it is tender, with just a bit of crunch. If you are using very small salad onions, you may be able to skip the baking step. Remove the onions from the oven and place them in a large shallow bowl.

Meanwhile, lay the asparagus horizontally across the grill grates and grill until done and charred in places, rolling them with the tongs to cook them evenly, 4 to 8 minutes, depending on the thickness of your asparagus. Remove the asparagus from the grill and add them to the bowl with the onions.

Pour the vinaigrette over the vegetables and gently roll them with a rubber spatula or your hands to coat evenly. Season to taste with a little more salt.

Arrange the onions and asparagus on a platter. Drizzle the Merlot balsamic decoratively over the vegetables. Using a vegetable peeler, shave the chunk of Parmesan into long thin shreds directly over the vegetables and grind some black pepper over the top.

LAMB CHOP T-BONES IN CRUSHED CHERRY MARINADE WITH TARRAGON MUSTARD

This chapter was inspired by Kay and Clay's annual Chinook Merlot release picnics. These events grew from the original, humble wienie roast in 1986 to mayhem in 1995 with multiple lambs and over one hundred guests at this tiny winery. The 1996 vintage release marked the end of these huge picnics, because the wine was in such short supply. The vines were ravaged by an early frost, which reduced the crop by two-thirds. Kay and Clay responded with smaller, more intimate gatherings in the subsequent years.

We still go on Father's Day every year, and now we bring the lamb—almost-2-inch-thick T-bones. Before we head over the mountains, I marinate the chops in olive oil, garlic, shallots, and rosemary. When we get to Kay and Clay's, we pick some cherries from their orchard to crush over the lamb chops and drizzle them with Merlot from a bottle from their cellar. The chops marinate for a few hours longer while we go swimming, or play boccie.

A kitchen tip: Marinate the chops in a sealable plastic bag instead of a pan or bowl.

FOR THE CHERRY MARINADE

1 cup sweet cherries such as Bing or Rainier, pitted (about 6 ounces)

6 garlic cloves, peeled

1 medium shallot, peeled and cut into quarters

2 tablespoons olive oil

½ cup Merlot

1 tablespoon chopped fresh rosemary

¼ teaspoon freshly ground black pepper

12 loin lamb chops, 4 to 5 ounces each, 1¼ to 1½ inches thick

FOR THE TARRAGON MUSTARD

2 tablespoons unsalted butter

½ cup finely chopped shallot

½ cup Dijon mustard

1 tablespoon coarsely chopped fresh tarragon

Kosher salt and freshly ground black pepper

A STEP AHEAD Make the mustard a few days ahead and store, covered, in the refrigerator.

To make the cherry marinade, put the cherries, garlic, and shallot in the bowl of a food processor and pulse until roughly pureed. Add the oil, wine, rosemary, and pepper and pulse until combined.

Put the lamb in a nonreactive pan and pour the marinade over it, turning to coat all sides. Cover and refrigerate for 2 to 4 hours.

To make the tarragon mustard, melt the butter in a sauté pan over medium-low heat. Add the shallot and cook slowly until soft and translucent, about 8 minutes, stirring occasionally. Turn the heat up to medium-high and continue cooking for a few more

minutes, stirring, until the shallot is caramelized golden-brown. Remove from the heat. Put the mustard in a small bowl and stir in the shallot and tarragon.

When you are ready to cook the lamb, fire up the grill for direct cooking. Remove the lamb from the refrigerator and allow it to come to room temperature. Remove the chops from the pan, shaking off the excess marinade, and season on both sides with salt and pepper. Grill the chops over a hot fire, lid off, vents open, turning them as needed, until done to your liking, about 15 minutes total for medium-rare, 125°F on an instant-read meat thermometer. The temperature will rise a bit as the meat rests. Transfer the meat to a platter and allow to rest 5 minutes.

Pass the platter of lamb chops and the bowl of tarragon mustard.

SEA SALT–ROASTED RED JACKET POTATOES

MAKES 6 SERVINGS

I like the brininess of sea salt; it tastes more like the ocean than regular salt. The smallest and best potatoes for this dish are "c" size and are often sold in 2- or 3-pound net bags. Either white or red works fine, but the reds are a little showier. The potatoes, if they're small, will be tender in less than an hour, but we like to cook them for the full hour in a hot oven to get them really browned and roasted. Substitute kosher salt if you prefer.

2½ pounds small red potatoes, washed and dried but not peeled
¼ cup olive oil
Sea salt and freshly ground black pepper

Preheat the oven to 450°F. Place an empty roasting pan in the oven to get hot, about 5 minutes.

Put the potatoes in a bowl and toss them with the oil. Season generously with salt and pepper.

Remove the hot roasting pan from the oven and pour in the potatoes. Use a rubber spatula to scrape all the oil and seasoning from the bowl to the roasting pan. Return the pan to the oven and roast for 1 hour, shaking the pan occasionally, until the potatoes are tender and the skins are browned and wrinkled. Check the seasoning and add more salt and pepper if desired. Transfer the potatoes to a serving dish and serve immediately.

MERLOT-POACHED APRICOTS AND CHERRIES

MAKES 6 SERVINGS

Many desserts are improved with a scoop of vanilla ice cream, and this one is no exception. If you have an herb garden, garnish each scarlet bowl of fruit with a rose geranium leaf, a sprig of anise hyssop, or other sweet herbs.

Buy a cherry pitter if you don't already own one; it's worth the small investment. A handheld cherry pitter is inexpensive and works just fine, but to make short work of a quantity of cherries, you may want to splurge on a countertop cherry pitter. It's not often I endorse a particular brand of equipment, but I just have to say that the Westmark Cherry Pitter, with an aluminum plunger and a plastic holder for the pitted cherries, is the best I've ever used.

2 cups Merlot or other dry red wine

¾ cup sugar

1 bay leaf

1 cinnamon stick, about 2 inches long

1 pound apricots, pitted and quartered

1 pound cherries, pitted

Vanilla ice cream

A STEP AHEAD You can make this up to a day ahead and store, covered, in the refrigerator.

Combine the wine, sugar, bay, and cinnamon in a heavy saucepan over medium-high heat and bring to a simmer, stirring to dissolve the sugar. Add the apricots and simmer for 5 minutes. Add the cherries and simmer for another 5 minutes. Drain, reserving both the fruit and the wine. Put the fruit in a bowl. Return the wine to the saucepan, bring it back to a boil, and boil until slightly reduced and syrupy. You should have 1½ cups. Cool the syrup, setting the bowl of syrup over a bowl of ice water to speed the cooling if desired. Discard the cinnamon stick and the bay leaf. Then pour the syrup over the fruit and refrigerate until cold.

Divide the fruit and the syrup among 6 shallow soup bowls. Put a scoop of ice cream in each bowl and serve with Kay's Merlot Biscotti.

KAY'S MERLOT BISCOTTI

MAKES ABOUT 2½ DOZEN

Kay gives us a tin of her pink, slightly crumbly, hazelnutty Merlot biscotti every Christmas. After fifteen years, I finally asked her for the recipe. Typically we wouldn't use a recipe that calls for food coloring, but Kay said that the wine tends to turn the biscotti gray, so she adds a drop or two of red food coloring. "Fresh-crop hazelnuts are really important," Kay states on the recipe card. She gets hers directly from Springbrook Hazelnut Farm in Oregon (see Sources, page 265).

If you're making this whole menu, you'll be opening some bottles of Merlot, and the 2 tablespoons called for in this recipe won't be a problem. But if you want to make these cookies and don't have an open bottle of Merlot in the house, use any red wine or even omit the wine altogether.

Because this dough is quite soft, you need to refrigerate it for several hours or overnight before shaping, so plan accordingly.

8 tablespoons (1 stick) unsalted butter, softened

¾ cup sugar

2 large eggs

1 teaspoon pure vanilla extract

2 tablespoons Merlot or other red wine

A few drops red food coloring, optional

2 cups all-purpose flour

1½ teaspoons baking powder

¼ teaspoon salt

¾ cup hazelnuts, toasted (see page 24) and coarsely chopped

A STEP AHEAD Make the dough up to a day ahead and store it, tightly wrapped, in the refrigerator. Store the baked cookies for up to 4 days in an airtight container at room temperature; or freeze the baked cookies, tightly wrapped, for about a month, then thaw at room temperature.

In a large bowl with an electric mixer or with a wooden spoon, cream the butter with the sugar. In another bowl, beat the eggs, vanilla, wine, and food coloring, if using. Add the egg mixture to the butter mixture and mix well.

In another bowl, stir together the flour, baking powder, and salt. Using a rubber spatula, add the dry ingredients and the chopped hazelnuts to the butter mixture, mixing until a soft dough is formed. Cover the dough with plastic wrap and refrigerate for several hours or overnight before shaping.

When you are ready to shape and bake the cookies, preheat the oven to 325°F.

On a well-floured surface, with floured hands, roll the dough into 2 cylinders about 1½ inches wide and 12 inches long. Flatten the cylinders slightly, place them about 2½ inches apart on a parchment-lined baking sheet, and bake until the tops are lightly browned, about 25 minutes. Remove from the oven and allow to cool for 5 minutes.

Carefully transfer the cylinders to a cutting board. Cut the cylinders on the diagonal into slices about ½ inch wide. Return the biscotti to the baking sheet, placing them with one of the cut surfaces down. Bake until lightly browned, about 25 minutes. Remove from the oven and allow to cool.

KAY AND CLAY'S WINE COUNTRY RESTAURANT GUIDE

One of the big differences between the Napa and Sonoma wine country in California and Yakima Valley wine country in Washington is that Yakima is not exactly chock-a-block with world class restaurants. But Yakima does have some great local food products. When Kay and Clay moved here in the late seventies, every farm wife had her own "secret" recipe for pickled asparagus, and Mrs. Hogue and Mrs. Tucker eventually made their versions locally famous. Chukar Cherries also got started in Prosser. The Twin City Foods plant in town processes potato products and makes the whole town smell like French fries. Tucker Cellars and Produce grows White Cloud Popcorn and sells it *cheap*. The restaurant scene in the area is a little sparse, but when Kay and Clay do go out to eat in the area, here's where they go:

❖ Burgers: Burger Ranch, for real ice cream milk shakes
1305 Meade Ave.
Prosser, WA 99350
(509) 786-2720

❖ Mexican food: El Caporal, for chiles rellenos and veggie burritos
624 6th St.
Prosser, WA 99350
(509) 786-4910

❖ Upscale northwest cuisine: Patit Creek, for green peppercorn steak and a glass of Walla Walla Washington wine
725 E. Dayton Ave.
Dayton, WA 99328
(509) 382-2625

❖ Wine Bar: The Barrel House, big selection of local wines and great Caesar salads
22 N. 1st St.
Yakima, WA 98901
(509) 453-3769

❖ Fine dining: The Dykstra House, homemade soups and bread, simple and delicious
114 Birch Ave.
Grandview, WA 98930
(509) 882-2082

SPRING CHICKENS

Some of my best restaurant memories are of great chicken dishes that I've had: the perfect roast chicken with the brittle, ultra-crispy skin and the moist meat Jackie and I ate at the well-worn bistro L'Ami Louis in Paris; the golden-brown panfried chicken at Stroud's in Kansas City, where their motto is "We choke our own chickens"; or the chicken with garlic shoots at Dim Sum A Go Go in New York's Chinatown.

In Seattle, when we get a hankering for fried chicken, we head to the legendary Alki Homestead, a West Seattle landmark. This huge log cabin was built originally as a private residence in 1902, just a hundred yards from the sandy Alki Beaches of Puget Sound. The view from Alki Beach, looking at downtown Seattle, is as good as it gets. Soon after, the homestead was sold to the Seattle Auto Club, which used it as a roadhouse for everyone to drive to in their new cars. Eventually, Doris Nelson purchased this grand estate, turning it into a full-time restaurant.

Alki Homestead couldn't be in better hands. Forty-two years later, Mrs. Nelson continues to nourish generations of grateful Seattleites with her melt-in-your-mouth fried chicken, steaming hot biscuits, and homemade apple pie. The lace doily–filled dining room is centered around a huge stone fireplace.

There are a lot of skinless, boneless breasts in the supermarket, but treat yourself to a whole chicken. Buy a couple of whole birds for the pan-browned and roasted chickens on this menu. Cut up the legs and the thighs. Take the breasts off. Add the backs and the necks to a pot of your own homemade chicken stock and use the stock to make the risotto. Flour and deep-fry the gizzards; drench them in Tabasco for a chef's treat. More important, if you have kids, teach them how to cut up a chicken. It's a life skill everyone should have.

MENU

HOMEMADE BIANCO ON THE
ROCKS WITH A TWIST

CHICKEN LIVER PÂTÉ WITH
PICKLED RHUBARB AND
BAGUETTE TOASTS

WARM SPINACH SALAD
WITH LARDONS, SHERRY
VINAIGRETTE, AND
FRIED EGGS

SPRING CHICKENS WITH
GREEN MARINADE

SWEET PEA RISOTTO

CANTINA DEL PINO DOLCETTO

ROSE'S BUTTERMILK CAKE
WITH BAY CRÈME FRAÎCHE
AND BRANDIED BING
CHERRIES

JOHANNES SELBACH
ZELTINGER HAMMELREICH
RIESLING

HOMEMADE BIANCO ON THE ROCKS WITH A TWIST

MAKES 6 SERVINGS

Bianco is an Italian wine-based aperitif with a complex herbal aroma in the style of vermouth. Lemon balm and lemon verbena can be found in farmers' markets and are easy to grow in your herb garden or in a pot on the windowsill. If you can't find either of these herbs, serve an Italian Bianco, a dry French vermouth, or Lillet Blanc on the rocks instead.

1 bottle Sauvignon Blanc
4 fresh lemon balm or lemon verbena sprigs
Four 2-inch strips lemon zest

Pour the wine into a pitcher, add the herbs and zest, and allow to steep about 30 minutes. Then pour the Bianco into ice-filled glasses and serve.

CHICKEN LIVER PÂTÉ WITH PICKLED RHUBARB AND BAGUETTE TOASTS

MAKES 6 TO 8 SERVINGS

Creamy and lush, chicken liver pâté is an old-fashioned classic that never goes out of style. Sometimes I take a big flat platter and spread chicken liver pâté out ¼ to ½ inch thick and then spread a topping over it, like a ½-inch layer of shiitake duxelles, or finely chopped shiitake mushrooms that have been sautéed in butter. This is a nice touch if you are having a lot of people, because everyone gets the flavor combination—a little of the pâté and a little of the topping—with every spoonful.

The pale pink rhubarb pickle adds some tang, sweetness, and spice to this dish.

½ pound chicken livers, trimmed

Kosher salt and freshly ground black pepper

9 tablespoons unsalted butter, softened

1 tablespoon olive oil

3 tablespoons minced shallot

¼ cup Cognac or brandy

2 teaspoons minced fresh thyme

2 teaspoons minced fresh flat-leaf parsley

Pickled Rhubarb

12 to 18 baguette toasts (see page 55)

A STEP AHEAD The pâté can be made up to 3 days ahead and stored, covered, in the refrigerator.

Season the livers on both sides with salt and pepper. Heat 1 tablespoon of the butter and the olive oil in a sauté pan over medium-high heat. When the fat is almost smoking, add the livers and sear them on both sides until nicely browned, about 2 minutes. The livers should be cooked medium-rare or medium, but not well-done. Transfer the livers to a plate. Return the sauté pan to medium-high heat, add the shallot, and sauté for a few minutes, stirring as needed, until softened. Remove the shallot from the pan and add to the plate with the livers. Pour the Cognac into the sauté pan and return to the heat for a moment, stirring with a wooden spoon to scrape up any browned bits, then pour over the livers and shallot.

When the livers and shallot have cooled to lukewarm, place them, along with the herbs, in the bowl of a food processor. Puree until very smooth while gradually adding the remaining butter, bit by bit. Season with salt and pepper to taste. Scrape the pâté into a small ceramic pot or earthenware dish, cover the surface directly with a piece of plastic wrap, and chill for at least 2 to 3 hours. Serve with the pickled rhubarb and the toasts.

PICKLED RHUBARB

Chicken liver pâté is very rich because of all the butter in it, so serving with this compote balances the fat and acid, the sweet and sour. Try serving this sweet, slightly spicy condiment with cured meats or roast duck.

½ pound rhubarb, sliced ½ inch thick (about 2 cups)

2 cups rice wine vinegar

1 cup firmly packed light brown sugar

½ cup granulated sugar

1 jalapeño pepper, thinly sliced crosswise on the bias

4 peeled fresh ginger coins (see page 46)

2 star anise

1 tablespoon whole coriander seeds, roughly crushed with a rolling pin or heavy pan

½ cinnamon stick, about 2 inches long

A STEP AHEAD Make this up to 2 days ahead and store, covered, in the refrigerator.

Place the rhubarb in a heatproof bowl.

Combine the vinegar, sugars, jalapeño, ginger, and spices in a saucepan over medium-high heat. Bring the pickling syrup to a boil, allow it to boil for about 3 minutes, then immediately pour the hot syrup over the rhubarb. Allow the rhubarb to cool to room temperature, then cover the bowl and refrigerate for several hours or overnight.

WARM SPINACH SALAD WITH LARDONS, SHERRY VINAIGRETTE, AND FRIED EGGS

MAKES 6 SERVINGS

A goat cheese omelet, or steak frites, or a frisée and lardon salad captures the essence of a Parisian bistro. To my mind, a forkful of this warm salad, with a bit of salty bacon and the yolk of a fried egg melting into and enriching the vinaigrette, is the epitome of Paris.

Be sure the spinach and frisée leaves and your bowl are at room temperature and not cold, or the bacon fat in the dressing may congeal on the cold leaves. Small, organic spinach leaves are nice here; buy the smallest and most tender heads of frisée you can find.

If you can handle it, have two nonstick sauté pans and fry all six eggs at once. Otherwise, cook the eggs in batches, transferring them to a warm plate as they are cooked. Instead of frying them, you can poach the eggs if you prefer.

You can also serve this salad as a light lunch. Or, for a less substantial starter salad, omit the fried eggs.

8 cups loosely packed spinach leaves, torn into pieces if the leaves are large (1 large bunch, about 12 ounces, or 4 ounces bagged ready-to-eat spinach leaves)

8 cups loosely packed frisée, stems trimmed, torn into bite-size pieces (1 medium head, about 6 ounces)

¼ cup sherry vinegar

1 tablespoon Dijon mustard

1 tablespoon plus 1 teaspoon honey

½ pound thick-sliced bacon, cut crosswise into ¼-inch-thick matchsticks

1 to 2 tablespoons unsalted butter, as needed, for frying the eggs

6 large eggs

6 tablespoons extra virgin olive oil

1 teaspoon minced garlic

Kosher salt and freshly ground black pepper

A STEP AHEAD The bacon can be cooked early in the day. The reserved bacon fat and drained bacon can be refrigerated until needed. Heat the bacon lardons in a hot oven for a minute or two before adding them to the salad.

Combine the spinach and frisée in a large bowl near the stove. In another small bowl, whisk together the vinegar, mustard, and honey. Put the bacon matchsticks (lardons) in a sauté pan over medium-low heat and cook until crisp, about 10 minutes. Drain the lardons, reserving 2 tablespoons of the bacon fat. Keep the bacon warm.

In a nonstick sauté pan, melt the butter over medium heat and cook the eggs either over easy or sunny side up. Set the eggs aside.

In a sauté pan over medium heat, gently heat the reserved bacon fat and the olive oil. Add the garlic and sauté for a minute or two, until aromatic. Carefully whisk in the vinegar mixture and

turn the heat to high. As the dressing begins to boil, keep whisking until it emulsifies. When the dressing is hot, remove the pan from the heat and immediately pour it over the spinach and frisée. Add the reserved warm lardons, season to taste with salt and pepper, and toss well.

Divide the salad among 6 warm plates, top each portion with a fried egg, and serve immediately.

SPRING CHICKENS WITH GREEN MARINADE

MAKES 6 TO 8 SERVINGS

For a couple of seasons, clubhouse manager Henry Genzalez hired me to bring trays and trays of food down for the Seattle Mariners' after-game meal. Considering that a bunch of millionaire players and managers were going to be eating this food, I started out cooking fancy restaurant dishes. But I soon found out that what most of the players really liked was chicken and steak. I must have cooked this chicken dish a couple of dozen times for them, and it remains one of my favorites.

These chickens marinate overnight in a thick green herb pesto before being pan-browned and then roasted. Substitute some of your favorite herbs for the ones specified in the recipe, but definitely use a few assertive herbs, like rosemary and marjoram. Be sure to serve the deliciously herby pan juices with the chicken.

2 chickens (about 3½ pounds each), cut into 8 pieces each (2 breasts, 2 legs, 2 thighs, and 2 wings), or 16 pieces total

FOR THE GREEN MARINADE

1 cup chopped scallion, white and green parts

½ cup chopped fresh flat-leaf parsley

½ cup sliced fresh chives

¼ cup chopped fresh tarragon

3 tablespoons chopped fresh rosemary

3 tablespoons chopped fresh marjoram

2 tablespoons chopped fresh thyme

2 tablespoons chopped garlic

1 tablespoon freshly grated lemon zest

2 teaspoons kosher salt

1 teaspoon freshly ground black pepper

¾ cup extra virgin olive oil

About ¼ cup olive oil, as needed, for browning the chicken

1 lemon, cut in half

A STEP AHEAD Make the marinade and marinate the chicken a day ahead.

Trim excess fat from the chicken pieces. Rinse them under cold running water, pat dry with paper towels, and place them in a nonreactive pan.

Combine the scallion, herbs, garlic, lemon zest, salt, and pepper in the bowl of a food processor and process until smooth, gradually adding the oil last to emulsify. The marinade will be very thick, like a pesto. Pour the marinade over the chicken pieces and coat the pieces on both sides. Cover with plastic wrap and refrigerate overnight.

To cook the chicken, preheat the oven to 450°F. Heat 2 large sauté pans over medium-high heat with about 2 tablespoons of oil

in each pan. If you don't have 2 large sauté pans, brown the chicken in batches. Remove the chicken from the marinade, reserving any excess marinade. Put the chicken pieces in the pans skin side down and sauté until the skin is nicely browned. Turn and brown the other side, adjusting the heat between medium and medium-high as necessary so you don't burn the chicken. When the chicken pieces are browned on both sides, 8 to 10 minutes total for each piece, transfer them to a roasting pan. Squeeze the lemon halves over the chicken and throw the lemon halves into the pan. Scrape any extra marinade into the roasting pan. Put the roasting pan in the oven and roast until the chicken is cooked, the juices run clear, and the thigh meat reads 175°F on an instant-read thermometer, 20 to 25 minutes. Remove the chicken from the oven.

Remove the chicken from the roasting pan and arrange on a platter. You can cut the chicken breasts in half first so your guests can choose both white and dark meat. Whisk the pan juices to break up any clumps of the marinade and drizzle a little over the chicken. Pour the rest of the pan juices into a gravy boat, discarding the lemon halves, and pass with the chicken.

NOTE: If you are making the whole menu, you can brown the chicken just ahead of the arrival of your guests and leave it at room temperature. Then, when you are ready to make the risotto, slip the pan of chicken into your preheated oven. The chicken and risotto will be ready at about the same time.

HOW TO CUT UP A CHICKEN

Remove the neck, heart, gizzard, and liver from the chicken. Cut off the fat and excess skin from the neck and tail ends.

Place the chicken on a work surface, breast side up, and cut off the wings at the first joint (closest to the breast). Then cut off the leg and thigh by cutting through the skin into the natural division between the leg and the body. Bend the leg away from the body and cut down between the thighbone joint and the hip socket. Cut the leg away from the body as close to the backbone as possible. Repeat with the other leg and thigh. Separate the drumstick from the thigh by cutting down through the joint that separates the two. Repeat with the other drumstick and thigh.

To remove the backbone, insert a large heavy knife into the chicken's cavity and cut down through the rib bones on each side of the backbone, chopping down through the collarbone to free the backbone completely. Or use kitchen or poultry shears to cut out the backbone.

Place the chicken on the work surface breast side up and use a large heavy knife or poultry shears to cut the breast in half, cutting through the breastbone. If you like, you can divide each half-breast in half, into two equal pieces.

SWEET PEA RISOTTO

MAKES 6 SERVINGS

Nothing says spring like the first fresh garden peas, also called *English peas*. The pea puree swirl garnish here is a fancy touch—it is the "peas" de resistance. But, if you prefer, you could skip it and put all the blanched peas in the risotto.

Arborio rice is Italian short-grain rice with a high starch content that makes risotto creamy. Always make risotto just before you serve it.

2 cups shelled fresh peas (from about 2 pounds English peas in the pod)

6 to 7 cups Chicken Stock (page 8), as needed

6 tablespoons unsalted butter, softened

¼ cup minced shallot

2 teaspoons minced garlic

2 cups Arborio rice

½ cup dry white wine

⅔ cup freshly grated Parmigiano-Reggiano cheese, plus more for passing at the table

2 tablespoons finely chopped fresh mint

2 tablespoons thinly sliced fresh chives

1 tablespoon finely chopped fresh dill

Kosher salt and freshly ground black pepper

A STEP AHEAD Blanch the peas and make the pea puree early in the day and store, covered, in the refrigerator. Allow the pea puree to come to room temperature before you use it over a bowl of hot water if desired. Have all your ingredients measured out and waiting by the stove, but make the risotto only when you are ready to serve it.

Bring a saucepan of lightly salted water to a boil and set up a bowl of ice water. Add the peas to the saucepan and cook until tender, 1 to 2 minutes. Drain the peas and immediately plunge them into the ice water. Drain the peas again. Reserve 1½ cups of the peas. Puree the remaining ½ cup of peas in a blender with about ⅓ cup or slightly more cold water until very smooth. Set the pea puree and the whole peas aside.

Put the chicken stock in a saucepan and bring it to a simmer. Melt 3 tablespoons of the butter over medium-high heat in a large sauté pan. Add the shallot and sauté for a few minutes, until translucent. Add the garlic and sauté for another minute, until aromatic. Add the rice and stir until the grains of rice are coated with butter. Add the wine and simmer, stirring, until most of the wine is absorbed. Start adding the simmering chicken stock, about 1 cup at a time, adding more chicken stock only once the rice has absorbed almost all of the stock already in the pan. Keep stirring the risotto frequently. Continue adding the stock in smaller amounts as the rice comes closer to being cooked. You may not need all the stock. After 20 to 25 minutes of this process, the rice should be cooked to the al dente stage. Taste a piece of rice to see if the grain is tender and edible with just a little bit of a bite in the center. When the rice is al dente, remove the risotto from the heat and stir in the remaining 3 tablespoons butter and the Parmesan. Add a little more of the simmering stock, about ¼ to ½ cup, to loosen the risotto and make it soupy and creamy in consistency. Add the fresh herbs, the reserved whole peas, and season to taste with salt and pepper.

Ladle the risotto into 6 large shallow soup bowls or onto a large platter. Use a spoon to drizzle the pea puree decoratively over the risotto. Pass more grated Parmesan at the table.

ROSE'S BUTTERMILK CAKE WITH BAY CRÈME FRAÎCHE AND BRANDIED BING CHERRIES

MAKES ONE 9-INCH CAKE, SERVING 8 TO 12

This is Jackie's favorite cake from one of our favorite cookbooks, *The Cake Bible* by Rose Levy Beranbaum. Jackie has made this light, tender, fluffy, and moist cake so many times I'm sure she could make it in her sleep. Instead of icing, Jackie insists on a light shake of powdered sugar, then she either serves the cake with the freshest fruit of the season or opens a jar of preserved fruit that she put up herself in the fall.

Rose has her own special technique for making cakes, and you have to do things exactly as she says. For example, the butter must be room temperature and soft; you must use cake flour and be sure to sift it *before* you measure. The correct way to measure the cake flour is to set the measuring cup on your counter, then sift the flour directly into the cup, sweeping the excess flour off the top of the cup with a metal spatula or knife. If you follow the directions carefully, this is an easy, quick, and almost foolproof cake. Instead of the brandied cherries, try fresh raspberries, blueberries, or lightly sugared sliced strawberries.

4 large egg yolks

⅔ cup buttermilk

1½ teaspoons pure vanilla extract

2 cups sifted cake flour

1 cup sugar

1 tablespoon baking powder

½ teaspoon salt

8 tablespoons (1 stick) unsalted butter, softened, plus a little more for buttering the pan

Confectioners' sugar

Bay Crème Fraîche

Brandied Bing Cherries

A STEP AHEAD Make the cake early in the day. Wrap with plastic wrap when the cake is completely cool and leave at room temperature. Sprinkle with confectioners' sugar right before serving.

Preheat the oven to 350°F. Butter a 9- by 2-inch round cake pan, line it with a circle of parchment paper, and butter the paper.

In a small bowl, combine the egg yolks, about a quarter of the buttermilk, and the vanilla. Set aside.

In the bowl of an electric mixer with the paddle attachment, or in a large bowl with a hand mixer, combine the flour, sugar, baking powder, and salt and mix on low speed for 30 seconds to combine. Add the butter and the remaining buttermilk and mix on low speed until moistened, then increase the speed to medium and beat on medium speed for 1½ minutes (or on high speed if using a hand mixer). Scrape down the sides. Add the egg mixture about a third at a time, beating for 20 seconds after each addition. Scrape down the sides. Scrape the batter into the prepared pan and bake until the center of the cake springs back when pressed lightly and a skewer inserted in the center comes out clean, 30 to 40 minutes. Remove from the oven.

Allow the cake to cool on a rack for 10 minutes. To unmold, run a small knife around the sides of the cake and place an inverted plate or a cardboard circle over the cake pan. Protecting your hands with a kitchen towel, invert the whole thing. The cake should slide right out onto the plate. Peel off the parchment paper, place another inverted plate over the cake, and, again, invert the whole thing. Do this gently—this is a tender and soft cake. Remove the top plate and the cake will be right side up. Allow the cake to cool completely, then sift confectioners' sugar evenly over the top.

Cut the cake into wedges and serve each wedge with a dollop of the crème fraîche and a large spoonful of the cherries and their syrup.

BAY CRÈME FRAÎCHE

MAKES ABOUT 1½ CUPS

Crème fraîche is similar in consistency to sour cream but with a less sour taste. You can purchase crème fraîche in many supermarkets or specialty cheese stores, or you can make your own. We flavor this version with bay leaves. California bay leaves, which have a stronger, more floral aroma than the Turkish variety, work well here. Or omit the bay leaves and use this recipe to make plain crème fraîche.

1½ cups heavy cream
¼ cup buttermilk
3 bay leaves
1 tablespoon plus 2 teaspoons sugar

A STEP AHEAD Crème fraîche will keep, covered and refrigerated, for a week or more.

Pour the cream into a clean container. Stir in the buttermilk and add the bay leaves. Cover the container with plastic wrap and leave out at room temperature for 2 to 3 days, until thickened. Remove the bay leaves, cover with plastic wrap, and chill for a few hours or overnight. Before serving, lightly whisk in the sugar.

BRANDIED BING CHERRIES

MAKES ABOUT 1 CUP

This is a quick dessert sauce of sweet cherries in brandy syrup. During cherry season, Jackie also likes to use the "Jubilee Cherries" recipe from her favorite preserving cookbook, Helen Witty's *Fancy Pantry* (Workman Publishing, 1986), to put up plenty of jars for the winter months.

Spoon the cherries and their syrup over a scoop of your favorite ice cream. You could also add one of these cherries to a Manhattan, instead of a maraschino.

⅔ cup sugar

1 vanilla bean, cut in half lengthwise

1 pound bing cherries, or other sweet cherries, stemmed and pitted, keeping the cherries whole

½ cup Cognac or other good-quality brandy

A STEP AHEAD You can make the brandied cherries up to a few weeks ahead and store them, covered and refrigerated. The flavor mellows and improves after a few days.

Combine the sugar and ½ cup water in a heavy saucepan over medium-high heat. Use a paring knife to scrape the seeds from the vanilla bean and add both the seeds and the pod to the pot. Bring to a boil, stirring to dissolve the sugar. Add the cherries and ¼ cup of the Cognac and simmer for 10 minutes. Remove from the heat and strain the cherries from the cooking liquid, reserving both the cherries and the liquid. Put the cherries and the vanilla bean pod in a heatproof bowl and return the liquid to the saucepan. Bring the liquid to a boil over medium-high heat and continue to boil until syrupy and reduced. You should have ½ cup syrup. Remove the pan from the heat and pour the hot syrup over the reserved cherries. Allow the brandied cherries to cool, then stir in the remaining ¼ cup Cognac. You can set the bowl of cherries over a bowl of ice water to cool them more quickly, if desired. Remove and discard the vanilla bean pod before serving.

CHRISTMAS EVE WITH THE DOWS

Christmas Eve Dinner is a communal affair, always celebrated with the Dows and the Hinkley-Teers. It's a really big dinner, the table loaded down with cherished favorites and fresh inspirations.

It's a big night, so we make a point of drinking out of big bottles. Peter Dow, Mike Teer, and I are all in the wine business, so we each eagerly scan our cellars for at least magnum-size bottles with the appropriate pedigree. We invariably start off with a couple of magnums of Laurent Perrier Rosé or Billecart Salmon Rosé or Louis Roederer Cristal. There's something magical about the combination of champagne and caviar punctuated by plump, briny Kumamoto oysters, still sleeping on the half shell.

I am not a religious person, outside of barbecue, but I do love the excitement of lighting the candles on the Dow's Christmas tree. This ceremony is not for the faint of heart because we're always afraid the tree is going to go up in flames, but for the twenty minutes that the candles are lit and the Christmas carols sung, we feel transported back into the time of Dickens. The kids, Molly Dow or Loretta, are in charge of picking out a Christmas story to be read aloud by the group. The girls get to open one present from each of us before we head back to the table for cheese and dessert.

The cheese course has always been Jackie's favorite. She discovered Epoisses, the runny, pungent cow's milk cheese from Burgundy, when we were in France fifteen years ago, and it has become a standard on the Christmas Eve cheese tray. Weeks in advance Jackie combs the city, searching out the best specimens, and sets them aside to ripen to sticky, gooey, stinky perfection. The kids usually hold their noses through this course, and windows must be opened to clear the air so as not to ruin the delicate aroma of Peggy Dow's silk persimmon pudding.

MENU

OYSTERS ON THE HALF SHELL, CAVIAR, AND CHAMPAGNE

LAURENT PERRIER ROSÉ

POL ROGER ROSÉ

OEUFS EN MEURETTE ON RUSTIC BREAD

ROAST DUCK WITH RIESLING, BLACK PEPPER, AND THYME

KING BOLETUS STUFFING

BROWN BUTTER KALE

BARTOLO MASCARELLO BAROLO

APPLE AND RADICCHIO SALAD WITH MAPLE MOLASSES PECANS

JACKIE'S RUNNING CHEESE TRAY

FIG BRIOCHES

HAMEL SYRAH

PERSIMMON PUDDING WITH PEAR BRANDY HARD SAUCE AND PEAR VANILLA SAUCE, SUGARED CRANBERRIES, AND SUGARED MINT LEAVES

HOT BUTTERED RUM

MORE CHAMPAGNE: ROEDERER CRISTAL

OYSTERS ON THE HALF SHELL, CAVIAR, AND CHAMPAGNE

See "How to Shuck Oysters," page 149.

See "American Caviar."

See "Jackie's Favorite Champagnes and Sparklers."

AMERICAN CAVIAR

Several years ago, after reading the umpteenth article about poaching in the Caspian Sea, and especially an article in the *New York Times* suggesting that 90-plus percent of all Russian caviar is poached, we decided to stop serving caviar at our restaurants altogether. Dale and Betsy at Seattle Caviar talked us into switching to environmentally friendly, sustainable Sterling caviar from Stolt Sea Farm in Elverta, California, which raises farmed white sturgeon.

White sturgeon is very similar to the species osetra from the Caspian Sea but is indigenous to the Pacific Coast of North America. The white sturgeon is one of the oldest species found on earth. White sturgeon caviar is a beautiful dark brown bead with a mild nutty taste balanced by a good ocean flavor.

It has become popular to garnish caviar service with capers, raw onions, sieved eggs, and sour cream. I, for one, think that's bunk. If I'm going to spend $40 for an ounce of caviar, I want to taste the caviar. I want to feel each egg burst on my tongue. I want to taste the salty freshness of well-handled roe. Maybe a little buttered brioche toast or something else fairly plain, but beyond that . . . fuhgedddaboutit!

SEATTLE CAVIAR

Dale and Betsy Sherrow

2833 Eastlake Ave. E.

Seattle, WA 98102

(206) 323-3005

www.caviar.com

To order Sterling caviar directly from Stolt Sea Farm:

www.sterling caviar.com

JACKIE'S FAVORITE CHAMPAGNES AND SPARKLERS

Billecart Salmon Rosé, France

Roederer Cristal, France

Philipponnat Clos de Goisses, France

Pol Roger Rosé, France (Winston Churchill's and Tom's favorite)

Roederer Estate, California

Mountain Dome, Washington (from Spokane, Jackie's hometown)

Argyle, Oregon

OEUFS EN MEURETTE ON RUSTIC BREAD

MAKES 8 SERVINGS

Our Christmas Eve dinners often take on a theme. It could be northern Italian, like the last one, which featured osso buco and risotto Milanese, or it could be Spanish with salt-grilled prawns and a crusty seafood paella. One year we explored Burgundy, and Peter Dow, our host, chose to make Oeufs en Meurette for the starter course, a classic Burgundian dish consisting of poached eggs on garlic toast with bacon, mushroom, and red wine gravy. Now this French standard starts all of our Christmas Eve meals, no matter what country we're cooking our way through. Yes, the eggs do turn pale purple when they are poached in the wine, and the sauce is purple as well. But the flavor is truly delicious, and it wouldn't be Christmas Eve without "the oeufs."

Peter doesn't use special equipment or fancy tricks when poaching eggs. He just cracks each egg against the side of the saucepan and drops it right into the wine, which should be simmering, not boiling. The simmering wine needs to be at a depth of about 1½ inches for poaching the eggs, so find a pan of

1 bottle dry red wine, such as Burgundy or Pinot Noir
2 bay leaves
8 large eggs
¼ pound thick-sliced bacon, cut crosswise into ½-inch-thick pieces
2 tablespoons unsalted butter
½ cup finely chopped onion
½ pound button mushrooms, wiped clean, tough ends of stems removed, cut into quarters
2 tablespoons all-purpose flour
1 teaspoon chopped fresh thyme
Kosher salt and freshly ground black pepper
8 Garlic Toasts, cut ¾ inch thick, made using broiler method (page 18)
8 small fresh thyme sprigs

A STEP AHEAD Poach the eggs and make the sauce up to a day ahead. Once the eggs are poached, place them in a container of cold, not hot, water. Cover the container with plastic wrap and place it in the refrigerator. Then strain the wine and make the sauce. Pour the sauce into a container, cool, then cover with plastic wrap and refrigerate. When ready to serve, reheat the sauce to a simmer over medium heat, stirring in a tablespoon or two of water if the sauce seems too thick. Reheat the poached eggs by lowering them into a pan of gently simmering water until they are warmed through, about 2 minutes, then remove the eggs with a slotted spoon and drain on a clean kitchen towel.

Pour the red wine into a saucepan, add the bay leaves, and heat to a simmer. The wine should fill the pan to a depth of at least 1½ inches. Break each egg into a small dish and slip it gently into the simmering wine, using as many of the eggs as will fit comfortably in your pan at one time. Allow the eggs to poach in the wine until the whites are firm, about 4 minutes, spooning the hot wine over the tops of the eggs occasionally. Using a slotted spoon, remove the appropriate size to hold the contents of a bottle of wine at that depth. A 9-inch sauté pan works well for poaching four eggs at a time.

Because this is a dish from Burgundy, I use a Burgundy wine or an Oregon Pinot Noir. It's perfectly okay to use button mushrooms for this recipe, or use cultivated mushrooms such as shiitakes.

the poached eggs from the saucepan and place them in a bowl of hot water to keep them warm while you finish the dish. Continue until all the eggs are poached. Pour the poaching wine through a strainer into a clean container and reserve.

In a large sauté pan, cook the bacon over medium-high heat until the fat is rendered and the bacon is starting to brown, then add the butter. When the butter melts, add the onion and mushrooms and sauté until the vegetables soften, 3 to 4 minutes. Sprinkle the flour over the bacon and vegetables, stir, and cook for a few minutes more. Add the reserved wine and the thyme. Bring to a boil and simmer until the sauce is thick enough to coat a spoon, 5 to 8 minutes. Season to taste with salt and pepper and remove from the heat.

Set out 8 shallow soup bowls and place a garlic toast in each bowl. Remove the poached eggs from the bowl of hot water with a slotted spoon and drain on a clean kitchen towel. Place an egg on top of each toast. Pour some of the sauce over each serving, dividing the mushrooms, onion, and bacon evenly. Garnish each serving with a thyme sprig.

NOTE: If you are making the entire menu, the oven may already be occupied with duck or stuffing when you are ready to use the broiler for making garlic toasts. In that case, broil the garlic toasts a few hours ahead and set them aside at room temperature. Before serving, reheat them in a 350°F to 400°F oven for a few minutes.

ROAST DUCK WITH RIESLING, BLACK PEPPER, AND THYME

MAKES 8 SERVINGS

Duck is my favorite bird to roast because it has silky dark meat all the way through. Duck has enough fat in its skin to baste itself while roasting, unlike chicken, but not so much, like goose, that it's overwhelming.

The two ducks called for here will provide each guest with one breast or one leg-thigh portion, which should be enough as part of a large Christmas Eve feast. If you think some of your guests will eat more, roast three ducks. Just be sure to use a roasting pan large enough for all the duck pieces, and you can proceed with the recipe without other changes, making the same amount of sauce. This recipe yields a generous amount of sauce so you and your guests will have plenty for both the duck and the bread stuffing.

Duck reheats beautifully, so making this dish a day or two ahead will free up your time considerably on Christmas Eve day. Since the duck is already quartered, you'll have no last-minute carving to do while your guests are at the table.

As you cook the ducks, plenty of duck fat will be rendered. Don't throw

2 tablespoons olive oil

2 medium onions, coarsely chopped

2 celery ribs, coarsely chopped

1 large carrot, coarsely chopped

2 bay leaves

6 fresh thyme sprigs

2 ducks, quartered (see page 243), to yield 4 leg-thigh portions and 4 breast-wing portions

Kosher salt and freshly ground black pepper

2 cups Riesling

2 tablespoons unsalted butter, softened

¼ cup all-purpose flour

4 cups Duck-Enriched Chicken Stock

1 tablespoon chopped fresh thyme

A STEP AHEAD Cook the duck and make the sauce a day or two ahead. Store both the duck and the sauce in the refrigerator, covered with plastic wrap. Reheat the duck as directed. Reheat the sauce to a simmer over medium heat, whisking occasionally.

Preheat the oven to 350°F. Put the oil in a roasting pan and place the pan on 2 burners over medium-high heat. Add the onions, celery, carrot, bay, and thyme and sauté, stirring as needed, until the vegetables start to brown, about 6 minute. Remove the roasting pan from the heat and set aside.

Score the skin of each duck breast by cutting 3 or 4 slashes in each direction in a crosshatch pattern with a sharp knife. (The breasts are much fattier than the leg-thighs, so you need to score only the breasts.) Season all the duck portions with salt and pepper on both sides. Place a large sauté pan over medium-high heat. A 12-inch sauté pan is the perfect size. If you don't have a pan this large, you will have to brown the duck in more batches or use 2 pans.

it away! Pour it into a container and save it for another use, just like you would use bacon fat, because flavorful fat like this should be treasured. It lasts a long time (weeks) in the refrigerator and even longer (months) in the freezer. (For a recipe using duck fat, see Duck-Fried Jo Jos, page 81.)

As soon as the pan is warm, place the leg-thigh portions in the pan, skin side down. You won't need any oil in the pan because as the duck heats it will begin to render plenty of fat, most of which you can pour into a container and reserve for another use. Cook the duck leg-thighs on the skin side only until golden brown, about 10 minutes, being careful of spattering fat. Transfer the duck leg-thigh portions, skin side up, to the prepared roasting pan. Pour off all but a film of fat from the sauté pan, then put the duck breasts, skin side down, in the sauté pan over medium-high

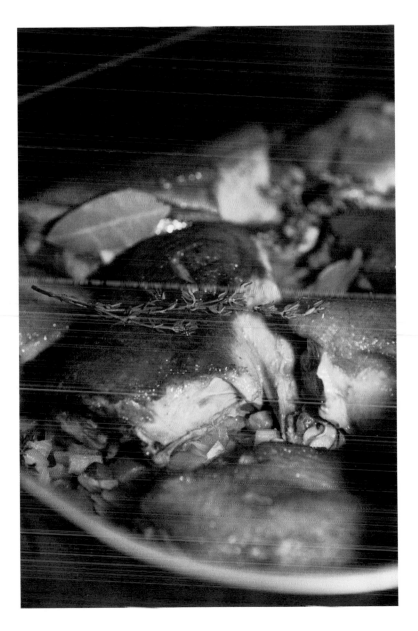

heat and brown them in the same manner. When the duck breasts are browned on the skin side, about 10 minutes, add them, skin side up, to the roasting pan. Pour off the fat in the sauté pan and reserve for another use. Pour 1 cup of the Riesling into the empty sauté pan and bring to a boil, stirring with a wooden spoon to scrape up any browned bits, then add this liquid to the roasting pan.

Cover the pan with foil and roast for 30 minutes. Remove the foil and continue to roast until the breasts are cooked through, about another 15 minutes. Transfer the duck breasts to a large plate and set them aside. When the duck breasts are cool enough to handle, I like to use a sharp knife to remove the breastbones to make them easier for my guests to eat. Continue to roast the legs until they are cooked through and an instant-read meat thermometer inserted into a thigh reads at least 165°F to 175°F, about an additional 15 minutes, then remove the pan from the oven. Remove the duck legs from the roasting pan, and set them aside on the plate with the breasts. Total roasting time for the duck breasts is about 45 minutes, and total roasting time for the legs is about 1 hour.

Scrape everything remaining in the roasting pan into a strainer set over a bowl and press on the debris to get all the juices. Discard the debris. Degrease the roasting juices either by pouring them into a gravy separator and pouring off the fat or by setting the bowl in a pan of ice water to cool for a while, then skimming all the fat off the top with a spoon or a small ladle. Set the defatted roasting juices aside for making the sauce.

To make the sauce, make a beurre manié by kneading together the butter and flour in a small bowl to form a smooth mixture, using your hands or a wooden spoon. Set aside. Pour the remaining cup of Riesling into a large saucepan over medium-high heat and bring to a boil. Add the duck-enriched chicken stock and the reserved roasting juices and bring to a simmer. Add the beurre manié to the simmering sauce bit by bit, whisking until smooth. Continue to cook the sauce until it is thick enough to coat a spoon, about 10 minutes. Add the thyme and season generously with salt and plenty of pepper.

To finish the dish, raise the oven temperature to 400°F and place a large ovenproof sauté pan over medium-high heat. Put the duck pieces in the pan, skin side down, and cook until the skin is golden and crispy, about 5 minutes. Flip the pieces and put the pan into the oven for another 5 to 10 minutes, until the duck is heated through. If you don't have a pan large enough to accommodate all the duck pieces, you can brown them in batches on the stove, then transfer them to a baking sheet and put the baking sheet in the oven.

Use a spatula to remove the duck from the pan or baking sheet and pile the duck, skin side up, on a platter. Pour the gravy into a sauceboat and pass with the duck.

NOTE: If you are making the duck-enriched chicken stock on the same day as the roast duck, preheat the oven to 450°F and get your stock started first. Then, while the stock is simmering, turn the oven down to 350°F and proceed with the roast duck recipe.

DUCK-ENRICHED CHICKEN STOCK

This is called a *double-strength stock,* because you're using chicken stock instead of water to make your duck stock. The yield is strikingly rich and delicious because the oven-roasted duck backbones add real depth of flavor. We use Riesling here to deglaze the pan because we're using it in the finished dish, but red wine works beautifully for a darker stock or sauce. It's easiest to remove fat from a chilled stock, so if you have time, chill the stock overnight before skimming.

Backbones, cut in half, necks, and wing tips from 2 ducks

1 onion, coarsely chopped

1 celery rib, coarsely chopped

1/2 large carrot, coarsely chopped

1 cup Riesling

6 cups Chicken Stock (page 8)

1 tablespoon plus 1 teaspoon black peppercorns

1 bay leaf

A STEP AHEAD Make the stock a few days ahead and store, covered, in the refrigerator. Or freeze the stock for several weeks. Bring the stock to a boil before using.

Preheat the oven to 450°F. Put the backbones, necks, wing tips, and all of the vegetables in a small roasting pan or a large sauté pan with an ovenproof handle and roast until everything is browned, about 40 minutes. Remove the roasting pan from the oven.

Using tongs and a slotted spoon, transfer the bones and the vegetables from the roasting pan to a large pot, leaving the fat behind. Pour off and discard the fat, then pour the wine into the empty roasting pan and place it on a burner over medium-high heat. Bring the wine to a boil and use a wooden spoon to scrape all the browned bits from the bottom of the pan. Remove the roasting pan from the burner and pour the wine into the pot. Add the chicken stock, peppercorns, and bay leaf to the pot. Bring to a boil over high heat, then reduce the heat and allow the stock to simmer for 1 to 1½ hours. Strain the stock through a fine-mesh strainer. Let the stock sit for 5 to 10 minutes, then skim off the fat, or refrigerate overnight and skim the fat the next day.

HOW TO QUARTER A DUCK

For the Roast Duck with Riesling, Black Pepper, and Thyme, you'll need 2 ducks. You can ask your butcher to quarter them for you, but be sure to ask for the backbones, necks, and wing tips so you can make the Duck-Enriched Chicken Stock.

Remove the necks, hearts, gizzards, and livers from two 5-pound ducks. Cut off the fat and excess skin from the neck and tail ends and cut off the wing tips. Reserve the neck and wing tips for the stock and discard the rest of the trimmings.

Place a duck, breast side up, on your cutting board and use your knife to cut off the leg and thigh by cutting into the natural division between the leg and the body. Bend the leg away from the body and cut down between the thighbone joint and the hip socket. Repeat with the other leg. To remove the backbone, insert a large heavy knife into the duck's cavity and, while holding the duck down with your other hand, cut down through the rib bones on each side of the backbone. Or, if you have poultry shears, place the duck breast side down and cut the backbone out with the poultry shears, cutting away from you. Cut the backbone in half and reserve for stock.

Place the duck breast side up and use a large heavy knife or poultry shears to cut the breast in half, cutting through the breastbone.

Repeat with the other duck. You now have four leg-thigh portions and four breast-wing portions from the two ducks. Carefully trim away excess skin and all visible gobs of fat from each duck portion.

KING BOLETUS STUFFING

MAKES 8 SERVINGS

When Jacques and Marie Joubert used to bring their chèvre into the restaurant every week it was usually accompanied by, depending on the season, something they had foraged for or grown themselves—gorgeous saffron-colored chicken eggs from their own coop, or maybe, after a trip hiking through the meadows of the Cascades, giant, squirrel-gnawed, boletus mushrooms with bronze caps the color of a well-worn penny and pearly white stems.

The Northwest's deliciously meaty boletus, "The King of Mushrooms," is closely related to Italy's porcini. If you can get your hands on fresh boletus or porcini mushrooms, use them in this recipe and omit the dried porcini. For the fresh mushrooms called for here, you can use cremini, button, shiitakes, oysters, chanterelles, or a combination. Duxelles is the French name for finely chopped cooked mushrooms.

We often serve this stuffing alongside roast chicken or goose and it has become a staple at our Thanksgiving table.

1 loaf European-style rustic bread, about 1 pound

3 tablespoons olive oil

Kosher salt and freshly ground black pepper

1 ounce dried porcini mushrooms

1 cup boiling water

8 tablespoons (1 stick) unsalted butter, plus more for buttering the pan

¼ cup minced shallots

1 pound mushrooms, cleaned, tough stems removed, finely chopped by hand or in the processor

½ cup finely chopped celery

½ cup finely chopped onion

⅔ cup toasted and chopped hazelnuts (see page 24)

⅔ cup dried cranberries or dried cherries, soaked in hot water 15 minutes and drained

¼ cup finely chopped parsley

1 tablespoon finely chopped fresh thyme

1 tablespoon finely chopped fresh sage

2 cups Chicken Stock (page 8), hot

A STEP AHEAD The unbaked stuffing can be covered with plastic wrap and refrigerated a day ahead. Bake as directed, allowing just a few minutes extra baking time.

Preheat the oven to 375°F. Butter a large shallow baking dish, such as a 9 × 13-inch pan, and set aside.

To toast the bread, cut the crusts off the loaf, then cut the bread into 1½-inch chunks. You should have about 8 cups of bread cubes. In a bowl, toss the bread with the olive oil, and season to taste with salt and pepper. Spread the bread out on a baking sheet and toast until golden, 15 to 20 minutes, stirring occasionally. Remove the pan from the oven and set aside. Reduce the oven temperature to 350°F.

To make the duxelles, place the porcini in a small heatproof bowl and pour the boiling water over them. Steep until soft, about 20 minutes. Rub the porcini to remove any grit, then remove them from the water, coarsely chop, and set aside. Strain the soaking liquid through a fine sieve or a cheesecloth-lined sieve into a small saucepan. Bring the soaking liquid to a boil over high heat, reduce the liquid until syrupy, and set aside. (You should have about ¼ cup porcini syrup.) Melt 5 tablespoons of the butter in a large sauté pan over medium-high heat. Add the shallots and cook a few minutes until softened. Add the finely chopped mushrooms and cook until softened. Add the porcini syrup and the chopped porcini, and season the mixture to taste with salt and pepper. Cook the duxelles until soft and pastelike, stirring occasionally and turning the heat down if needed to prevent scorching as the liquid evaporates, 15 to 20 minutes total cooking time. Remove the duxelles from the heat and set aside.

Melt the remaining 3 tablespoons butter in a sauté pan over medium heat and sauté the celery and onion until soft but not brown, about 5 minutes. Remove from the heat.

In a large bowl, combine the toasted bread, the duxelles, the celery and onion, the hazelnuts, cranberries or cherries, herbs, and chicken stock. Stir everything together well. Season with salt and pepper to taste. Spread the mixture in the prepared pan. Cover the pan with foil. Bake for 30 minutes, then remove the foil, and bake another 35 minutes until the top is crusty and golden. Serve the stuffing directly from the baking dish.

NOTE: If you are making the whole menu, you may need to turn the temperature up to 400°F in order to reheat the Roast Duck with Riesling, Black Pepper, and Thyme (page 238) while your bread stuffing is still baking in a 350° oven. Just keep an eye on the stuffing and reduce the baking time slightly if necessary, removing it from the oven whenever it is hot and the top is golden.

BROWN BUTTER KALE

Leafy greens like kale have many virtues, not the least of which is that most of the prep work can be done ahead—trimming, washing, blanching, and chopping. All you need to do at the last minute is toss them in some browned butter.

There are many varieties of kale. We like the narrow dark blue-green leaves of Lacinato kale; sometimes called black, Tuscan, or dinosaur kale, but use any variety you like. The blanching time may vary, depending on the thickness of the kale leaves.

2½ pounds kale
8 tablespoons (1 stick) unsalted butter
Kosher salt and freshly ground black pepper
Lemon wedges

A STEP AHEAD Blanch, squeeze, and chop the kale a few days ahead. Store in the refrigerator, covered with plastic wrap.

Stem and wash the kale, shaking off any excess water. In a large pot of boiling salted water, cook the kale until tender, 5 to 10 minutes. Drain the kale in a large colander, then let cold water run over it until it is cool enough to handle. Using your hands, squeeze most of the water out. It does not need to be squeezed completely dry. Then roughly chop the kale.

Melt the butter in a very large sauté pan (or divide between 2 pans if you don't have a large enough pan) over medium-high heat. Allow the butter to bubble and turn golden brown, with a toasted fragrance. Watch carefully—this will take only a few minutes. Add the kale to the pan and stir it around until it's mixed with the butter and warmed through. Season to taste with salt and pepper and remove from the heat. Pile on a platter and garnish with lemon wedges to squeeze over the kale.

APPLE AND RADICCHIO SALAD WITH MAPLE MOLASSES PECANS

MAKES 6 TO 8 SERVINGS

Granny Smith, Braeburn, Akane, Cameo, Gala, Fuji, or Sweet 16 —any flavorful apple can be thinly sliced for this festive red and green salad with sweet, spicy nuts. If the salad is not going to be followed by a cheese tray, try crumbling some blue cheese over the top.

You can substitute either baby spinach leaves or mâche for the arugula.

1½ teaspoons minced shallot

2 tablespoons sherry vinegar

1½ teaspoons honey

1½ teaspoons Dijon mustard

6 tablespoons pure olive oil

Kosher salt and freshly ground black pepper

12 cups loosely packed arugula leaves, washed and dried

½ medium head radicchio, cored, leaves separated, washed, dried, and torn into bite-size pieces

1 Belgian endive, sliced in half, cored, and cut into ½-inch strips

1½ medium apples, cored but not peeled

¼ lemon

Maple Molasses Pecans

A STEP AHEAD Make the vinaigrette a few days ahead and store it, covered, in the refrigerator. Wash and dry the arugula and radicchio and keep them refrigerated, covered with a damp kitchen towel, for up to 1 day ahead. Cut the Belgian endive and the apples when you are ready to serve the salad.

To make the vinaigrette, combine the shallot, vinegar, honey, and mustard in a small bowl. Gradually whisk in the olive oil. Season to taste with salt and pepper.

In a large bowl, combine the arugula, radicchio, and endive. Cut the apples into thin slices and add them to the bowl. Toss with enough vinaigrette to coat everything lightly and season to taste with salt, pepper, and a squeeze of lemon.

Divide the salad among 8 salad plates or pile into a large shallow decorative bowl and garnish with the pecans.

MAPLE MOLASSES PECANS

MAKES ABOUT 2 CUPS

Easy to make, and with just the right amount of sweetness, these lightly candied nuts also make a welcome addition to a cheese tray, or scatter a few over your pumpkin pie at Thanksgiving. Adding the butter to the pecans after they come out of the oven keeps them from sticking together.

2 tablespoons honey

2 tablespoons pure maple syrup

1 teaspoon molasses

1 teaspoon pure vanilla extract

Pinch of kosher salt

½ pound pecan halves

1 tablespoon unsalted butter, melted

A STEP AHEAD The pecans will keep for at least 4 days in an airtight container at room temperature.

Preheat the oven to 375°F and line a baking pan with a piece of parchment paper sprayed with vegetable oil spray. Or line your baking pan with a flexible nonstick baking sheet such as Silpat and omit the vegetable oil spray.

Combine the honey, maple syrup, molasses, vanilla, and salt in a large bowl. Add the pecans and toss to combine well. Spread the pecans in a single layer on the prepared baking sheet. Bake for 15 minutes, stirring the nuts with a wooden spoon halfway through the cooking time. Remove the pecans from the oven and pour them into a bowl. Stir in the melted butter, then spread the pecans out on a clean baking sheet lined with parchment to cool.

JACKIE'S RUNNING CHEESE TRAY

During the holiday season, Jackie keeps a "running" cheese tray. Starting at Thanksgiving and running all the way through New Year's, Jackie searches out the best cheeses, and every day or so, she adds a new one to her tray. This is the perfect nibble when guests stop by for a holiday visit or as a course in a fancy dinner. Here are some of her favorites. Serve your cheeses at room temperature for the best flavor.

Epoisses: a strong smelling, washed rind cow's milk cheese, from Bourgogne and Champagne-Ardennes, France

Colston Bassett Stilton: one of the great blue cheeses of the world, rich and crumbly, from Nottinghamshire, England

Sally Jackson Chestnut Leaf–Wrapped Sheep Cheese: semisoft sheep's milk cheese with a deliciously pungent aroma, from Oroville, Washington

Montgomery Farmhouse Cheddar: cow's milk cheese with deep flavor and buttery texture, from Somerset, England

Humboldt Fog: ripened goat's milk cheese with a layer of ash in the center and under the exterior white mold, from Cypress Grove Chèvre, McKinleyville, California

FIG BRIOCHES

MAKES 24 SMALL BRIOCHES

These golden little breads, though not classic brioche, are light, buttery, and easy to make. Mix the dough and form the brioche the day before and impress your guests by serving them warm right from the oven, alongside a cheese tray or as part of a special Christmas breakfast.

You'll need two mini-muffin pans for this recipe.

½ cup milk

¼ cup sugar

2 teaspoons active dry yeast

4 large egg yolks, beaten

8 tablespoons (1 stick) unsalted butter, melted, plus softened butter for buttering the bowl and muffin tins

1 cup finely chopped dried figs (about 5 ounces)

1½ teaspoons freshly grated orange zest

1 teaspoon kosher salt

2 cups all-purpose flour

FOR THE EGG WASH

1 large egg yolk

A STEP AHEAD Prepare the brioche to the step where the mini-muffin pans are filled with balls of dough. Cover the pans with plastic wrap and refrigerate overnight. Remove the pans from the refrigerator, uncover, and allow the dough to rise in a warm place until soft and puffy, 1 to 1½ hours. Brush with egg wash and bake as directed.

Combine the milk and sugar in a small saucepan and heat just to lukewarm, about 100°F. Don't get the milk too hot, or it may kill the yeast. Remove the pan from the heat and stir in the yeast. Set the pan in a warm place and allow the yeast to proof for about 10 minutes. Scrape the yeast mixture into a large bowl and stir in the egg yolks, melted butter, figs, zest, and salt. Gradually add the flour, about ½ cup at a time, stirring well with a rubber spatula or a wooden spoon for several minutes, until the dough is smooth. The dough will be soft and sticky. Place the dough in a buttered bowl and cover tightly with a piece of plastic wrap. Place in a warm, draft-free spot and allow the dough to rise until doubled, about 1½ hours.

Meanwhile, butter 2 mini-muffin pans and set aside.

Turn the dough out onto a lightly floured surface, lightly flour the top of the dough, and flour your hands. Punch the dough down and knead for several minutes, until it is smooth and elastic. Using a knife, cut the dough into 24 equal pieces. Roll each piece of dough into a ball and place each ball in the well of a mini-muffin pan. When the muffin pans are full, set them in a warm, draft-free place to rise for about an hour, until the balls of dough are puffed over the tops of the muffin pans.

Preheat the oven to 375°F. To make the egg wash, lightly beat the egg yolk with 1 tablespoon water in a small bowl. Brush the top of each brioche with some of the egg wash. Bake the brioche until golden brown, 15 to 20 minutes.

Pile the brioche in a napkin-lined basket and serve them warm from the oven as an accompaniment to the cheese tray. You could also serve them at room temperature, but they are best the same day they are baked.

PERSIMMON PUDDING WITH PEAR BRANDY HARD SAUCE AND PEAR VANILLA SAUCE, SUGARED CRANBERRIES, AND SUGARED MINT LEAVES

MAKES ONE 9-INCH CAKE, SERVING 8

Peggy Dow's persimmon pudding is an old-fashioned dessert—soft, very moist, and almost like a custard, with the spicy sweet flavors of gingerbread and pumpkin pie. There are many recipes for steamed persimmon pudding, but this version is extra-easy because it's baked in the oven. We've dressed up the pudding for Christmas with two sauces, sugared cranberries, and mint, but you could also serve it more simply with a dollop of Sweetened Whipped Cream and a sprinkle of pomegranate seeds.

In the fall and winter, two varieties of persimmons are commonly found in American markets—Fuyus and Hachiyas. Fuyus are round and squat, with a tomato shape, and you eat them when they are ripe but still firm and crisp. Hachiya persimmons, with their elongated acorn shape, are the ones to use for this recipe. Hachiyas taste unpleasantly astringent until they are completely ripe. When truly

4 very ripe Hachiya persimmons

3 tablespoons unsalted butter, melted, plus a little softened butter for the pan

2 cups buttermilk

3 large eggs

¾ cup firmly packed light brown sugar

¼ cup granulated sugar

1 teaspoon pure vanilla extract

1 cup all-purpose flour

1 teaspoon baking powder

1 teaspoon baking soda

1 teaspoon ground cinnamon

½ teaspoon ground allspice

¼ teaspoon freshly grated nutmeg

Pinch of salt

Pear Brandy Hard Sauce or Sweetened Whipped Cream (page 69)

Pear Vanilla Sauce

Sugared Cranberries

Sugared Mint Leaves

A STEP AHEAD The pudding can be made up to a day ahead. If you are making the pudding ahead, unmold it onto something that can go into the oven, such as a cardboard circle or the bottom of a springform pan. Allow the pudding to cool completely, then wrap in plastic wrap and leave at room temperature. Before serving, unwrap the cake and transfer it to a baking sheet. Loosely cover the pudding with foil and reheat in a 350°F oven until warm, 15 to 20 minutes.

ripe, their skins become translucent and their flesh collapses into a jelly. Occasionally you will find very ripe Hachiyas in the market, but often you need to ripen them at home, which may take a few days, a few weeks, or even a month. Persimmons are usually available starting sometime in October, so you can buy them ahead. As each one ripens, pop it into a sealable plastic bag and toss it in the freezer. Thaw your persimmons when you want to make this pudding.

Preheat the oven to 350°F. Butter a 9-inch cake pan, line the bottom with a circle of parchment paper, and butter the paper.

To make the persimmon puree, cut the persimmons in half, scrape out the soft flesh with a spoon, and puree the flesh until smooth in a food processor. You should have about 1½ cups puree.

In a large bowl, using a whisk, combine the persimmon puree, butter, buttermilk, eggs, sugars, and vanilla. Whisk until smooth. In another bowl, mix together the flour, baking powder, baking soda, spices, and salt. Add the dry ingredients to the wet ingredients and mix until just combined. Scrape the batter into the prepared cake pan. Bake until a skewer inserted in the center of the cake comes out clean, 50 to 60 minutes. Remove from the oven and cool for on a rack 10 minutes. The pudding will sink as it cools.

To unmold the cake, run a thin knife around the cake to loosen it. The top surface of the pudding may be sticky when it is hot, so place a piece of lightly buttered wax paper over the cake pan, then cover with an inverted plate or a cardboard circle. Protecting your hands with a kitchen towel, invert the whole thing. The pudding should slide out onto the wax paper–lined plate. Peel off the circle of parchment, then place another inverted plate or cardboard circle over the pudding. Again, invert the whole thing. Remove both the top plate and the piece of wax paper and the pudding will be right side up. The pudding will be very soft with some syrupy liquid collecting on the plate. Allow the pudding to cool for 10 to 15 minutes, then cut into wedges.

Set out 8 dessert plates and, using an offset spatula, place a wedge of warm pudding on each. Put a dollop of pear brandy hard sauce on top of the pudding and ladle some pear vanilla sauce next to it. Garnish with the sugared cranberries and mint leaves.

PEAR BRANDY HARD SAUCE

MAKES ABOUT 1 CUP

My Grandma Fogarty's hard sauce with Jack Daniel's whiskey always tickled my taste buds. This is a similar version but made with pear brandy. This classic dessert sauce is best at room temperature so it's soft and creamy. Dollop some over a warm piece of persimmon pudding or any steamed Christmas pudding, so it starts to melt a little as you serve dessert.

Clear Creek Pear Brandy is an intensely fruity eau-de-vie made in Oregon from fresh pears. Use it or another fruit brandy such as Poire Williams from Switzerland or eau-de-vie de poire from Alsace. Or use a good-quality Cognac or other brandy.

12 tablespoons (1½ sticks) unsalted butter, softened

1½ cups confectioners' sugar

3 tablespoons Clear Creek Pear Brandy or other good-quality brandy

A STEP AHEAD Pear Brandy Hard Sauce can be made several days ahead and stored in the refrigerator. Bring it to room temperature before serving.

In the bowl of an electric mixer using the paddle, or in a bowl with an electric hand mixer, cream the butter. Gradually beat in the confectioners' sugar. Add the brandy and beat until fluffy. Serve at room temperature.

PEAR VANILLA SAUCE

MAKES 1½ CUPS

Fragrant ripe pears and equally fragrant vanilla beans are perfect flavor companions. Try serving this sauce with a gingerbread or spice cake.

2 ripe pears (about 8 ounces each)

1 cup sugar

1 vanilla bean, sliced in half lengthwise

A STEP AHEAD Make the pear sauce 3 or 4 days ahead and store, covered, in the refrigerator.

Peel the pears and cut them in half lengthwise. Trim out the stem and blossom end and remove the core using a melon baller or paring knife. Slice the pear halves lengthwise about ¼ inch thick. Combine 2 cups water and the sugar in a saucepan. Using a paring knife, scrape the seeds from the vanilla bean and set them aside, then add the scraped-out pod and the pears to the saucepan. To keep the pears submerged while they poach, put a piece of parchment or wax paper on the surface and weight it with a plate or small lid. Place the saucepan over medium-high heat. When the liquid comes to a boil, turn the heat down to simmer. Poach the pear slices until they are completely tender, about 15 minutes, depending on the ripeness of the pears. When the pears are very tender, remove the saucepan from the heat and allow them to cool in the liquid.

Drain the pears, discarding the vanilla pod and reserving the poaching liquid. Place the pears and the reserved vanilla bean seeds in the bowl of a food processor. Puree, adding about ½ cup of the poaching liquid to make a smooth sauce, similar to a thin applesauce. Discard the remaining poaching liquid or reserve for another use.

Scrape the pear sauce into a small bowl, cover, and chill.

SUGARED CRANBERRIES

MAKES 2 CUPS

These tasty, sparkly red berries add a festive touch to the Persimmon Pudding or any other holiday dessert. Save the simple syrup used to steep the berries in the refrigerator for sweetening holiday drinks.

2 cups sugar

2 cups cranberries

A STEP AHEAD Prepare the cranberries a day ahead and leave them uncovered, at room temperature, in the pan of sugar.

Combine 1 cup water and 1 cup of the sugar in a saucepan and bring to a boil over high heat, stirring to dissolve the sugar. When the syrup is at a rolling boil, add the cranberries. Immediately remove from the heat and cover the pan. Allow the cranberries to steep for 15 minutes, then strain the cranberries from the syrup.

Spread the cranberries in a single layer on a wire cooling rack, discarding any that may have burst, and allow to dry for 30 minutes to an hour.

Pour the remaining cup of sugar into a shallow pan. Add the cranberries and stir them around to coat with the sugar, separating any clumps with your fingers.

SUGARED MINT LEAVES

These frosted leaves are better to look at than to eat, unless you're a die-hard mint fan.

1 small bunch fresh mint

1 egg white

About 1 cup sugar

A STEP AHEAD Prepare the leaves a day ahead and leave them on the rack at room temperature.

Pick off as many mint leaves as you will use for garnish. Using a whisk, beat the egg white in a small bowl until frothy. Pour the sugar into a shallow pan. Using a pastry brush, brush both sides of each leaf with egg white. After each leaf is brushed, dredge it on both sides in the sugar, then place the sugared leaf on a wire cooling rack. Allow the leaves to dry at room temperature for about 2 hours.

HOT BUTTERED RUM

MAKES 1 SERVING

With a batch of Hot Buttered Rum Mix (below) in the freezer, you can whip up a warm, fragrant mug at a moment's notice for holiday visitors or just to get yourself in the mood for trimming the tree.

Rubbing orange zest around the rim of each mug gives you a fresh little hit of orange when you take a sip. Mount Gay or Myers's rums are good, dark, soulful rums for this drink.

2 tablespoons Hot Buttered Rum Mix
1 shot rum (1¼ ounces)
⅔ cup boiling water
1 strip orange zest

Put the Hot Buttered Rum Mix and the rum in a 1-cup heatproof glass mug. Stir. Add the boiling water and stir again. Twist the strip of zest and rub it around the rim of the glass, then drop it in.

HOT BUTTERED RUM MIX

MAKES 1⅓ CUPS, ABOUT 10 SERVINGS

Twenty-five years ago I was sous chef at the Second Landing Restaurant on Bainbridge Island, across the sound from Seattle. My friend Kim Tomlinson, who was the pastry chef, made the best hot buttered rum that I had ever tasted. I knew she used vanilla ice cream as the base, and I've been trying to duplicate her recipe ever since. Maybe I should just call her, but it's more fun to taste the drinks while testing the recipe.

8 tablespoons (1 stick) unsalted butter, softened
1 cup vanilla ice cream, softened
6 tablespoons packed light brown sugar
1 teaspoon ground cinnamon
½ teaspoon ground ginger
A few gratings of fresh nutmeg

A STEP AHEAD You can store this, well covered, in the freezer for about a month.

Put the butter in the bowl of a food processor and pulse until smooth. Add the ice cream, brown sugar, and spices and process until combined. Don't worry if the mixture looks a little grainy; it will melt when you use it. Scrape the mixture into a container, cover, and store in the freezer until needed.

EQUIPMENT

Whether it's a $15 cherry pitter or a $300 stand mixer, the perfect tool will make the job easier and a lot more fun.

THERMOMETERS

I prefer an instant-read meat thermometer to check the internal temperature of meats, fish, and poultry. You don't keep this kind of thermometer in the meat while it's cooking. Insert the stem end into the meat and you'll get an instant reading, on either a dial or a digital display. If you're going to do any deep frying, a candy/frying thermometer, which reads up to 400°F, is invaluable, and it's useful to have one that will clip to the side of the pan. The thermometer that you put on your barbecue grill should read up to 600°F or better.

TIMERS

A good timer costs only a few bucks, but it is indispensable. I like the kind that contains three timers in one so you can keep track of several things going on at your big dinner at the same time.

MANDOLINES AND SLICERS

Sometimes you need to cut food into very thin slices, like slicing potatoes for potato chips. A sharp knife will work, but the job will be easier and faster on a mandoline or slicer. A French stainless-steel mandoline costs about $150, but you can find a perfectly ser-

viceable plastic slicer that will do the trick for $40 or less in kitchenware shops, Japanese specialty stores, or by mail order. At home I still use the cheap plastic slicer I bought years ago in Chinatown. It's best to buy a slicer that comes with a safety guard, because it's dangerously easy to cut your fingers.

STRAINERS, RICERS, FOOD MILLS

I like having a variety of sieves and strainers. I use a very fine-mesh one for straining all the debris from an elegant sauce and a coarser double mesh one for straining the big pieces out of stocks or the juice from a can of tomatoes or for forcing food through to make a puree.

A flat wire-mesh basket attached to the end of a long metal handle is great for scooping food out of hot oil or boiling water. An inexpensive Chinese mesh spoon is called a *spider* because it looks like a wire spiderweb attached to a bamboo handle.

A food mill is great for fluffy mashed potatoes and will also remove the skins from pureed berries or tomatoes. When making a puree, the food mill's blades will push the food through the metal plate faster than you can do the job with a strainer and a rubber spatula.

PARCHMENT PAPER OR FLEXIBLE NONSTICK BAKING SHEETS

Sheets of heat-resistant parchment paper are used to line baking pans for nonstick baking. A flexible nonstick baking sheet (such as Silpat) does the same job and has an even better nonstick surface than parchment. The nonstick baking sheet may seem expensive (about $25), but it can be used over and over and is easily available by mail order (see Sources, page 265).

ICE CREAM MAKERS

This is not an essential tool, but it's fun to have an ice cream maker. You can spend several hundred dollars on a state-of-the-art machine with a self-enclosed freezer, or you can buy an old-fashioned bucket and churn that freezes the ice cream with a mixture of ice and salt. There are also several well priced ice cream makers on the market that operate by chilling the machine's canister in the freezer the night before you churn the ice cream. Some of these machines are hand-cranked, and some have electric motors to do the work for you.

RICE COOKERS

If you buy a rice cooker with a nonstick bowl, you'll probably never cook rice in a saucepan again. This machine will cook rice perfectly and keep it warm for a long time. There are expensive versions with a lot of bells and whistles, but I find a moderately priced model does the job nicely.

WOKS

You'll find a wide variety of mostly inexpensive woks in Chinatown stores and somewhat more expensive versions in kitchenware stores. Searing foods in a wok has a unique feel compared to a skillet or sauté pan. The shape of the wok concentrates the heat, and the thin metal conducts the heat quickly. You need to stir the food or shake the wok while you're stir-frying to keep the food cooking evenly and not burning in the hot spots, but shaking and tossing the food around is the fun part. Even if you're inexperienced at this, the food is less likely to be tossed out of a deep wok and onto the floor than out of a shallow skillet. A wok is also great for deep frying since you can use less oil to get the depth you need due to the cone-shaped bottom. A wok also makes a great steamer when you put a few inches of water in the wok and a Chinese bamboo steamer basket and lid on top.

CLEAVERS

I like to rummage around Chinese hardware stores for their great selection of cleavers, but you can also buy them at knife stores, kitchenware stores, or by mail order (see Sources, page 265). For Chinese-style cooking I use a good, heavy cleaver to chop cooked crabs through the shell

and cooked ducks and chickens through the bone. For slicing and dicing vegetables, I use a thinner, stainless-steel cleaver.

RUBBER SPATULAS

Every restaurant kitchen stocks a supply of small and large rubber spatulas. They're the perfect tools for thoroughly mixing food and scraping it out of bowls, and I use them just as frequently at home. There's a new material that they're using these days to make great, nonmelting plastic spatulas. These are the kind to buy if you're in the market for new ones.

WHISKS

An ordinary whisk works well for emulsifying things like vinaigrettes. I really like to have a balloon whisk for hand-whipping cream or egg whites, because it adds air more quickly. Those newfangled "ball whisks"—open-ended whisks with little metal balls on the ends—are handy for making gravy. The balls get into the corners of the pan, and the whisk can't collect debris in the middle.

MICROPLANE GRATERS

We now have four different microplane graters in our home kitchen, and Jackie likes to say these nifty supersharp tools have changed her life. The fine grater is perfect for zesting citrus or grating Parmesan. The ribbon grater gives you cool-looking curlicues of Parmesan. The big-holed grater is good when you need a coarser

grate, and the final one has a cutting blade almost like a mandoline or slicer. I think our enthusiasm for these tools is proven by the fact that we gave sets of microplane graters to three different friends for Christmas this year.

ROASTING PANS

A heavy, well-designed roasting pan is a beautiful thing. The important thing is to have a roasting pan you can put directly over the burners, as well as in the oven, for browning meats before roasting and making sauces and gravies afterward. At home I have a nonstick-coated All-Clad roaster. When you deglaze, every little browned bit releases from the pan and adds more flavor to your sauces and gravies.

STAND MIXER

When you're looking at an expensive piece of equipment, like the KitchenAid 5-quart mixer—which is the standard in all of our kitchens, at the restaurants and at home—think about the price spread over the twenty years you'll be using it. If the mixer costs $300, that's $15 a year, well worth every cent. This machine is a workhorse and a real pleasure to own if you like to bake. Besides mixing and whipping batters and doughs, you can buy all kinds of attachments, like meat grinders and sausage stuffers.

FOOD PROCESSOR

This handy piece of equipment has become almost de rigueur in home kitchens, though you can often use a blender to do a similar job. Mainly I use the blade attachment of my processor for making mayonnaise, pastry doughs, purees, and pesto. I find the slice and dice attachments fairly useless; they just seem to sit around the kitchen in the way. For slicing, it's better to use a mandoline or a knife. Jackie loves our little mini-processor, for chopping up a few cloves of garlic or a handful of nuts.

CHERRY PITTER

Not essential, but very, very nice to have whenever you need to pit cherries or olives.

NONSTICK FRYING PANS

Get the chef's style that has a metal handle with a removable rubber sheath that can go right in the oven. Get a small 7- or 8-inch pan and a large 10- or 12-inch pan. I always use a nonstick pan for bacon. All the little brown bits that would stick to the bottom of a regular skillet stick to the bacon instead, and you get *all* the flavor.

SAUTÉ PANS OR FRYING PANS

I like to have these in a few sizes, 7 or 8 inches, 10 inches, and 12 inches. I prefer a heavy pan from a top-quality brand like All-Clad.

STOCK/SOUP POT

You need at least one big pot for soups and stocks, holding at least 12 quarts. It's helpful if it's stainless steel, with a thick bottom, so when you're cooking anything with acids, like tomato sauce, you won't have a metallic flavor and you won't scorch the bottom. Whenever Jackie and I make a big pot of soup, we make enough to put 8-ounce containers in the freezer so Loretta can just pop one in the microwave for lunch.

SCRAPER

A metal scraper with a wood or plastic handle, also called a pastry scraper or a bench scraper, is great for transferring ingredients, portioning out dough, and scraping down your cutting board. You can also use your Chinese cleaver as a bench scraper. After you're done slicing, just scoop every-thing up on the flat blade and carry it right to the pan. A flexible plastic scraper, also called a bowl scraper, works like an extension of your hand—perfect for mixing doughs.

OYSTER KNIVES

It's helpful to have a couple of different oyster knives around. For the small yearlings or Olympias, a good 2-inch-bladed sharp-pointed knife works best. For the larger oysters, the 4 inch blade works well.

CITRUS ZESTER/CHANNEL KNIFE

Both of these small tools are handy for removing zest from a piece of citrus. The five little holes of a citrus zester shave lemon, lime, or orange zest into fine slivers. If you want thicker strips of zest for garnish, when making lemon twists for a cocktail, for example, use a channel knife, which has one larger hole that cuts the zest into wide, deep strips.

INGREDIENTS

Spend half your time buying the best ingredients and the rest of the time trying not to screw them up. This is a motto we live by.

CHEESE

I buy the best-quality cheese I can find from either a specialty cheese store or a "gourmet" supermarket with a really good cheese department. If you need grated cheese, buy a wedge or chunk and grate it yourself right before you need it.

OLIVE OIL

Olive oil is the oil most frequently put to use in my kitchen. Extra virgin olive oil results from the cold-pressed first pressing of the olives. I use extra virgin olive oil when I'm looking for intense, fruity, assertive, olive flavor. Pure olive oil has a milder flavor that won't dominate a dish. It's also more economical for general cooking and has a higher smoke point, so it's better for frying. Whenever I think it's important to use extra virgin or pure olive oil in a particular recipe, I specify. Otherwise, I leave the decision up to you.

VEGETABLE OIL

When I don't use olive oil, I use canola, grapeseed, or peanut oil for clean, neutral flavors and high smoke points.

SALT

Kosher salt is the salt I use most frequently in my kitchen. It has a less harsh and salty taste than table salt, and it's easier to add by hand because of the coarse texture. I also sometimes enjoy the flavor of sea salt and special salts such as the French fleur de sel. Sea salt may seem expensive, but you don't use very much, so it's a small luxury. Sea salt, kosher salt, and table salt have different degrees of saltiness relative to each other. Be sure to taste when substituting another type of salt in these recipes.

RICE

For Asian-style cooking, I prefer California-grown Japanese short-grain rice, such as Niko Niko Calrose brand, for its flavor and slightly sticky quality. Basmati is a long-grain Indian rice with a lovely fragrance. Arborio is Italian short-grain rice with a high starch content that makes it perfect for risotto.

VINEGAR

I like to use good-quality white, red wine, and sherry vinegar. Don't buy the cheapest brand at the supermarket or you'll ruin your cooking with harsh flavors. Even expensive vinegar is still pretty affordable and worth a few extra dollars. I sometimes use Champagne vinegar or rice wine vinegar for their more delicate, less acidic qualities.

STAR ANISE

This star-shaped seed pod with a sweet flavor and aroma is one of my favorite spices. You can steep the pods in hot liquids to release the flavor, or you can crush them with a rolling pin or in a spice grinder.

CHINESE CHILE GARLIC SAUCE

There are many bottled Asian-style chile sauces on the market. We like Lan Chi brand, which is made with chile peppers and oil with a nice garlic kick.

SAMBAL OELEK

This Indonesian condiment of ground fresh red chiles usually mixed with salt, vinegar, and a little sugar can be found in well-stocked supermarkets and Asian specialty stores.

CHINESE WHEAT NOODLES

These noodles are available fresh and dried in well-stocked supermarkets and Asian specialty markets.

CHINESE FERMENTED BLACK BEANS

Fermented and salted soybeans flavor many classic Chinese dishes. They have a winey, salty taste and go especially well with seafood. Usually they are chopped a bit to release their flavor.

SPRING ROLL WRAPPERS

It's very difficult for the home cook to make ultra-thin egg roll wrappers by hand, so this factory-made product (also called "spring roll pastry"), available at Asian specialty stores, is the best alternative. There are usually twenty to twenty-five square, paper-thin wrappers to a package. If they are frozen, thaw before using.

WILD MUSHROOMS

Farmed "wild" mushrooms like shiitake and oyster mushrooms, and cultivated mushrooms that people think of as wild, like portobello and cremini, are widely available in supermarkets. I usually prefer them to white button mushrooms. If you have access to foraged wild mushrooms in your area, buy them only from someone you can trust. Don't experiment with something unfamiliar and don't take chances.

DRIED CHILES

I prefer the flavor of pure ground chile powders, such as ancho or chipotle, to the mixed chile powders available in supermarkets. Whole and ground dried chiles are available in specialty spice stores, well-stocked large supermarkets, and also by mail order (see Sources).

SOURCES

UWAJIMAYA
519 6th Ave.
Seattle, WA 98104
(206) 624-6248
(800) 889-1928
www.uwajimaya.com
Asian ingredients of all kinds, woks, cleavers, rice cookers, etc.

SPRINGBROOK HAZELNUT FARM
30295 N. Hwy. 99W
Newberg, OR 97132
(503) 538-4606
Hazelnuts

HOLMQUIST HAZELNUT ORCHARD
9821 Holmquist Rd.
Lynden, WA 98264
(360) 988-9240
Hazelnuts

PENZEYS SPICES
(800) 741-7787
www.penzeys.com
Pure ancho and chipotle chile powders, other ground chiles, and other spices

WORLD SPICE MERCHANTS
1509 Western Ave.
Seattle, WA 98101
(206) 682-7274
Fax (206) 622-7564
Dried chiles, ground and whole, smoked paprika, dried herbs, and spices of all kind

VALRHONA
(310) 277-0401
Valrhona chocolate

SCHARFFEN BERGER CHOCOLATE MAKER
(800) 930-4528
www.scharffenberger.com
Scharffen Berger chocolate

WEBER
(800) 446-1071
Hardwood chips, hardwood charcoal, chimney starters, and thermometers for charcoal grills

WALLA WALLA GARDENER'S ASSOCIATION
210 N. 11th St.
Walla Walla, WA 99362
(800) 553-5014
Walla Walla sweet onions

SOSIO'S FRUIT AND PRODUCE
1527 Pike Place
Seattle, WA 98101
(206) 622-1370
Local wild mushrooms, peppers, peaches

EL MERCADO LATINO
1514 Pike Place
Seattle, WA 98101
(206) 623-3240
Dried chiles and other South and Central American products

CHUKAR CHERRY COMPANY
PO Box 510, 320 Wine Country Rd.
Prosser, WA 99350
(800) 624-9544
chukar@chukar.com
Dried cherries

To order **RUB WITH LOVE** or **SEATTLE KITCHEN** products:
www.tomdouglas.com
Tom Douglas' spice rubs and barbecue and teriyaki sauces for meat, poultry, and fish

MUTUAL FISH
2335 Rainier Ave. S.
Seattle, WA 98144
(206) 322-4368
Dungeness crab, whole salmon, local oysters

BAVARIAN MEATS
1920 Pike Place
Seattle, WA 98101
(206) 441-0942
Ham hocks, bacon, other smoked meats

REDHOOK ALE BREWERY
14300 N.E. 145 St.
Woodinville, WA 98072
(425) 483-3232
www.redhook.com
Information on finding Redhook in your area

PIKE AND WESTERN WINE SHOP
1934 Pike Place
Seattle, WA 98101
(206) 441-1307
Northwest wines

CHINOOK WINERY
PO Box 387
Prosser, WA 99350
(509) 786-2725

COLUMBIA CREST WINERY
PO Box 231
Paterson, WA 99345-0231
(509) 875-2061

CLEAR CREEK DISTILLERY
1430 NW 23rd Ave.
Portland, OR 97210
(503) 248-9470
www.clearcreekdistillery.com
Fruit-based brandies such as pear brandy and grappas

THE WINE ENTHUSIAST
(800) 356-8466
www.wineenthusiast.com
A wine essence tasting kit that lets you taste and identify the nine principal components of wine such as sweet, bitter, tannic, oak, flowery, and fruity

SUR LA TABLE
84 Pine St.
Seattle, WA 98101
(800) 243-0852
Catalog available
Kitchenware, flexible nonstick baking sheets, high-quality pots, pans, and knives, thermometers, ice cream machines. Also serving platters and Asian-inspired plates, bowls, ramekins, and chopsticks.

WILLIAMS-SONOMA
(800) 541-2233
www.williamssonoma.com
Catalog available
Some specialty food products such as fine chocolates, cheeses, demiglace. High-quality pots and pans, slicers, knives, kitchen thermometers, whisks, spatulas, other hand tools, ice cream machines, serving platters.

WASHINGTON WINE COMMISSION
(206) 667-9463
www.washingtonwine.org
Winery tour information

THE SPANISH TABLE
1427 Western Ave.
Seattle, WA 98101
(206) 682-2827
Fax (206) 682-2814
Smoked paprika, Spanish olive oils, olives

SCHROEDER'S BAKERIES, INC.
(800) 850-7763
www.schroedersbakery.com
Corrugated cake rounds in assorted sizes

MORE THAN GOURMET
(800) 860-9385
Demiglace Gold

D'ARTAGNAN
280 Wilson Ave.
Newark, NJ 07105
(800) 327-8246
www.dartagnan.com
Duck fat, duck demiglace, and other specialty duck products, whole ducks and whole squabs

FRAN'S CHOCOLATES
(Seattle's Queen of Chocolate)
2594 NE University Village
Seattle, WA 98105
(206) 528-9969
www.franschocolates.com

INDEX

greens:
    collard, down-home,
        155–57
    garlic, on toast, 54–55
grill(ed):
    asparagus and Walla Walla
        onions with Merlot
        balsamic, 207–8
    corn relish, heirloom
        tomatoes and basil
        vinaigrette, 75–76
    lamb skewers with red wine
        and honey glaze,
        132–33
    oysters with horseradish
        butter, 148–49
    ripe Camembert, in grape
        leaves with sweet cherry
        chutney, 205–6
    shrimp and garlic-stuffed black
        olive skewers, 134–36
    whole salmon on, stuffed with
        sea salt, onion and
        lemon, 19–21

H

ham hock stock, 157
hard sauce, pear brandy,
    persimmon pudding
    with pear vanilla sauce,
    sugared cranberries,
    sugared mint leaves and,
    252–58
hard watermelon lemonade,
    147
hazelnut rice salad with parsley
    and artichokes, 22–24
heirloom tomatoes, grilled corn
    relish, and basil
    vinaigrette, 75–76
homemade Bianco on the rocks
    with a twist, 218

honey:
    and red wine glaze, grilled
        lamb skewers with,
        132–33
    sweet goat cheese turnovers
        and pistachios and,
        139–41
horseradish butter, grilled oysters
    with, 148–49
hot buttered rum, 259

J

Jackie's running cheese tray, 249
jam:
    blueberry, in blueberry
        cornmeal crostata,
        120–22
    Syrah, vine-roasted squab
        with, 77–79
Jarlsberg cheese, fried, with tartar
    sauce, 187–89
jo jos, duck-fried, 81

K

kale, brown butter, 246
Kay's Merlot biscotti, 214–15
king boletus stuffing, 244–45

L

lamb:
    chop T-bones in crushed
        cherry marinade with
        tarragon mustard,
        209–10
    skewers, grilled, with red wine
        and honey glaze, 132–33

lardons, warm spinach salad with
    sherry vinaigrette, fried
    eggs and, 221–22
lemon:
    glaze, cornmeal rosemary cake
        with, 180–81
    vinaigrette, for charred squid
        skewers on garlic toast
        with arugula, 110–13
    vinaigrette for grilled
        asparagus and Walla
        Walla onions with Merlot
        balsamic, 207–8
    whole salmon on the grill
        stuffed with sea salt,
        onion and, 19–21
lemonade, hard watermelon,
    147
lobster, broiled, spaghetti *aglio e
    olio* with crusty bread
    crumbs and, 91–92

M

mac and cheese salad with
    buttermilk dressing,
    118
macaroons, coconut, 49
mango sorbet, 48
maple molasses pecans, apple and
    radicchio salad with,
    247–48
marinade:
    chermoula, for charred squid
        skewers on garlic toast
        with arugula, 110–13
    crushed cherry, with tarragon
        mustard, lamb chop
        T-bones in, 209–10
    Greek, 136
    green, spring chickens with,
        223–24
martini, Pop Pop's perfect, 170

pistachios, sweet goat cheese turnovers and honey and, 139–41
pit-roasted pork spareribs, 150–52
Pop Pop's perfect martini, 170
pork:
    slow-roasted, with caraway onion gravy, 192–95
    spareribs, pit-roasted, 150–52
    sticky finger ribs, 40–42
    see also bacon
potato(es):
    red jacket, sea salt–roasted, 211
    russet, for duck-fried jo jos, 81
    smashed Greek, 138
potato chips, russet, Mom's crab dip on, 12–15
prawns, how to devein, 33
pudding, persimmon, with pear brandy hard sauce and pear vanilla sauce, sugared cranberries, and sugared mint leaves, 252–58

ribs:
    removing membrane from, 42
    spare-, pit roasted, 150–52
    sticky-finger, 40–42
rice:
    aromatic steamed, 47
    lemony, grape leaves stuffed with mint and, 128–29
    salad, hazelnut, with parsley and artichokes, 22–24
Riesling, roast duck with black pepper, thyme and, 238–42
ripe Camembert grilled in grape leaves with sweet cherry chutney, 205–6
risotto, sweet pea, 226–27
roast(ed):
    chicken, five-spice, 43–45
    duck with Riesling, thyme and black pepper, 238–42
    pan, wild mushroom, 17–18
    peppers, fresh corn crêpes with goat cheese, ancho chile sauce, avocado-tomatillo salsa, fresh corn salsa and, 59–64
    pit-, pork spareribs, 150–52
    sea salt–, red jacket potatoes, 211
    slow-, pork with caraway onion gravy, 192–95
    vine-, squab with Syrah jam, 77–79
romaine salad with pickled cucumbers and red cabbage, 190–91
rosemary, cornmeal cake with lemon glaze, 180–82
Rose's buttermilk cake with bay crème fraîche and brandied cherries, 229–31
rouille, smoked paprika, 178
rum, hot buttered, 259

S

salad:
    apple and radicchio, with maple molasses pecans, 247–48
    chop, with corn, snap peas, and bacon, 116–17
    green bean, with tiny cherry tomatoes and feta, 130–31
    hazelnut rice, with parsley and artichokes, 22–24
    mac and cheese, with buttermilk dressing, 118
    parsley, 136
    radicchio, on caramelized fennel tart, 171–74
    romaine, with pickled cucumbers and red cabbage, 190–91
    salmon, sandwiches, 20
    spinach, warm, with lardons, sherry vinaigrette, and fried eggs, 221–22
salmon:
    salad sandwiches, 20
    whole, on the grill, stuffed with sea salt, lemon, and onion, 19–21
    wines with, 21
salsa, avocado-tomatillo, fresh corn crêpes with goat cheese and roasted peppers, ancho chile sauce, fresh corn salsa and, 59–64
sandwiches, salmon salad, 20
sangria, Sauvignon Blanc peach, 109
Santorini-tinis, 127
sauce:
    ancho chile, fresh corn crêpes with goat cheese and roasted peppers, avocado-tomatillo salsa, fresh corn salsa and, 59